THE EXPENSE
OF GREATNESS

THE EXPENSE
OF GREATNESS

By

R. P. BLACKMUR

Gloucester, Mass.

PETER SMITH

1958

Acknowledgments are made to *The Partisan Review*, *The Kenyon Review*, *The Virginia Quarterly Review*, and *The Southern Review* where these essays first appeared, with the exception of those on T. E. Lawrence and on Criticism which are new.

CONTENTS

The Everlasting Effort

A Citation of T. E. Lawrence

"Either forced good or forced evil will make a people
cry out with pain."
—Feisal to Lawrence in *Seven Pillars*.

In thinking of T. E. Lawrence we are bound up in the
web of action and event—of the war, the air force, the
motor cycle—which made the man a legend while he yet
lived, a myth, and almost a Cause, lost but lurking: as
who should call a king great because his country per-
ished during his reign. The fate of Arabia, of Europe,
the no less irrelevant fate of Lawrence himself: these as
they work together to the merest look of recognition
make the image that goes before us—Will o' the Wisp if
you will—in our present adventure, shared or imminent.
Lawrence wrote it down himself in the introduction to
the Oxford text of the *Seven Pillars of Wisdom*: "We
were wrought up with ideas inexpressible and vaporous,
but to be fought for. We lived many lives in those
whirling campaigns, never sparing ourselves any good or
evil: yet when we achieved and the new world dawned,
the old men came out again and took from us our victory, and remade it in the likeness of the former world
they knew. Youth could win, but had not learned to
keep, and was pitiably weak against age. We stammered
that we had worked for a new heaven and a new earth,
and they thanked us kindly and made their peace. When

we are their age no doubt we shall serve our children so." Lawrence wrote it down as a statement of fact, but on the advice of Bernard Shaw omitted it from later editions; for Lawrence was docile, in the very measure of his scrupulousness, and in imagination as well as act, to those whom he admired. He walked always with pebbles in his boots.

But he put it down and we put it back. It is there: all the power—of persuasion, of enactment—that comes from the ability to put things down: the power without which Lawrence could not have become a legend or a myth, for without that power he could not have revealed his cause, its strength, its weakness, its necessity. At least he could not have done so in our western world, however it may be in the east; for in the west the old men habitually obliterate every power short of the rational imagination: imagination rising from a Cause through the written word. Lawrence would have been made nothing or wholly falsified, as at the Peace Conference or in the newspapers, if he had not written a book. Whether fable or fact, there is justice in the tale that the first manuscript of the book was stolen from the train at Reading Station, presumptively by the agents of the old men, almost as soon as it had been written, in November 1919 when the old men had taken over the world again not to let it go: we may think they recognised with what, someday, policy could not cope. Which is so. The subtitle of the book calls it A Triumph. Lawrence may have meant it, ironically enough, as the liberation of the Arab nations; for us only the third step in irony is needed to make it mean the liberation of the actual, Arab and otherwise, by the imaginative power of the written word; for so only has it transpired.

Let us turn away from the action of event and policy, the plot of the book, and turn directly, as Henry James would say, for the sake of the moral involved, to the book itself: first to the prose style, the general means of the writer, then to the whole sensibility which it both enriches and feeds on. Event and policy will return; indeed, they will never have been absent, only abjured for the time being—as in the diagnosis of bodily ills and resources one abjures the personality one wishes to save, which yet inhabits the body, at the least look, pat and regardless.

It may be as well to begin with an emphasis upon Lawrence's own view of himself as a craftsman: his love of the minute mechanics of writing and his aspiration towards major form—towards what he called, along with many, the architecture of his book. The emphasis cries for plain citation. Here are a few sentences and phrases isolated from the letters, of which the first set deal with words.

"That frenzied aching delight in a pattern of words that happen to run true. . . . My deepest satisfaction [is] in the collocation of words so ordinary and plain that they cannot mean anything to a book-jaded mind: and out of some such I can draw deep stuff. . . . Prose depends on a music in one's head which involuntarily chooses & balances the possible words to *keep tune* with the thought. The best passages in English prose all deal with death or the vanity of things, since that is a tune we all know, and the mind is set quite free to think while writing about it. . . . Only occasionally in things constantly dwelt upon, do you get an unconscious balance, & then you get a *spontaneous* and perfect arrangement of words to fit the idea, *as the tune*. Polishing is an attempt, by stages, to get to what should be a single combined stride. . . . The worst of being a habitual translator is that one gets in the way of trying to squeeze every sponge dry—and so few authors ever really *intend* all the content of their sponges. Words get richer every time they are deliberately used . . . but only when deliberately used: and it is hard to be conscious of each single word, and yet not at the same time self-conscious. . . . What you say about the emphasis I get on simple words like Moon or chocolate bisquits, mayn't it be partly because I do try & feel every article and emotion that comes into the book? I tie myself into knots trying to re-act everything, as I write it out. It's like writing in front of a looking-glass, and never looking at the paper, but always at the imaginary scene. That, and a trick of arranging words, so that the one I care for most is either repeated, or syllable-echoed, or put in a startling position."

So much for the craft of words. The citations are emphatic, it seems to me, of the high degree in which Lawrence was a deliberate craftsman. It is not easy to make the emphasis as plain with regard to the more formal aspects of craft, because the citations seldom appear in compact phrases or sentences. Any reader of the Letters may find for himself instance after instance of Lawrence's effort to shape his books for sequence and balance and drama.

The chief labour that went into *The Mint*, for example, seems to have been the labour of re-arranging its items so as to reach a satisfactory pattern. As it happens, there is one passage about *The Mint* compact and self-complete enough to quote. "You are right about the absence of flowers in *The Mint*. There is a severe beauty in some buildings, which would only be reduced if creepers were grown over them. I tried—deliberately—for that. You see, as I suppose every writer who reads it will see—how deliberate the construction and arrangement of *The Mint* is. I called its proportions the worst side of *The Seven Pillars*: and was determined that (what Siegfried Sassoon calls the architectonics of) whatever else I wrote should be, at any rate, calculated." We shall see later the irredeemable fault which made the proportions of *The Seven Pillars* what Lawrence called their worst side. Meanwhile we can note that Lawrence was quite aware of the worth of a few flowers on even the severest of buildings; for he continued the letter just quoted with this paragraph. "Your liking for the first-afternoon-football-match pleases me. That page was meant like a seat for anyone tired with the idea of effort. So was the whole third book put in like a benediction after a commination service: and the very occasional landscapes and lyric paragraphs, between stresses."

Finally, just as a general statement selected from among many for the ambiguity at its centre—for just that ambivalence and sense of defeated judgment which has afflicted so many writers—there is this paragraph, taken from the letter containing the quoted passage about words as sponges. "I mustn't slip again into the technique of writing. Writing has been my inmost self all my life, and I can never put my full strength into anything else. Yet the same force, I know, put into action upon material things would move them, make me famous and effective. The everlasting effort to write is like trying to fight a featherbed. In letters there is no room for strength."

This is the declaration of vocation at the strongest

value Lawrence ever reached: the co-operative sentiment of doubt was here no stronger than the sentiment of vocation. Conviction, which alone makes mastery possible, he never reached; for reasons of sensibility which it will be the main effort of these notes to show. His general sentiment was more nearly at the level of the following statement, which he made in a letter to Robert Graves shortly before he died. "Almost I could be an artist, but there is a core that puts on the brake. If I knew what it was I would tell you, or become one of you. Only I can't."

The everlasting effort nevertheless went far before the brake was felt. It was forced writing, seldom discovered writing, never the writing of momentum. Lawrence *forced* his eyes into the looking-glass with all the impetuosity which is characteristic of the complex dread of letting go, of missing, and of going forward. His writing acquired ease, I think, only in the sense that impetuosity became a habit. Usually his best effects are conspicuously either struck off or seized at, snatched from a near physical collision of his sensibility with the object. How strong his predilection was for violence of imagery is perhaps suggested by his choice of a first paragraph for *Revolt in the Desert*. It is taken from the second paragraph of chapter VIII of *Seven Pillars*, where the first, in a more composed writer, would have served more masterfully. "When at last we anchored in Jeddah's outer harbour, off the white town hung between the blazing sky and its reflection in the mirage which swept and rolled over the wide lagoon, then the heat of Arabia came out like a drawn sword and struck us speechless."

It is an excellent passage in its kind, but it is quoted

here because of the initial position Lawrence assigned to it in the *Revolt*: which leads us immediately to understand in *Seven Pillars* that it is the violence of the first two pages there that gives them their principal relevance to the book, for, without the yoking consideration of violence, they deal with matters not otherwise explored. I refer particularly to the description of casual homosexuality among the Arab troops. A "cold convenience" he called it, and proceeded: "Later, some began to justify this sterile process, and swore that friends quivering together in the yielding sand with intimate hot limbs in supreme embrace, found there hidden in the darkness a sensual coefficient of the mental passion which was welding our souls and spirits in one flaming effort. Several, thirsting to punish appetites they could not wholly prevent, took a savage pride in degrading the body, and offered themselves fiercely in any habit which promised physical pain or filth."

The reader will remember that these sentences occur in a general consideration of the Arab Revolt and Lawrence's relation, as an alien Englishman, to it. They come down like a fist struck on a table during an otherwise steady argument, without significance to it but the contrary, yet forcing attention upon it beyond the confines of logic. Memory is invested; whether the shock or the argument is better remembered is no question, the association is permanent: kept, say, as the sense of smart. This mode of persuasion is well recognised, whether in conduct or in art; is often the deliberate substitute for mastery (the more inviting because in the instance it amounts to mastery); and Lawrence furnishes an extreme, perhaps a heroic, example of a writer for whom it constituted a chief resource. It overcame in the act one of his major obstructive obsessions—which we shall come to in another form; it overcame his sense of "many humiliating material limits" by declaring that there were "no moral impossibilities," and overcame too, by enacting it, that "physical shame of success" which was the reaction to victory. It gave him the means to say, or partly say, what he at once knew and did not know, otherwise unsayable.

If his reliance on this mode marked a limit, in the sense of barrier rather than boundary, to the major aspect of sensibility, and was the outward sign of an inward cripplement, it yet gave him for detail—for any detail short of the largest—a constant principle of growth; and made, indeed, an excellent showing forth of his own observation, "that the rules of action were only snares of action till they had run out of the empty head into the hands, by use."

There are at least three easily separable sub-species of writing in which Lawrence reached through the rules of his mode into handy use. One is the expression of atmosphere, landscape, setting, through imagery which, by coupling close observation, that might be dead, with far-fetched simile, that might often be *distrait*, gave a created effect of actuality. The strain of sensibility becomes thus equivalent to the tension of the object. Citation of this species is easy because brief examples offer. One is the figure of the heat and the drawn sword quoted above. Another, especially apt here, is when Lawrence remarks of tactics that nine tenths are teachable, "but the irrational tenth was like the kingfisher flashing across the pool, and in it lay the test of generals." He proceeds immediately, and here is the characteristic interesting point: "It could be ensued only by instinct (sharpened by thought practicing the stroke) until at the crisis it came naturally, a reflex." The reader will note how vivid, and useful, and how created out of whole cloth is General Kingfisher. Again, when Lawrence told the Arabs of Allenby's successes: "My hearers' minds drew after me like flames. Tallal took fire, boasting." Here the apposition seems at first sight so logical that no amount of analysis—which the reader may make for himself—will reduce its aptness to the level of yoked superficies where logically it belongs. What was created by the first stroke cannot afterwards be cut down, except by an uncalled for act of will. *Seven Pillars* is full of such strokes, some simple and some complex, e.g., balls of dead thistle "careered like run-away haycocks across the fallow"; an airplane "climbed like a cat up the sky"; and "black-white buildings moving up and down like pistons in the mirage"—which last gains its virtue perhaps precisely because it will not bear analysis at all.

One of the slightly more complex examples of this type of trope may be cited, an example where it is the sensibility rather than the language that betrays the signs of force in our present sense. It seems that "to an Arab an essential part of the triumph of victory was to wear the clothes of an enemy." Thus the dead were stripped naked. After one such victory Lawrence went out onto the field:

"The dead men looked wonderfully beautiful. The night was shining gently down, softening them into new ivory. Turks were white-skinned on their clothed parts, much whiter than the Arabs; and these soldiers had been very young. Close round them lapped the dark wormwood, now heavy with dew, in which the ends of the moonbeams sparkled like sea-spray. The corpses seemed flung so pitifully on the ground, huddled anyhow in low heaps. Surely if straightened they would be comfortable at last. So I put them all in order, one by one, very wearied myself, and longing to be of these quiet ones, not of the restless, noisy, aching mob up the valley, quarrelling over the plunder, boasting of their speed and strength to endure God knew how many toils and pains of this sort; with death, whether we won or lost, waiting to end the history."

Here what was seen—better, what Lawrence forced himself to see—is the trope of imagination. The language itself is calm and reserved; the overt attitude is controlled: but the vision is violent, an extreme effort to exhibit a face of that aspect of life which is intolerable from within rather than from without. It is an example of Yeats' "uncontrollable mystery" of which the terms always have to be created since they cannot exist. *Convenit esse deos et ergo esse creaemus.* Yeats—of whom Lawrence said that his later work was the ash of poetry—returned to the image of the Christ-child; Lawrence straightened the bodies of the immediate dead. One arrives where one is driven.

It is not easy to cite either of the other two principal sub-species in Lawrence's practice in his natural forced mode. The difficulty is partly in length and partly in clear identification. The best citations will therefore be fragmentary and themselves forced. One sub-species is to be found in the series of Arab portraits that extend through *Seven Pillars*—the full-dress characterisations of such men as Hussein, Feisal, Abdulla, and Auda, given sometimes all at once, but more often a page or so at a time as the history called for comment. My point is that these portraits are marvellous forced creations, quite removed from but parallel to their unrealiseable originals: pictures Lawrence kept with him, let us say, to remind himself of the complete men with whom he had to deal —preach to, persuade, and command.

The connection between the picture and the man is analogous to that between the minds that drew after Lawrence like flames and Tallal taking fire, not logical but putative. For Lawrence, they were limited acts of forced attention, for us they are created possibilities of human character, violent and incomplete, not open anywhere to analysis. They are characters not achieved or discovered, but asserted. Lawrence lacked the power, or the rare abiding charity, to make, or even to see, character complete; but he had inexhaustibly the power to make a willed substitute for it. To put it unkindly, his Arabs, and his Englishmen, and himself, too, all play character parts; they all work on formulas, however unpredictable and unusual; but, to make it praise, the formulas are intensely felt and the working out all fits into the game recorded. Two things need hardly be added, one that these remarks have no bearing on Lawrence's private intuition of character, which may have been perfect, but apply only to what he put down; the second, that what he did put down has only a lesser value, in the experience of character, than the productions of those who have put down, not so much more, but what was more complete. What is said here only makes another clue to help us discriminate the class of writer to which Lawrence belongs. Let us say merely that he was a man of feelings, which are fundamental, and of emotions, which are sometimes perfect products of feelings; but that, as a writer, he was governed by a driven and imperfect intellect, an intellect not ever his in the sense that his feelings were his, and not ever completing his feelings as his emotions might have completed them, and, as he knew, they were meant to. It is a matter of dominance, of hierarchy, of productive order, and not a matter of whether or not he owned the various talents; which he did, uneasily.

The remaining, or third principal sub-species in which Lawrence shows himself characteristic of his mode, has been saved till now because its great complexity is everywhere based on the relative simplicity of the first and second sub-species, and because it makes up, if we can cite it, evidently the very blood-stream of his imagination: the medium—the food and the habitat—of what he had to say. It will be understood that we speak really of the whole *Seven Pillars* and of *The Mint*, too, at least by extension, and that it is merely to focus attention that we bring up on a single passage: namely, chapters thirty-one to thirty-three of *Seven Pillars*.

These chapters contain Lawrence's account of his journey from Wejh to Wadi Ais to find out why Abdulla had done nothing with his army for two months. During the journey he is sick with dysentery, boils on his back and heavy fever, commits judicial murder, and discovers the major strategy by which the Arab revolt can be successfully conducted. The sickness—the physical suffering and the biological dismay—together with a concomitant sense of landscape and quotidian actuality may be said here to furnish what I. A. Richards calls the co-adunating power of imagination and so give meaning and location to the murder, and the strategy, and compose, on top, a new meaning possible to these pages alone. Certainly not the sickness only, and impossibly the landscape only, made these images their fertile apposition. Lawrence's wilderness had need to be spiritual as well as physical before it could breed vision out of observation, and the pang of conceptual feeling needed a direct base in bodily pain before it could be forced, by imagination, into emotion or, as it happened, the plot of action.

We can say if we like, looking for the technical aspect of these chapters, that we have just an example of old-fashioned straight-forward first-person narrative, limited by the historical facts and enriched by the forced data of a special sensibility. Lawrence went, was sick, did murder, and conceived strategy; these things were so; this is how they were seen; no more. But this is to remove both the sense of the deliberate artist and of the driven intellect, which furnish the true setting of the narrative and produce the true meaning. So far as Lawrence was aware of his writing—and in terms of precision of feeling he was supremely aware—what he wrote was not narrative at all, but a re-seizure, highly selective and deeply canalised, of the focal material of experience: to which the mere narrative line can never be more than apposite. That is why the sickness and the landscape count for so much, while the narrative counts relatively for so little in defining the murder and enforcing the strategy come upon. Any other narrative would have done as well or as poorly; for Lawrence did not compose by narrative means, the story does not come first. In fact the composition comes the other way round: the story, the events, serve to enrich and to prune a little the native superabundance of the sensibility engaged. The events, say, served as a mechanical closing focus—the iris of a camera—upon the actual material of experience, just as his intentions, the residual pattern or habituated eyesight of his sensibility served as the evaluing focus. They reduced, and thereby concentrated, the scope of his attention sufficiently to permit the valuing act to occur.

This is, I think, the only way Lawrence knew how to write; it explains the predominance of the fragmentary and the violent over the evidently integrating and reserved factors in two books which had the express aim of presenting whole pictures. Wholeness, for Lawrence, lay in the sensibility; so far as its elements could be expressed, they would make a unity that might be taken as complete if taken at all: the unity of obsession.

The problem of Lawrence, if there needs to be a problem, is the problem of the obsessed sensibility, which beyond or beneath its obsessions is disparate, without conviction, altogether homeless, nearly lost. What can it make for itself, what must it miss? With these questions, locked as they must be in the arms of *Seven Pillars* and *The Mint*, the remainder of these notes is concerned.

Nothing could better introduce the bottom sensibility of *Seven Pillars* as we think back on it and feel into it than the first paragraph of Doughty's *Arabia Deserta*. The reader will remember that Lawrence leaves his proper story with an account of the first days after the Arabs' triumphant entry into Damascus. "A new voice hailed me of an old friend," said Doughty, "when, first returned from the Peninsula, I paced again in that long street of Damascus which is called Straight; and suddenly taking me wonderingly by the hand 'Tell me (said he), since thou art here again in the peace and assurance of Ullah, and whilst we walk, as in the former years, toward the new blossoming orchards, full of the sweet spring as the garden of God, what moved thee, or how couldst thou take such journeys into the fanatic Arabia?'"

Lawrence called his book A Triumph; and so it was; but of the imagination, and terminating in an ambiguous, intolerable, because somehow alien emotion—an emotion the counterpart of which is raised somehow in the phrasing of Doughty's paragraph. In his Introduction to *Arabia Deserta*, Lawrence quotes Doughty that "if one live any time with the Arab he will have all his life after a feeling of the desert," but there is a richer phrasing in Doughty than that, which marks better the substantive feeling in Lawrence's emotion. "Here is a dead land, whence, if he die not, he shall bring home nothing but a perpetual weariness in his bones."

A part of the man died, as a motive cancelled out, and survived only as emotion, so powerful or so pervasive, being now groundless and without object, that it sometimes alienated all that had survived. Emotion which has lost its motor is the true disease and disorder of spirit, infecting like the ragged, ejaculatory after-weakness of violence every remaining movement in the degree of its initial force. This Lawrence knew, or partly knew; for there is a tailpiece to the Triumph, which doubles while undermining its value. "The strongest motive throughout had been a personal one, not mentioned here, but present to me, I think, every hour of these two years. Active pains and joys might fling up, like towers, among my days: but, refluent as air, this hidden urge re-formed, to be the persisting element of life, till near the end. It was dead, before we reached Damascus."

It had died; but death is a partial act in these senses, a mere pruning punctuation or breach of order; and what survives is re-enforced, sometimes in the direction of integration, sometimes not; but always leaving disruptions, gaps that may be found: which are the present object of search, though if we find them we shall probably not realise them, so embedded they must be in the continuing pattern of the man: so much a general stain of the sensibility, not anywhere startling stigmata. For it needs to be emphasised that only sensibilities of great strength and of a deep-seated order are capable of devastating weakness and actual disorder, and we are likely in looking at a man like Lawrence to mistake at critical points the one aspect for the other, just because of the greatness and the strength involved. That is why the matter is here introduced by the indirect means—assays of bias— of unconnected quotations, in the hope that the atmosphere they make when taken together will suggest to the reader the substantive feeling that brought them to mind: our feeling of Lawrence's emotion—a feeling full of ignorance and waywardness and imprecision—is all we can expect to manage, short of the attempt to share the emotion itself, which is a pathetic tame-goose chase not here to be commended however commonly self-applauded. It will be quite enough to absorb the full power of attention if we simply feel what disturbed and deprived Lawrence and drove him on, in his life and in his writing, to acts and images—to the unrelenting deed and deliberate vision—that he could not abide.

Except Swift, Lawrence is the least abiding writer of magnitude in English (short of Shakespeare in *King Lear*), and like Swift chose in his difficulty the subject-matter of his art. The type is not uncommon outside the arts; the world is full of men and women who practice distraught endurance and press for chances to make stoicism absolute and dull. It is imagination that animates endurance into a vice and makes stoicism, as Henry Adams called it, a form of moral suicide; imagination concentrates endurance into a supreme kind of attention, and compels stoicism to declare the values it destroys. In this respect—in this type of sensibility—imagination operates analogously to religion upon the world which both deny; only, if as in Lawrence the imagination be without religion, the balance of heaven is lacking, the picture projected is incomplete and in an ultimate sense fails of responsibility. It is thus, I think, that we get from Lawrence a sense of unsatisfied excitement, inadequate despair, and the blank extreme of shock. But it is excitement, is despair, is shock; made actual; disturbing us; finding room within us in our own tiding disorder. On the imaginative level, perhaps on the moral level—or on any level except the social—order is only a predicament accepted. It is the strength of an imagination like Lawrence's that it removes the acceptance and leaves the predicament bare. The weakness, which is basic only, lies in the absence of any effective anterior conviction to supply a standard of disclosure; and there, it is suggested, is the limitation, the constriction, the stress, the missing urge, which we feel chiefly as a dislocated but dominant emotion throughout Lawrence's work. To change the context from religion to sensibility or character, the weakness amounts to an immaturity in the compositional habit, which Lawrence, had he gone on living in this slow age—slow in growth, not revolution—might well have made up for. The late letters, written as he left the Air Force, show intimations of the recovery of conviction; and, more important, looking back, his work had all along shown quick material enough to require any amount of composition, the deepest degree of conviction.

This is not all, and exhausts nothing, this weakness. To repeat for emphasis, the weakness is basic only; and in the worlds of the mind what is basic is not necessarily conclusive, what totters at the bottom does not always fall: the towers of imagination fling up, like Lawrence's active pains and joys, out of quicksand, and stand, firm in light and air. It may be there is a type of imagination, of which Lawrence would be an exemplar, incapable equally of the bottom reality and the top ideal, yet tortured by both, which exhibits its strength solely in the actual confronting world—the flux—and is confounded only in those terminals which, so to speak, it could never reach. Surely there is nothing that so illuminates the validity of imagination as when we find ourselves assenting to an imaginative process whose beginnings shift under us as we look for them and whose ends we must feel as alien. Something like this is the case with Blake (to whom it is noteworthy here that Lawrence when young was much attracted), with Donne, El Greco, Proust, Baudelaire, but which is not the case, to make a rough standard of comparison, with Shakespeare, the early Tolstoi, Mann, or Dante, where assent is carried one way or another beyond the actual. When we think of Lawrence we do not think of Shakespeare, but we might well think of Baudelaire and again of Proust. Writers like Shakespeare shape, predict, and sometimes embody our sensibilities, so vast their work is. Writers like Lawrence dislocate, unseat, but always stretch and freshen our sensibilities. The difference is not in subject-matter or in expressive ability but in a limitation of imaginative process under the control of a distracted attention. That is why at distraught moments or times, writers like Lawrence seem especially rewarding: we see in them the minutia—the actuality—that is distraught. Distress seems better than any placation because more *immediately* honest. Besides, there is the recurrent, fearful question—more an emotion than a question—whether distraction is not as far as the mind can go.

It may some day be said that such an unconvicted belief was idiosyncratic of the experiment of our times. What else the suicidally distrustful epidemic ideologies, everywhere about us, that may be said rather to rage than to prevail, to promote rather than to meet catastrophe. Even this day—late summer 1940—shows chiefly the clinical picture of shock. It is almost nowhere the tragic sense, it is almost everywhere the perfidious sense that is encouraged. It is not impossible that a combination of these characters of the public sensibility may explain the extraordinary popularity of *Seven Pillars*, which must number by now a million readers. The public understands everything but the indictment, feels everything but the loss. Lawrence expressed—glamour is the refluent air in which it was received—an image on the great level of what many men would like to be so long as they know they cannot. That Lawrence showed also the actuality, which was part of his greatness, and that in his showing was a full sense, in Eliot's phrase for the poet's advantage, of "the boredom, the horror, and the glory," which is the rest of his greatness, together make the value both behind and beyond the popular fashion. His weakness—his radical distraction—only qualifies and canalises the value.

Both the value and its qualifiers will clear up considerably if we measure the force of *The Mint*. In that work Lawrence recounted the daily life of an enlisted man in the Air Force during the first months of training, and followed it with an account of a short period some time later, at another post, when the burden of fatigue drill had been replaced, to a degree, by school-work, and the

individual soldier participated in his work instead of submitting, so far as compulsion could go, to personal obliteration and the exhaustion of sensibility. The tale is flat
autobiography, composed, Lawrence said, entirely of
notes made at the time, later re-arranged, but textually
unaltered; nothing was taken out and nothing added. It
constitutes, in the first part, a record of animal debasement, and in the second much shorter part the intimation
of spiritual release through a disciplined and surrendered
life. It is thus an essay in moral immolation and intellectual asceticism, religious in prompting, escapist in enactment; so that its final significance, while religious, is the
significance of an irrational, restricted religion; which is
to say that it is abnormal in the sense of being *merely*
individual. It is the perfect fruit, true to sport, of Lawrence's enlistment in the Air Force, which took the influence of a Prime Minister to bring about.

It is not easy to discuss a work which cannot be
counted as familiar to more than a few hundred persons
and from which it is forbidden to quote; confidence
which cannot be checked ought not to be felt in the
critic, and certainly cannot be demanded by him. But
there are several aspects of *The Mint*, related closer than
cousins to aspects of *Seven Pillars*, that may be emphasised without recourse to the text. These are the aspects
that show in Lawrence the development, or deepening,
of his identity, and by the connections exhibited persuade qualities otherwise overlooked—in the *Letters* or
Seven Pillars—to transpire: and these just the illuminating
qualities we want.

The first of these aspects is the overt theme, fresh-
pressed in the title, which had by temperament obsessed
Lawrence for years, and which by his enlistment he

strove to enact and by his book to express: it was a question. What was the intrinsic value of the common coin pressed by the mint of His Majesty's Armed Forces? The extrinsic value varied about a norm from war to war and peace to peace; the intrinsic would be found partly in the transformation of material wrought by the pressure of the mint, and partly in what, if anything, remained unmodified, and was indeed brought out and firmed by the minting process. The difference between the civilian and the enlisted man was extreme. The civilian, for example, is presumed to choose and exalt his leaders, and is able to change them: he shapes the purposes of his society. The enlisted man is degraded beneath the level of choice and is expected, except in liquor and sex on leave, to reduce his personal abilities to a minimum: he exists to serve a purpose shaped beyond barriers which he cannot hope to cross except by his suicide as a soldier. Yet the material of which soldier and civilian are made is identical. How does the civilian become a soldier, and what keeps him so—what bars the restoring suicide—once he is there? There must be a deep and complex struggle involved, and some reward, not in sight but positive, some compensating, some fructifying release from the personality that has been lost. The interim period—the minting—will be an agony wilfully maintained and attended, at least in peacetime, though it is not commonly understood or enjoyed as such. Lawrence himself had perhaps not at first thought of the experience as an agony—the obsession was too close—but when the word was offered him he snatched it. David Garnett, after reading the typescript, wrote that as the *Seven Pillars* was a Triumph, *The Mint* was an agony, and Lawrence wrote back: "You have it in one word. I should have written *an agony* after the Title," and indeed, two weeks later, writing to Jonathan Cape, he referred to his "second book *The Mint*, an agony of the Royal Air Force." An agony it was.

Lest the reader think that the agony had entirely a dramatic or religious emphasis—which is merely the emphasis we keep—it should be observed that Lawrence had also the motive of reforming and lightening the waste burden of discipline on enlisted men, just as he worked for the abolition of the death penalty for military cowardice. The practical concern was distinguishable from the imaginative concern, but not separable: his integrity, like his humanity, was touched in different ways. We see the involvement clear in chapter CXVIII of *Seven Pillars*, which is towards the end, just before the entry into Damascus, when some Indian troops worked in conjunction with Lawrence and the Arabs. Lawrence had not been close to any body of "civilised" troops for some time, and the contact struck him. "My mind felt in the Indian rank and file something puny and confined; an air of thinking themselves mean; almost a careful, esteemed subservience, unlike the abrupt wholesomeness of Beduin. The manner of the British officers towards their men struck horror into my bodyguard, who had never seen personal inequality before." Two pages further on is a passage which ties *The Mint* and *Seven Pillars* together, and on all levels, in the centre of Lawrence's sensibility.

"But these others [British, Australian, Indian as compared to Arabs] were really soldiers, a novelty after ten years' irregularity. And it came upon me freshly how the secret of uniform was to make a crowd solid, dignified, impersonal: to give it a singleness and tautness of an upstanding man. This death's livery which walled its bearers from ordinary life, was sign that they had sold their wills and bodies to the state: and contracted themselves into a service not the less abject for that its beginning was voluntary. Some of them had obeyed the instinct of lawlessness: some were hungry: others thirsted for glamour, for the supposed colour of a military life: but, of them all, those only received satisfaction who had sought to degrade themselves, for to the peace-eye they were below humanity. Only women with a lech were allured by those witnessing clothes; the soldiers' pay, not sustenance like a labourer's, but pocket-money, seemed most profitably spent when it let them drink sometimes and forget."

The significance of this passage and what led Lawrence to write it would be worthless to any reader not aware, as Lawrence was aware, of the other side, of the theory and practice of war in the mass—of compound or social war. Lawrence showed his awareness often enough, but nowhere more clearly than when, in a paper called "The Evolution of a Revolt," he compared regular armies with his Arab bands with regard to discipline. One paragraph needs to be quoted entire. "Consequently we [the Arabs] had no discipline, in the sense in which it is restrictive, submergent of individuality, the lowest common denominator of men. In regular armies in peace it means the limit of energy attainable by everybody present: it is the hunt not of an average, but of an absolute, a 100-per-cent. standard, in which ninety-nine stronger men are played down to the level of the worst. The aim is to render the unit a unit, and the man a type, in order that their effort shall be calculable, their collective output even in grain and bulk. The deeper the discipline, the lower the individual efficiency, and the more sure the performance. It is a deliberate sacrifice of capacity in order to reduce the uncertain element, the bionomic factor, in enlisted humanity, and its accompaniment is *compound* or social war, that form in which the man in the fighting line has to be the product of the multiplied exertions of the long hierarchy, from workshop to supply unit, which maintains him in the field."

Here is the overt justification, the administrative logic—with its *preliminary* disregard of the human material—for the humiliation of the self which must precede either humility or grounded pride: the hell through which alone access is afforded to paradise or personal triumph. But the overt is never enough for the intensive sensibility; for what is overt is incapable, construed alone, of minting the soul: that which drives forwards or outwards from within, searching a pattern to fill out, a circulating system to follow. Faith, philosophy, fanaticism—some vehicle of conviction—serves indifferently to supply the deficiency, blood to the veins, inward justification: and *declares* the material to be minted. Lawrence lacked such a vehicle, except insofar as others by some mode or vestigial habit of their own, assumed that he possessed one. One might say in passing that Lawrence constantly reached out for the precarious support of those who made such assumptions; that on the whole, Jacob's Ladder led downwards, each rung clutched with inhuman resolution, let go with utter weakness. It is as if the faculty of attention craved, was satiated, and then disgorged. We say that Dante was a master of disgust; lacking St. Thomas and Aristotle, Lawrence is a master of disgorgement—but not alone of what was disgusting, but also of what might otherwise, swallowed, have been delight. *The Mint* is a running example of such disgorgement—of the continuous cultivation of the intolerable; like Baudelaire's poems about corpses—evil in the bestial, flaunted sense—without Baudelaire's intermittently recurring spiritual control, but with a mastery of the actuality which Baudelaire never reached. Lawrence could have cried with Baudelaire, and indeed did many times, *Je jalouse du Néante;* but the nothingness was worn with a difference. Baudelaire's nothingness was of insensibility, and he longed unavailingly for the haven of *Nombres et des Êtres,* Pascal's refuge of mathematics and mysticism. Lawrence's nothingness was rather represented by complete disgorgement of the details of sensibility. Nowhere in Lawrence is the least presence felt of *Luxe, calme, volupté,* nor is there any place, even in the furthest ideal offing, where all is order. Baudelaire was damned; Lawrence deprived; both exposed themselves deliberately and at a maximum tension to the sense of their fates. Another way of putting it may be risked: that Baudelaire was reminded always of original sin—of radical imperfection; where Lawrence was engaged always in terminal sin—ultimate inadequacy. Thus we are furnished with another version of the effect of the lack of conviction: a deeply engaged perfidy to the experience which produces the last as well as the least sentiments. Lawrence put it all down, again and again: the very inner press of *The Mint,* the imaginative outcropping motive of *Seven Pillars,* and occasionally as a bitter bossed rubric in the Letters. Let us put them together, with a letter, as both more self-conscious and it maybe thereby the less candid, coming first.

Lawrence wrote a series of letters to Lionel Curtis during 1923 when he was in the Tank Corps—the very worst period of the minting—and in one of them, evidently in answer to an urgent plea that he leave the army and come to his senses, there is the following passage. "And the blackness of your letter? Because it tempts me to run away from here, and so doing it marches with my wishes against my will. Conscience in healthy men is a balanced sadism, the bitter sauce which makes more tasteful the ordinary sweets of life: and in sick stomachs the desire for condiment becomes a craving, till what is hateful feels therefore wholesome, and what is repugnant to the moral sense becomes (to the mind) therefore pure and righteous and to be pursued. So because my senses hate it, my will forces me to it . . . and a comfortable life would seem now to me sinful. . . . When I embarked on it, a year ago, I thought it a mood and curable: while today I feel that there is no change before me, and no hope of change." In a letter of two weeks previous, after describing both his hatred of and submission to bodily activity, he went on: "This sort of thing must be madness, and sometimes I wonder how far mad I am, and if a mad-house would not be my next (and merciful) stage. Merciful compared with this place, which hurts me, body and soul. It's terrible to hold myself here: and yet I want to stay here till it no longer hurts me: till the burnt child no longer feels the fire."

Thus the resolution, the devouring appetite, as it appeared to Lawrence when addressing a friend in the combined terms of self-justification and expiation. What the food was, and condiment as well as food, cannot be reproduced here, though it comes as near objective justification as possible; for *The Mint* may be read only privately, and, in this country, in the Congressional Library; but a neighbor taint of it may be presented, a leaf which brew in the same pile.

Lawrence left behind him some pencilled manuscript,

called *Leaves in the Wind*, meant to be notes for a final section of *The Mint;* some of these are printed in Garnett's edition of the Letters, and of these one may be examined for our present purpose: to characterise the process of minting to which Lawrence yielded himself for some twelve years; but, more, to vitalise the references made here to the book itself, which was finished during the first three or four. The passage chosen finds Lawrence in the troopship *Derbyshire* on the way to India, as sentry in Married Quarters posted in the corridor leading to the women's latrine. The stench is bad; there is a splashing in the latrine, and peeping in Lawrence discovers the drain is clogged and the floor awash. The Orderly Officer makes a visit at this moment, and Lawrence tells him about the latrine:—"The grimy-folded face, the hard jaw, toil-hardened hands. An ex-naval warrant, I'll bet. No gentleman. He strides boldly to the latrine: 'Excuse me' unshyly to two shrinking women. 'God,' he jerked out, 'flooded with shit—where's the trap?' He pulled off his tunic and threw it at me to hold, and with a plumber's quick glance strode over to the far side, bent down, and ripped out a grating. Gazed a moment, while the ordure rippled over his boots. Up his right sleeve, baring a fore arm hairy as a mastiff's grey leg, knotted with veins, and a gnarled hand: thrust it deep in, groped, pulled out a moist white bundle. 'Open that port' and out it splashed into the night. 'You'd think they'd have had some other place for their sanitary towels. Bloody awful show, not having anything fixed up.' He shook his sleeve down as it was over his slowly-drying arm, and huddled on his tunic, while the released liquid gurgled contentedly down its re-opened drain."

I think it will be clear from this passage—which is not

entirely exemplary—that the drive behind it was not simple disgust, nor even the forced will of disgusted attention; there is a drive towards satiation, toward a complete absorption of the material in hand upon the outer film of the whole sensibility. The risibilities, too, are somewhat engaged, and the sense of verbal decoration. There is here that sentiment which is the posthumous and irresponsible achievement of shock: even sentimentality in reverse. Lawrence was rather vain of his achievements in this line: he realised perfectly the effect of his hospital chapter in *Seven Pillars*, which is queried up several times in letters; and the quality here meant to be emphasised may be illustrated by a few sentences from that chapter, followed by a sentence of Lawrence's own comment.

"I stepped in [from blazing sunlight to a shuttered lobby], to meet a sickening stench: and, as my eyes grew open, a sickening sight. The stone floor was covered with dead bodies side by side, some in full uniform, some in underclothing, some stark naked. There might be thirty there, and they crept with rats, who had gnawed wet red galleries into them. A few were corpses nearly fresh, perhaps only a day or two old: others must have been there for long. Of some the flesh, going putrid, was yellow and blue and black. Many were already swollen twice or thrice life width, their fat heads laughing with black mouth across jaws harsh with stubble. Of others the softer parts were fallen in. A few had burst open, and were liquescent with decay." The scene proper ends with this sentence: "The trench was too small for them, but so fluid was the mass that each newcomer, when tipped in, fell softly just jellying out the edges of the pile a little with his weight."

The reader who can separate himself from the subject-matter, which is extremely adhesive, should notice the vocabulary: the relish with which words were found to present the horror. The relish is the cement; the condiment of which Lawrence wrote to Curtis as desired by the sick stomach; condiment which not only promotes the appetite but forces feeding beyond capacity.

There are other examples on different or higher levels of tension, as it were, of the moral morass, to which we shall come. Here the concern is to point the difference between the quality of the text as quoted and the quality of Lawrence's feeling about it. In the latter was no relish. Writing to Edward Garnett, who had evidently complained more than once because Lawrence had omitted the chapter from *Revolt in the Desert*, Lawrence argues himself right in these terms: "No, I have not changed ground on the hospital chapter. I have been firm from the start that it was totally unsuited, because of its power, its bitterness, its length, its late position, for inclusion in a popular abridgment. I kept my horrors further back, where the blood was hot, and let the book just run down to its conclusion. . . . To overweight the last pages with matter emotionally more powerful than anything in the body of the book would be to finish up with a bang. Whereas the bang comes in the third act, properly."

Disregarding Lawrence's obvious over-estimation of the chapter (in another, earlier letter to Edward Garnett he thought that the *inclusion* of the chapter would have prevented the *Revolt* from being a best-seller), it is yet plain that Lawrence put an excess value on the expression of physical disgust and the revulsions, guided by the attending mind, of the flesh, without or with but little respect for the intrinsic significance of the agent. This is another point in the distinction between him and Baudelaire; for the latter even in his most exorbitant submissions to casual evil knew with *what* disciplined imagination he was submitting and thereby always extracted from the grossest material at least a connection and often an intensification of *that* imagination. Lawrence was driven perhaps further: to exploit the grossest material on those terms only in which it actually declared itself and regardless of the terms, if any, of the envisaging imagination. Hence—with a lack of control equalling the lack of conviction—the presence, which must either be ignored like vulgarity or taken as intrusive impertinence, of the "relishing" words in the passages quoted above. Lawrence called *The Mint* pure observation; but like most pure observation it had better be called uncontrolled or ungrounded idealism.

Which is a phrase, this last, that gives us a foothold of transition to what seems to me a central declaration, along the lines already laid down, of the intent, scope, and magnitude of Lawrence's sensibility. The declaration is double, to be discerned in an apposition made by the critic, rather than by Lawrence, to establish as well as state the identity of the two ends, expressive and receptive, of the engaged sensibility. Let us remark, as a renewed clue for attention, that Lawrence was severely addicted to all that we think of in the phrase, trial by ordeal; which is meant not only as a convenient summary of moral attitude, but also to suggest that the emotion of justice, and the feeling of justness, appeared to Lawrence chiefly masked as annihilation.

Both passages come from *Seven Pillars,* and the first carries as running heads to its two pages the phrases "Midnight Sermon" and "A Full Conversion." Lawrence had come back from the "clarifying wilderness" to find that his allies, the Serahin, were lacking in spirit to continue the revolt. Lawrence exhorted them in "a halting, half-coherent speech, struck out desperately, in our extreme need, upon the anvil of those white minds round the dying fire." The second and third paragraphs out of four in which the speech is recounted are here quoted.

To be of the desert was, as they knew, a doom to wage unending battle with an enemy who was not of the world, nor life, nor anything, but hope itself; and failure seemed God's freedom to mankind. We might only exercise this our freedom by not doing what lay within our power to do, for then life would belong to us, and we should have mastered it by holding it cheap. Death would seem best of all our works, the last free loyalty within our grasp, our final leisure: and of these two poles, death and life, or, less finally, leisure and subsistence, we should shun subsistence (which was the stuff of life) in all save its faintest degree, and cling close to leisure. Thereby we would serve to promote the not-doing rather than the doing. Some men, there might be, uncreative; whose leisure was barren; but the activity of these would have been material only. To bring forth immaterial things, things creative, partaking of spirit, not flesh, we must be jealous of spending time or trouble upon physical demands, since in most men the soul grew aged long before the body. Mankind had been no gainer by its drudges.

There could be no honour in a sure success, but much might be wrested from a sure defeat. Omnipotence and the Infinite were our two worthiest foemen, indeed the only ones for a full man to meet, they being monsters of his own spirit's making; and the stoutest enemies were always of the household. In fighting Omnipotence, honour was proudly to throw away the poor resources that we had, and dare Him, empty-handed; to be beaten, not merely by more mind, but by its advantage of better tools. To the clear-sighted, failure was the only goal. We must believe, through and through, that there was no victory, except to go down into death fighting and crying for failure itself, calling in excess of despair to Omnipotence to strike harder, that by His very striking He might temper our tortured selves into the weapon of his own ruin.

There are so many things of interest here—things so alien or so fundamental to our common experience—things fundamental *made* alien—that it is hard to determine where the seat of interest stands. Death as leisure; subsistence as the stuff of life; failure as goal; human despair as God's ruin. Let us take them, and the rest, as they work together; for it is, or ought to be, Lawrence's relation to the whole that counts most. Is it not a relation to the feeling of conviction?—conviction by debasement?—conviction without humility?—debasement that comes, as Lawrence says, by "the slow humbling of the Serahin" which ended in "their flashing eagerness to ride with us whatever the bourne." Here is where the seat of conviction shakes; and mastery is felt as self-nullity.

It is, the whole passage, the labour of the sensibility to bear, on its own, the new thing. That is to say, only by an intensive denial can you come *down* to affirmation. (There is another route, not down; but Lawrence was incapable of taking it.) One thinks, perhaps this is the heritage of Christianity tottering; the heritage irrecoverable except in terms of close denial. But might it not be more appropriate to think, *That* half of Christianity always tottered, and only existed by tottering. The ascetic insight, brought into the western world, must needs totter; partly because of its alienship in a temperate climate makes it a forced growth, so that it essentially wrings away from its unnatural soil; partly, and rather, because the other half—of Christianity, of the human spirit—constantly leaps into the saddle. There is no one like your European ascetic for awareness of the sensual, for riding upon it and being ridden, for spurring and being rowelled. If the merely ascetic, which is here to say the personal, aspect of the insight is dropped, the whole man or at least the whole sensibility emerges, restored to that balance wherein asceticism is of the heart rather than the brain, is the motor rather than the motivation. Lawrence could not drop it; his brain needed it to get on with; but he transformed it, using it on uncommon considerations —death as leisure and creation, the flesh as drudge. Hence both the force and the incoherence of his reactions.

It is as if a man needed to be insane in order to act, needed to destroy himself in order to express himself. We see him here, above, in the passage quoted, bringing men (and most himself) to the point of action by denying every worth to action except the worth of failure. The goal is *hubris* through denial, through *abandonment* as an actively and resolutely secured state. Faith, to him, could not be the substance of things hoped for, but of things conceived as impossible. There is here, it may be, the rancour of experience when understood through an ungrounded idealism. It is the nothing-heart at work, humbled, in the pejorative and oppressive sense, by the blind pride of its own heroism: without humility; and to say so reminds us again of Baudelaire, and the distinction we made between him and Lawrence. It makes itself again. Baudelaire's cry,

> Et mon esprit, toujours du vertige hanté,
> Jalouse du néant l'insensibilité

was very different from Lawrence's because based on a conviction, inherited and mastered. Lawrence's conviction was unequal to his experience; or his experience was superior to his conviction. In either case, he could only judge experience by annihilating its values.

If his exhortation to the Serahin represented the maximum value of sensibility on the high plane of action, we have hardly to turn a page to find its maximum value on the bottom plane of personal reaction. It is exactly the same driven, committed asceticism which led Lawrence to the imaginative recapitulation *and* sensual actualisation of the collective sexual assault made on him in the Turkish station, which might otherwise, as commonly, have just horribly happened, but which to Lawrence meant that the citadel of his integrity "had been irrevocably lost." The reader will remember the narrative—the stripping and the knife, the whip, the delicious warmth—and will know that Lawrence did not *mean* any of the words in his summary declaration, except in terms of his ascetic recapitulation. Yet one knows through them what he did mean: human defilement as final humiliation. If we put this together with the final pride of the midnight sermon to the Serahin, they will make what perhaps is the measure of Lawrence's contribution.

It is not an inch measure nor a yard stick, but a compass bearing: the focus of scope, great enough initially to absorb any amount of attention, wide enough eventually, one thinks, to command a full horizon, though it need not be just the closing night horizon Lawrence himself actually envisaged, but perhaps—however *manqué, deraciné*, and without term—still the horizon Lawrence once said—for imagination—that he desired to show. Writing to Edward Garnett in 1922 in answer to a letter of praise for *Seven Pillars*, he made his best intention plain. "Do you remember my telling you once that I collected a shelf of 'Titanic' books (those distinguished by greatness of spirit, 'sublimity' as Longinus would call it): and that they were *The Karamazovs, Zarathustra,* and *Moby Dick.* Well, my ambition was to make an English fourth." One barrier to satisfaction—perhaps the only barrier—was in the limiting factor of subjectivity. Lawrence wrote always about himself, the individual who, ultimately, could not cope,—with nothing, no plan or frame or conception, to fit himself into to make his tale objective in immediate import. His plain ambition is, as it were, untested; he could not steer for it, whether instinctively or deliberately; which is the difference in value between his books, and his life, and the books of the "Titans" he desired so to emulate. The ungrounded idealism which was fatal to him as a man comes out in his writing as compositional weakness, and is indeed the rough counterpart to what we feel as the lack of an abiding conviction. What is meant here by composition is the sum of those inner modes and outward manners by which the materials of experience are set together so that they make a whole so secure that the mere intention of the writer becomes immaterial to the book. In Lawrence, the intention everywhere counts, which is to say is questionable: uncomposed. It was his only operative weakness; other weaknesses hardly count, hardly exist, so tenaciously, with such strength of sensibility, did he fasten upon just those major aspects of experience which he could not compose. Few with that strength *and* that weakness— for it is a weakness that inhabits especially the whole class of great but eccentric sensibilities—few in the measure of Lawrence have done more. Not Melville, certainly not Nietzsche; only Dostoevsky on Lawrence's list, and he by that inexhaustible charity of imagination which produced, quite superior to the insult, the injury, and the humiliation which attracted Lawrence to him, a vast host of what we call "characters." Characters are an end-product, an objective form, of imaginative composition, and their creation depends on the deepest-seated of human convictions, so humanly full of error, by the occasion of genius so superhumanly right. When we say that Lawrence never produced a character, not even his own, if we add that he produced nevertheless almost everything that makes for character, we have said very nearly what is necessary. It was his everlasting effort.

The Shorter Poems of
Thomas Hardy

Both for those who enjoy the bulk of Thomas Hardy's poems and for those whose genuine enjoyment of a few poems is almost overcome by a combination of depression and dismay at the bulk, the great need is some sort of canon—a criterion more for exclusion than for judgment. At the general enjoyers this essay is not directly aimed; nor is it meant to be as irritating as it will seem because it names what it discards more clearly than it specifies what it keeps. It is meant rather to be a help—a protection, a refuge—for those who see in Hardy's poetry a great art beaten down, much of it quite smothered to death, by the intellectual machinery by means of which Hardy expected it to run and breathe free.

However abnormal, the condition is far from unusual. If we may say that in Shelley we see a great sensibility the victim of the early stages of religious and philosophical decay in the nineteenth century, and that in Swinburne we see an even greater poetic sensibility vitiated by the substitution of emotion for subject matter, then it is only a natural step further to see in Hardy the consummate double ruin of an extraordinary sensibility that had been deprived of both emotional discipline and the structural support of a received imagination. Hardy was a free man in everything that concerns the poet;

which is to say, helpless, without tradition; and he therefore rushed for support into the slavery of ideas whenever his freedom failed him. The astonishing thing is—
as with Shelley and Swinburne to a lesser degree—that
he was able to bring so much poetry with him into a pile
of work that shows, like a brush heap, all the disad-
vantages of the nineteenth-century mind as it affected
poetry, and yet shows almost none of the difficulties—
whether overcome, come short of, or characteristic—
belonging to the production or appreciation of poetry
itself. The poetry is there—permanently; and it is our
business to get at it. What obstructs us is man-made,
impermanent, and need not have been there at all. It is
a thicket of ideas, formulas, obsessions, indisciplined
compulsions, nonce insights, and specious particularities.
That is, it is accidental, not substantial, and can be
cleared away; then we can come at the feeling, the conviction, the actuality, that are there, not underneath,
but throughout the body of poetry.

Everybody who has read a volume of Thomas Hardy's
verse retains a secure impression, like the smart of a blow,
of what it was like. Everybody who has read the Apol-
ogy prefixed to *Late Lyrics* knows that Hardy and many
of his reviewers disagreed as to what made the blow
smart. The reviewers referred to unrelieved pessimism;
Hardy insisted he was no pessimist, was applying ideas
to life, and that the smart came from "exacting a full
look at the worst." That the reviewers were right on
instinct, ignorantly and with the wrong slogan, and that
Hardy was also right, with an equivalent ignorance
and a misapprehension of *his* slogan, is a part of what
these notes are meant to show as a basis for exclusion.
We are committed then to a study of ignorance in

poetry. Specifically, we are bound to segregate examples of those ideas which Hardy applied, like inspection stickers, to those stages of activity which most appealed to him as life, and then to see what happened to the poetry as a consequence.

What Hardy meant by his submission to Arnold's phrase about poetry's being a criticism of life—and that is what his own phrase amounts to—is neither always clear nor always consistent. But he did use ideas and did apply them, and we may provisionally say what the practice amounted to. Hardy seems to have used the word *idea* to represent a pattern of behavior, judgment, or significance. He wrote as if his ideas had an authority equal to their availability, and as if that authority were both exclusive and sufficient. If you had the pattern everything else followed and followed right. Pattern was the matrix of experience. If you could show experience as pattern, you showed all that could be shown; what would not fit, what could not be made to fit the pattern, did not count. Further, Hardy's idea-patterns were not heuristic, not designed to discover, spread, or multiply significance, but were held rather as rigid frames to limit experience so far as possible and to substitute for what they could not enclose. This is the absolutist, doctrinaire, as we now call it totalitarian, frame of mind: a mind of great but brittle rigidity, tenacious to the point of fanaticism, given when either hungry or endangered to emotion: a mind that seems to require, whether for object or outlet, eventual resort to violence. For only by violence, by violation, can experience be made to furnish it satisfaction.

We are familiar with the consequences of this frame of mind in religion, in politics, and in what passes for

THE EXPENSE OF GREATNESS

philosophy. We should also be familiar with it in the chores of daily life: the life we get over with as so much blind action, but which yet needs its excuse, its quick, quibbled justification. We are not familiar with it in the works of rational imagination—at least not as a dominant value or as a source of strength. When we see it, we see it as weakness, as substitution, precisely as work not done: as, at its best, melodrama, and at its worst, dead convention or the rehearsal of formula; and that is what we see in the great bulk of Hardy's verse. The very frame of mind that provided the pattern of his writing provided also, and at once, the terms of its general failure: leaving success, so far as his conscious devotions went, an accident of escape from the governing frame. Concern is in the end with the success, and will show it no accident; in the meantime with the considerations that make it seem so.

It is worth mentioning that the effect of the great liberating ideas of the nineteenth century upon Hardy's ideas was apparently restrictive and even imprisoning. The inductive ideas—the opening areas of experience—associated with the names of Huxley and Mill and Darwin and Arnold, Maxwell and Kelvin, Acton, Lecky, Bellamy, and Marx; all this affected Hardy if at all mostly as so much dead deductive limitation: a further measure for the cripplement of human sensibility. It is this effect that we have in mind I think when we refer to Hardy's stoicism, his pessimism, or to any of the forms of his addiction to a mechanically deduced fate. His gain from the impact of the new sciences and the new democracy, and from the destruction of dead parts of religion by the Higher Criticism, was all loss in his work: a loss represented by what we feel as the privation of his humanity.

· 40 ·

To push the emphasis an inch, it sometimes seems that his sensibility had lost, on the expressive level, all discrimination of human value, human dignity, and the inextricability in the trope of human life, of good and evil. It was a terrible privation for his work, and he bore it—that was his stoicism—without ever either the smile or the revulsion of recognition; he bore it, as a practical writer, by making various mechanical substitutions: keeping the violence without the value, the desperation without the dignity, the evil without the good—so far as these operations could be performed without mortality—as the basis of substitution.

It is in these substitutions that we find the obsessive ideas that governed the substance and procedure of the great bulk of the poems. Some of these obsessions—for they lost the pattern-character of ideas and became virtually the objects of sensibility rather than the skeleton of attention—have to do with love, time, memory, death, and nature, and have to do mainly with the disloyalty, implacability, or mechanical fatality of these. Some are embedded in single words and their variations; some in tones of response; some in mere violence of emotion; some in the rudimentary predictive pattern of plot; again many in complications of these. The embedded forms, in turn, largely control by limitation, by asserting themselves as principles of exclusion more than by their force as agents of selection, what is actually noted, observed, represented in the poem in question. Were one master of the counters Hardy uses, one could, so much does the production of his poems follow the rules, once the poem was begun, play the hand out for him to the end. Almost the only objective influence consistently exerted upon his verse is the influence of meter; from which indeed his happiest and some of his most awkward effects come. There remain, of course, besides, neither objective nor otherwise, but pervasive, the fermenting, synergical influence of words thrown together, and the primary influence of the rhythm of his sensibility; that double influence in language used, which a skillful poet knows how to invoke, and which *is* invoked in just the degree that he has the sense of the actuality wanted already within him, when it shows as the very measure of his imagination and the object of his craft, but which, in the poet who, like Hardy, has violated his sensibility with ideas, comes only adventitiously and in flashes, and shows chiefly as the measure of imagination missed.

Neither what is adventitious nor what is missed can be dealt with at length. Our waking concern must be with what is plotted, excreted, left as sediment—with what is used. In running over the thousand odd pages of Hardy's verse, feeling them as mass if not as unity, we wake at once, under the obsessive heads listed above, especially to the obsession of what will here be called crossed fidelities as of the commanding, determining order for the whole mass—though not of the poems we most value. By crossed fidelities I mean the significant subject matter of all those poems dealing with love, young, mature, or married, or with the conventional forms of illicit sexual passion, in which at least one and often all the represented characters commits, has committed, or longs to commit fraud upon the object of fidelity, or else loses the true object by mischance, mistake, or misunderstanding, or else discovers either in the self or the object through mere lapse of time or better acquaintance some privy devastating fault. Surely no serious writer ever heaped together so much *sordid* adultery, so much *hap-*

hazard surrender of human value as Hardy did in these poems, and with never a pang or incentive but the pang of pattern and the incentive of inadequacy, and yet asked his readers to consider that haphazard sordor a full look at the worst—a tragic view of life—exacted with honesty and power.

How it came about is I suppose simple. Hardy had a genuine insight into the instability of irresponsible passion and the effect upon it of conventional and social authority. *Jude* was his clearest expression of that insight, and *Tess* the deepest, though neither touches for imaginative strength and conviction, for expensiveness of moral texture as opposed to cheapness, *Cousine Bette*, *Madame Bovary*, or *Anna Karenina*. But he had the insight, and saw it strike home; therefore he applied it. Unfortunately, he had to a great degree what can only be characterized as a scandalous sensibility. Seeing or guessing the vast number of disorderly, desperate marriages in the world he knew, he applied his combination of insight and observation almost solely to the scandalous pattern—precisely as Antony and Cleopatra, Solomon and Sheba, are heard of in smoking rooms and country stores, only without the dirt or the relish, just the pattern. The pattern as it is repeated more and more barely becomes at first cynical and then meretricious. Hardy mistook, in short, the imaginative function of insight just as he fell short of the imaginative value of convention. Insight is to heighten the significance *of* something; it reveals the pattern *in* the flesh, the trope or forward stress of life. Convention is to determine how the value of that forward stress, so embedded, so empatterned, is received. In works of imagination they make a dichotomy where if either branch is dead the vitality of the

tree is impaired. You cannot express, you cannot dramatize human life unless your insight and your convention
—your simplifications of substance—are somehow made to
seem the very form of that life. Your handy formula will
not do, unless you every time, by the persuasive force
of your drama, carry it back to the actual instance of
which, in your case of instruments, it is the cheap abstraction. That, again, is the skill of the artist; that he
knows how to invest any formula, however barrenly
presented—like that of *Lear*, say—with enough of the
riches of direct sensibility to make it actual and complete
for sense and interest; when insight and convention and
formula become, as they properly ought to be, all afterthought.

Here is a handy juncture to introduce an image from
the early Hardy, before he undertook to substitute his
own formulas·for those traditionally available, and leant
naturally upon the strength of his predecessors to buttress
his effects. One of the earliest dated poems is the series
of four Shakespearean sonnets called "She to Him."
They are facile in mood and mode: it is the jilted lover
addressing the beloved after the fashion of Shakespeare
or Sidney or Drayton in easy iambics stretched out for
meter and rhyme and composed largely on the *when* and
then scheme. We have the Sportsman Time, Life's sun-
less hill and fitful masquerade, and we have a good deal of
desolated martyrdom supporting a deathless love—all
properties so dear because so adequately ominous to the
young sensibility, and all used well enough to make, for
the reader, a good journeyman's exercise, and show,
in the poet, positive promise. What we see in these
sonnets is, with one exception, the traditional body of
poetry absorbing, holding, expressing the individual ap-

prentice until, if he does, he finds the skill and the scope to add to that body. The exception leaps out: one of the best tropes Hardy ever produced and perhaps the only one of similar excellence in its kind.

> Amid the happy people of my time
> Who work their love's fulfilment, I appear
> Numb as a vane that cankers on its point,
> True to the wind that kissed ere canker came: . . .

Grant its point, which is universally easy, and the metaphor is inexhaustible: it stretches, living, in every direction through it theme. The lines are well enough known and have been quoted before, for example in Symons' early essay on Hardy's verse, and too much ought not to be made of them here, yet they are so startling in Hardy's general context that it seems plausible to look for some other explanation of their appearance than the accidental.

The theory of accidents in poetry like that of idiopathy in medicine is only a cloak for inadequate observation and explains nothing. Language in the form of poetry is as objective as a lesion of the meninges; only we get at the objectivity by different jumps of the inspecting imagination. The appearance of Hardy's trope, if it was not accidental, was, let us say, due to the fertility of the form which he was practicing; the form dragged it out of him. Not the metrical form alone, not any aspect of it separately, but the whole form of the Elizabethan sonnet taken as a mode of feeling and the composition of feeling—that was the enacting agent. The generalized trope of the mind was matrix for the specific trope of sensibility. Precisely as we are able, as readers, to respond to the form—the energizing pattern of music and meaning—of this special type of sonnet as something felt, so Hardy in this figure was able to work from his own feelings into the form *as a poet:* he made something, however fragmentarily, *of* the form. The test of manufacture is that both speed and meaning are absolute, at once in terms of themselves and in terms of the form they exemplify. The tautology between form and significance is absolute within the limits of language and inexhaustible within the limits of apprehension. It might be put that Hardy was here almost only the transmitting agent of an imaginative event that occurred objectively in the words and the pattern of the words; when the true or ultimate agency might be thought of as lying in the invoked reality of the whole form. It is the tradition not only at work, but met, and used. Doubtless Hardy had read a good deal of Elizabethan and Jacobean poetry, and got from his reading the themes as well as the means of his early poems; certainly in this poem, for two lines, he got the full authority of the form at once as a cumulus and as a fresh instance. Authority, then, is the word of explanation that we wanted, and we may take it in two senses: the principle of derived right and as the very quality of authorship which has as its perfection the peculiar objective virtue of anonymity. That is one's gain from tradition: anonymous authority. We shall come at it later in these notes otherwise and expensively derived.

Meanwhile it is a good deal of weight to heap on two lines; the pity is that it cannot be generally heaped over the whole body of Hardy's verse. That is the privative fact about most of Hardy's verse: he dispensed with tradition in most of his ambitious verse; it is willful where it should be authoritative, idiosyncratic where it should be anonymous; it is damaged—Mr. Eliot would say it is damned—by the vanity of Hardy's adherence to his personal and crotchety obsessions. It is so by choice, but not exactly by discrimination; rather choice by a series of those chances to whose operation in the moral field Hardy was so warmly addicted. (We might risk it parenthetically that Hardy was incapable of the act of choice precisely as he was incapable of discerning the ideal which would have made choice necessary.) Hardy never rejected the tradition of English poetry; probably, indeed, if he thought about it at all, he thought he followed it and even improved it by his metrical experiments. What he did was more negative than rejection. He failed to recognize and failed to absorb those modes of representing felt reality persuasively and credibly and justly, which make up, far more than meters and rhymes and the general stock of versification, the creative habit of imagination, and which are the indefeasible substance of tradition. Put another way, it is the presence of that achieved tradition which makes great poems resemble each other as much as they differ and even "sound" so much alike; and to its absence is due both the relative unreality and incompatibility of minor poetry—especially in its failures. But, to return to Hardy in relation to the major modes of tradition, no poet can compose the whole of his poetry himself, and if he does not go for help to poetic authority he will go elsewhere, substituting the extra-poetic for the poetic as much as may be necessary all along the line just to get the poem on paper. Hardy's elsewhere was not far off: it was in his own head: in his own ideas taken as absolute and conceived as persuasive by mere statement. The result was that he was relieved of the responsibilities of craft; and the worse result for the reader is that, lacking the persuasiveness of craft—lacking objective authority—the validity of the poems comes to depend on the validity of the ideas in that vacuum which is the medium of simple assertion. What we have is the substitution of the authoritarian for the authoritative, of violence for emotion, frenzy for passion, calamity by chance for tragedy by fate.

Hardy, of course, could not have accepted any such description of his intellectual behavior towards his verse. What he thought he did was, to repeat, to apply his ideas pretty directly to life; and it probably never occurred to him that his practice involved any substitution —or thereby any weakening, any diminution of either life or idea—of intellectual or emotional predilection for actual representation. Judging by his practice he did not know what substitution was, and evidently felt that he quickened the life and heightened the reality of his poems by making their action—what they were meant to show—so often hinge upon an unrepresented, a merely stated idea. In short, and this is what we have been leading up to, what Hardy really lacked was the craft of his profession—technique in the wide sense; that craft, which, as a constant, reliable possession, would have taught him the radical necessity as it furnished the means, of endowing every crucial statement with the virtual force of representation. The availing fount of that enabling craft springs from the whole tradition of poetry. Just as we say that his mastery of the particular, limited tradition of seventeenth-century metaphysical poetry enabled Henry King to compose his "Exequy," so we may say that every poet writes his poetry only as his poetry embodies what is necessary of the whole tradition. The same is true of reading poetry, but on a lesser level; where we often call the mastery of tradition the cultiva-

THOMAS HARDY

tion of taste, and ought sometimes to call it just getting
used to what a poem or body of poetry is about. In
Hardy's case, the interesting fact is that he sometimes
possessed the tradition and sometimes did not; and the
fertile possibility is that possession or lack may explain
what otherwise seems the accident of success or failure.

To his ideas as such, then, there is no primary objection. The objection is to his failure to absorb them by
craft into the representative effect of his verse. Indeed,
from a literary point of view, all that is objectionable
in Hardy's ideas would have been overcome, had they
been absorbed; for they would have struck the reader
as consequences instead of instigators of significance.
It is the certification of craft, that what it handles it
makes actual: objective, authoritative, anonymous. The
final value of a poet's version of the actual is another
matter, which literary criticism may take up but with
which it ought not to be preoccupied. The standards
engaged in the discernment of value cannot be exclusively literary standards. Here, at least for the moment,
let us stick to those values which can be exemplified in
terms of craft.

Some of Hardy's best effects—which should be kept
in mind while looking at his worst—come when his triple
obsession with death, memory, and time makes by mutual
absorption something of a trinity. It is an absorption
which excludes both that "full look at the worst" which
he wanted his poems to exact, and also the mechanical
crux of what we have called crossed fidelities. Then
the business of the poet proceeded free of the violation
of ideas. and the ideas became themselves something
seen or felt. Here is the nubbin of what is meant, from
the poem "One We Knew."

THE EXPENSE OF GREATNESS

She said she had often heard the gibbet creaking
  As it swayed in the lightning flash,
Had caught from the neighbouring town a small child's
    shrieking
  At the cart-tail under the lash. . . .

With cap-framed face and long gaze into the embers—
  We seated around her knees—
She would dwell on such dead themes, not as one who
    remembers,
  But rather as one who sees.

There is a dignity of tone, and a sense of release in the
language, in the poems of this order, which give them
a stature elsewhere beaten down: the stature of true or
fundamental poetic piety. Since the effect is produced
as the series of details, it needs to be shown in the full
length of such a poem as "She Hears the Storm."

> There was a time in former years—
>   While my roof-tree was his—
> When I should have been distressed by fears
>   At such a night as this!
>
> I should have murmured anxiously,
>   "The pricking rain strikes cold;
> His road is bare of hedge or tree,
>   And he is getting old."
>
> But now the fitful chimney-roar,
>   The drone of Thorncombe trees,
> The Froom in flood upon the moor,
>   The mud of Mellstock Leaze,
>
> The candle slanting sooty wick'd,
>   The thuds upon the thatch,
> The eaves-drops on the window flicked,
>   The clacking garden-hatch,

And what they mean to wayfarers,
   I scarcely heed or mind;
He has won that storm-tight roof of hers
   Which Earth grants all her kind.

The true piety here exemplified consists in the celebration of the feeling of things for their own sake and not for the sake of the act of feeling; and the celebration becomes poetic when the things are so put together as to declare their own significance, when they can be taken to mean just what they are—when the form, the meter, the various devices of poetry merely provide the motion of the meaning. In this poem and in others of its class, Hardy obtains objective and self-sufficient strength precisely by *reducing* his private operative means to a minimum, by getting rid of or ignoring most of the machinery he ordinarily used altogether. Instead of applying ideas to life—instead of turning the screws to exact meaning—he merely took what he found and let the words it came in, put it together. Doubtless, if asked, he would have said that the poem came on inspiration, and would have valued it less highly as craft for that reason. He evidently preferred to assault his material with an emotion, preferably violent, and an idea, preferably distraught, in either hand. At any rate, something such was his regular practice, so long continued—over sixty years—that it seems certain he could never have noticed that his poems produced more emotion and even developed more nearly into ideas, when he came to them, as it were, quite disarmed.

This is no argument for what is called inspired writing, as inspiration is commonly understood. It would be a better account of the matter to say that there was more work, far more attention to the complex task of uniting diverse and disparate detail, in the preparation of "She Hears the Storm," or in a single line like "My clothing clams me, mire-bestarred," than in a whole handful of those poems deliberately critical of life. It is simply that Hardy was unaware of the nature of poetic work, or of how much he did in spite of himself, or of how vastly much more was done for him in those remote, impressionable, germinal areas of the sensibility —that work which transpires, almost without invocation and often beyond control, to show as both fresh and permanent in what we choose to call *our* works of imagination. The final skill of a poet lies in his so conducting the work he does deliberately do, that the other work—the hidden work, the inspiration, the genius—becomes increasingly available not only in new poems but in old poems re-read.

The only consistent exhibition of such skill in the last century is in the second half of the career of W. B. Yeats. In prose there are others—Mann, James, Gide, possibly Proust, and perhaps Joyce. But these are not our concern and we need not think of them except to buttress the force with which we come back to the example of Yeats as it sits beside the example of Hardy. Yeats was addicted to magic, to a private symbolism, in much the same way, and for similar reasons, that Hardy was addicted to his set of ideas. Each had been deprived by his education, or the lack of it, of an authoritative faith, and each hastened to set up a scaffold out of the nearest congenial materials strong enough and rigid enough to support the structure imagination meant to rear. It was, and remains, a desperate occupation for each; for the risk was that the scaffold might become so much more important than the poetry as to replace it, and the mere preliminary labor come to be the sum of the work done. Such is indeed the condition of most ambitious poetry seriously regarded, and not only in our own day with its invitation to privation but even in the ages of faith. The poetic imagination is seldom able either to overcome or to absorb the devices by which alone it undertakes it greater reaches. Shakespeare is perhaps the only poet in English whose work habitually overcame its conscious means; which is why we say it is so good a mirror looked at generally, and why, looked at specifically, we say it is all in the words. None of it, where it is good, transcends anything or is about anything: it is itself, its own intention as well as its own meaning. Hence the evident fact that it cannot be imitated except ruinously. You can use Shakespeare but you cannot imitate him; for the imitable elements in his work are either vestigial or unimportant. Yeats' poetry rarely overcame its means, but it usually absorbed them in his best work so that they became part of its effect. The devices of his private symbolism can be discriminated but they cannot be disengaged from the poems where he used them; the devices, that is, are partly what the poems are about, and to the degree that they are discriminated, whether for or against, they limit the vitality —the meaning—of the poems in which they occur. You need to know beforehand what Yeats meant to do, and that knowledge delimits the poem and makes it precarious. It is the key that may be lost. With the key, the poetry of Yeats may be both used and imitated; for the discriminated symbolism, once made objective in Yeats' poems, can be put to similar use elsewhere. Hardy's poetry, relatively, almost never either overcame or absorbed its means. On the contrary, the more ambitious the poem, the more the means tend to appear as the complete substitute for the poem; so that what should have been produced by the progression of the poem never appears except in the form—or formula—of intention. Thus Hardy's ambitious poetry may be imitated, and often is, but cannot be used, which is why the imitations are bad. For in the class of poems we speak of, the imitable elements—all that goes by rote, by declaration, by formula, all that can be reduplicated—constitute almost all that is actually in the words. The rest—what Hardy wanted to write about—is only imputedly present and never transpires except as the sympathetic reader, entertaining similar intentions and inviting identic emotions, finds himself accepting the imputed as actual. It may be observed that such readers are common and inhabit all of us to the great detriment of our taste but to the great benefit, too, of our general sensibility; which brings us to the problem of approach central to all our reading, not only the reading of poets like Hardy where it is necessary to show great good will, but also poets like Yeats where it is less necessary, and poets like the best of Shakespeare where it may impede reading in the proper sense.

If we were not initially ready to accept an author's formula we could never discover what he had done with or in spite of it. There is the benefit. The evil lies in that sloth of mind which finds acceptable only those formulas which are familiar, or violent, and which insists on recognizing just what was expected—or "desired"—and nothing else. In this confusion of good and evil—of good will and sloth—lies one aspect of the problem of approach. As Hardy himself did not know, neither does the reader know how far in a given poem sloth or good will is responsible for the initial effect. We look at a poem that has all the airs and makes all the noises of setting considerable matters in motion. Does it so? or is it merely about the business of searching for a subject to use the airs and noises on? If the latter, does it after all succeed, by divine accident, in catching the subject by the throat or tail? or is it windmill fighting—a whirling, a whirring, and all gone? Certainly the fine lines and passages that vein bad poetry are come at—written and read—somewhat that way; and we need not value them less for that—though we need not thereby value more the slag in which they occur. The economical writ does not run in our experience of poetry, as any library or the best anthology will show. We put up with what we get, no matter what the expense and wastage, in order to use what little we can discover.

Discovery is judgment, and the best judgment is bound to falter, either allowing the poem too little through a deficiency of good will, or accepting as performance what was only expected through undiscriminated sloth, or on both sides at once by overlooking the poem's stretches of plain good writing—writing in the language that, as Marianne Moore says, "cats and dogs can read." Take Hardy at his face value and you may falter in the first or second fashion, depending on whether his machinery repels or fascinates you. Take him seriously, and you are liable to the third error; he gets in his own way so much of the time, you do not notice when his poems go straight, or if you do you think the instances not his but anonymous and ignore them when for that very reason you ought to value them most. Anonymity is the sign of the objective achieved at the blessed expense of the personal, whether in the poet or the reader, and is just what to look for when the bother is done. It is only in its imperfections, which distract us as revery or literary criticism, that good poetry fails to reach the condition of anonymity. Only then can there be anything like unanimity between the poem and its readers. For it is a curious thing that when the author pokes his head in so does the reader, and straightway there is no room for the poem. It is either cramped or excluded.

Fortunately for purposes of elucidation, Hardy gives us many versions of his favorite themes. Most of them appear on aesthetically impoverished levels, but occasionally there is a version, enriched both aesthetically and morally, that reaches into the anonymous and objective level. Let us take, for example, a group of poems occurring in *Satires of Circumstance*, all coming pretty much together in the book, and all on Hardy's principal obsessed theme of crossed fidelities. If we select the appropriate facts to emphasize about them, we should have some sort of standard, a canon of inclusion as well as exclusion, to apply roughly throughout the mass of Hardy's work. The poems chosen are called "The Telegram," "The Moth-Signal," "Seen by the Waits," "In the Days of Crinoline," and "The Workbox."

All these deal one way or another with conflicting loyalties—crossed fidelities—in the double field, as Hardy commonly takes it to be, of love and marriage. The skeleton in the closet of marriage is love, and is often articulated in the light of the honeymoon. Thus in "The Telegram" the bride either deliberately or distractedly declares to the groom that her true love is not for him but for someone else who, she has just learned by telegram, lies ill and perhaps dying. The bride, stung by the roused apprehension of death, shows her falsity by proving an anterior allegiance to which, in turn, by the fact of marriage, she had already been false. To any wakened sensibility the situation cries out for treatment, promising from the riches of feeling involved, a tragic perspective brought to the focus of emotion. I will not say Hardy preferred, but at any rate he used the violence of ill-chosen circumstance as the sole agent of discovery and engine of emotion. The fatalized, which is to say mechanized, coincidence of the telegram and the honeymoon, seizes on precisely its capacity for riches and no more. It is one of those instances where everything depends on the joint operation of the reader's good will and sloth. If he accepts beforehand the first five stanzas of the poem as somehow both equivalent to Hardy's intention and a furnishing forth of his (the reader's) general store of emotion, then the sixth stanza—what Hardy *made* of the poem—will seem a sufficient delivery of riches. It is the groom who speaks:

What now I see before me is a long lane overhung
With lovelessness, and stretching from the present to the
grave.
And I would I were away from this, with friends I knew
when young,
Ere a woman held me slave.

On the other hand, if he persuades his taste to operate—if he is interested in the creation or sedimentation of poetic emotion rather than the venting of his own—he will reject not Hardy's formula but what Hardy did with it, or more exactly he will reject what the formula did to the possibility of a poem. It let the poem down, up to the last stanza—let it down in all but a line or so to about as low a level of writing as a poem can touch and survive at all. The two passably good lines, it may be observed, have no intimate connection with the movement of the poem but merely serve to give a setting: representing a kind of objective circumstance as compared to the chosen circumstance of the telegram.

—The yachts ride mute at anchor and the fulling moon
    is fair,
And the giddy folk are strutting up and down the smooth
    parade, . . .

In short, it would seem that where Hardy felt his formula at work he apparently felt no need to employ more than the most conventional stock phraseology. Yet where the formula did not apply he was quick to write as a poet should. Coming now to the last stanza, quoted above, we see that it cheats the sensibility that it ought to have enriched. It is neither guaranteed by what went before, nor does it itself, working backward, pull the poem together. It is something added, not something made; something plainly a substitute for what, whatever it was, ought to have been there. There is no quarrel with the generalness of its statement; its rhythm is strong and invigorates the worn imagery; but it plainly misses with its lame last line any adequate relation to the emotion the poem was meant to construct. Because it would serve as well as an appendage to some other poem as it serves for this, it fails here. Without any intention of rewriting Hardy's intended poem, but just to tinker with the poem as it is, let us try altering the last line to read: "Ere a man had made me slave"; which would give the words to the bride instead of the groom, and makes poetic sense if not a good verse. Better still would be the deletion of the last line and the substitution of plural for singular personal pronouns in the remaining three lines of the stanza. Either of these stanzas would compel the final stanza both to work back into and draw sustenance from the rest of the poem. Neither change, nor any similar change, could redeem the plain bad writing, but at least all six stanzas would then make an effect of unity for the written aspect of the poem. The unwritten poem—the undeclared possibility—must be left to those with so much superflous sloth of good will as to *prefer* their poems unwritten.

"The Moth-Signal," the next poem on our list, shows in its first half the immediate advantage of being relatively well-written as verse, and therefore, just in that well-writtenness, shows the parts of the poem yoked together in a proper poetic conspiracy up to the very end. Here a husband reads, a moth burns in the candle flame, a wife waits and watches. After a light word or two, the wife goes out to look at the moon while the husband goes on with his reading "In the annals of ages gone,"—a phrase which prepares for what follows objectively, as the *idea* of the burned moth (not the image, which is imperfect) prepares for what follows symbolically and dramatically. At point, as the quality of the thought begins to strain a little, the quality of the writing begins to slip.

> Outside the house a figure
>   Came from the tumulus near,
> And speedily waxed bigger,
>   And clasped and called her Dear.
>
> "I saw the pale-winged token
>   You sent through the crack," sighed she.
> "That moth is burnt and broken
>   With which you lured out me.

> "And were I as the moth is
> It might be better far
> For one whose marriage troth is
> Shattered as potsherds are!"

The metaphor, with straining, becomes inexact with relation to the emotion; both fall mutually out of focus,
as that point of strain where inner tension snaps is
reached; and the poem ends, like "The Telegram," in-
adequately to its promise—which is to say awkwardly.

> Then grinned the Ancient Briton
> From the tumulus treed with pine:
> "So, hearts are thwartly smitten
> In these days as in mine!"

It is a question, perhaps, whether "The Moth-Signal"
is one of those poems that "exact a full look at the
worst" or rather instances one of those humorous poems
which Hardy said he put in to lighten the burden of
that look. There is a tradition, however poor in itself
yet honored because ancient, that allows the humorous
poet to overlook what would have otherwise been the
exigencies of his craft; so that if this is a humorous poem,
then it is plain why the rhyme-sounds were allowed to
knock both sense and motion out of kilter in the second
half of the poem. Perhaps the second half decided to be
humorous. Perhaps only the last stanza. If the poem
is not to be taken as humorous but as serious with a
quality of levity—or low level poetic wit—meant to tie
it together in the reader's response, then one or two suggestions may be made about the order in which the units
of perception are arranged. The grinning Briton ought
not to be where he is; if anywhere, he should appear
after the first stanza quoted above. The reader may

try the transposition and see. But then the poem would lack an ending, a rounding off? Not at all, the ending already exists, occupying a place where it does no good but merely kills time while the wife leaves the house. It is the stanza preceding the stanzas quoted above. If it is shifted to its natural terminal position, the poem will come to a proper end with the transposed Briton even deeper in mind. In its present situation the first line of the stanza reads, "She rose," that is, to go out. Now we want her back among her potsherds, so we will put it merely:

> [When she returned, unheeding]
>   Her life-mate then went on
> With his mute and museful reading
>   In the annals of ages gone.

The point is not that these tinkerings and transpositions actually improve the poems—they may, or may not —but that the poems so lack compositional strength, which is what is meant by inevitability, that they lay themselves open to the temptation of re-composition.

The next poem, "Seen by the Waits," carries the moral progress of this order of Hardy's poetry one step further backwards—into the arms of deliberate, unvarnished anecdote. A wait, it should be said, is a band of musicians and singers who play and sing carols by night at Christmas and the New Year in the expectation of gratuities. There are many waits in Hardy's poems, put there partly because he loved them and their old music, and partly because they made excellent agents of observation and even better foils to what they observed. The observation was the gratuity. In this poem the waits play by moonlight outside the manor-lady's window, and looking up see her image in a mirror dancing "thin-draped in her robe of night," making "a strange phantasmal sight." The poem ends:

> She had learnt (we heard when homing)
> That her roving spouse was dead:
> Why she had danced in the gloaming
> We thought, but never said.

Here again the sloth of good will can accept the manufactured observation as genuine if it likes. There is indeed a kind of competence about the poem, as about so many of Hardy's poems based upon his obsessive formulas, that strikes as more astonishing the more you realize what it misses or overlooks: the competence, precisely, of the lyric exercise joined *mechanically* to a predetermined idea, without that attention to language—the working of words among themselves—that makes competence mastery and the mechanical juncture organic. It is not a quibble but a conviction that you cannot, without sublime inspiration, make out of bad writing—"glancing to where a mirror leaned . . . robe of night" or, in the context, the word "gloaming"—out of such verbal detritus you cannot make a good poem. "In the Days of Crinoline" is another case in point, but from a slightly different angle. If "Seen by the Waits" remains an unactualized anecdote because carelessly written, "In the Days of Crinoline" remains at its low poetic level because no amount of competence could have raised the conception as taken, the *donnée* from which it springs, to a higher level. It remains versification because there was nothing in it to make poetry of. The *donnée* is on the plain scandal level—almost the limerick level—of the cuckolded vicar, and should have appeared in a bawdier *Punch* or a less sophisticated *New Yorker*, where the pat competence of its rhyme scheme and final smacking gag might shine like mastery. Substance and form are for once indistinguishable (through *not* inextricable) because both are trick, and no more. The vicar complacently lets his wife go off to her lover because she wears a plain tilt-bonnet. Once out of sight she draws an ostrich-feathered hat from under her skirts where she then pins her dowdy hood, reversing the operation when she returns home.

> "To-day," he said, "you have shown good sense,
> A dress so modest and so meek
> Should always deck your goings hence
> Alone." And as a recompense
> He kissed her on the cheek.

What we have been showing is, to repeat, a variety of the ills brought upon Hardy's verse by the substitution of formula for form and of preconceived or ready-made emotion for builded emotion—emotion made out of the materials of the poem. The track through this exhibition has been downwards, but it has nevertheless been leading up to the sight of a poem in which the formula is no longer a formula but a genuine habit of seeing, and in which the emotion, however ready-made it may have been for Hardy, yet appears to come out of and crown the poem. The formula discovers the form; the obsession makes the emotion; which are the preliminary conditions to good poetry where they affect the matter at all. For the whole emphasis of practical argument is this: that it is not formula or obsessed emotion that work evil but the fact of stopping short at them, so that they subsitute for what they actually spring from. But here is the poem, called "The Work-box," which it would be unfair not to quote complete.

"See, here's the workbox, little wife,
  That I made of polished oak."
He was a joiner, of village life;
  She came of borough folk.

He holds the present up to her
  As with a smile she nears
And answers to the profferer,
  " 'Twill last all my sewing years!"

"I warrant it will. And longer too.
  'Tis a scantling that I got
Off poor John Wayward's coffin, who
  Dead of they knew not what.

"The shingled pattern that seems to cease
  Against your box's rim
Continues right on in the piece
  That's underground with him.

"And while I worked it made me think
  Of timber's varied doom;
One inch where people eat and drink,
  The next inch in a tomb.

"But why do you look so white, my dear,
  And turn aside your face?
You knew not that good lad, I fear,
  Though he came from your native place?"

"How could I know that good young man,
  Though he came from my native town,
When he must have left far earlier than
  I was a woman grown?"

"Ah, no. I should have understood!
  It shocked you that I gave
To you one end of a piece of wood
  Whose other is in a grave?"

"Don't dear, despise my intellect,
   Mere accidental things
Of that sort never have effect
   On my imaginings."

Yet still her lips were limp and wan,
   Her face still held aside,
As if she had known not only John,
   But known of what he died.

This is about the maximum value Hardy ever got
by the application of this idea—this formula and this
obsession—to life; and it amounts, really, in the strictest
possible sense of a loose phrase, to a reversal of Hardy's
conscious intent: here we have the application to the
idea of as much life as could be brought to bear. To
define the value is difficult. Like many aspects of poetry
it can best be noted by stating a series of negative facts.
The poem has no sore thumbs; since its emotion is self-
created it maintains an even tone and speed. It is without violence of act and assertion; the details presented
are deep and tentacular enough in their roots to supply
strength without strain. The coincidence upon which
the release of emotion depends seems neither incredible
nor willful; because it is prepared for, it is part of the
texture of the feelings in the poem, and therefore seems
natural or probable. There are no forced rhymes, no
wrenchings of sense or meter; there was enough initial
provision of material, and enough possible material
thereby opened up, to compel—or tempt—the poet to
use the full relevant resources of his craft. Put positively, the formula fitted the job of work, and in the
process of getting the job done was incorporated in the
poem. It is still there; it still counts, and shapes, and
limits; but it is not a substitute for any wanted value: it

is just the idiosyncrasy of the finished product—the expression on the face—in much the same sense that the character of a wooden box is determined by the carpenter's tools as much as by his skill.

All this is to beg the pressing but craven question of stature, which requires dogmas that are not literary dogmas to answer, and is therefore not primarily within the province of these notes. In a secondary sense it is not hard to see—one cannot help feeling—that even at its maximum executed value, this formula of production limits the engaged sensibility more than the consequent release is worth; which may be a matter of accident not of principle; for other formulas, when they become habits of seeing and feeling, expand the sensibility in the very terms of the control that the formulas exert. The general formula of ballad-tragedy, for example, as in "The Sacrilege," allows and *demands* a greater scope in music and therefore, possibly, makes a wider range of material available for treatment. Certainly "The Sacrilege," "The Trampwoman's Tragedy" and "A Sunday Morning Tragedy" are poems of wider scope and excite deeper responses than even the best of the crossed-fidelity lyrics, despite the fact that they rest upon substantially similar ideas. The double agency—musical and compositional—of the refrain is perhaps responsible; for the refrain—any agency at once iterative and variable about a pattern of sound—is a wonderful device for stretching and intensifying the process of sensibility. Yeats and Hardy are the great modern masters of refrain; Hardy using it to keep the substance of his ballads —what they were actually about—continuously present, Yeats using it to develop and modify the substance otherwise made present. Returning to the crossed-fidelity formula, it is the difference between the concrete poetic formula—so concrete and so poetic that, like rhyme, it is almost part of the language, an objective habit of words in association—and the abstract intellectual formula, which is a reduction, a kind of statistical index, of the concrete and poetic, and which requires, for success, re-expansion in every instance. Hardy, lacking direct access to all that is meant by the tradition of craft, condemned himself, in a great part of his serious poetry—in over two hundred poems—to the labor of remaking the abstract as concrete, the intellectual as actual. That he had a naturally primitive intelligence, schematized beyond discrimination, only made the labor more difficult. Success—I do not mean greatness but just the possible limited achievement—came about once in ten times. About twenty of these lyrics reach more or less the level of "The Workbox"; none of them reach the level achieved in certain poems which escape the formula altogether. Yet they make—not the twenty but the whole lump of two hundred—the caricature by which Hardy's shorter verse is known; which is why so much space has been here devoted to them. Caricature is the very art of formula.

The true character beneath the caricature and which made the caricature possible—the whole fate of Hardy's sensibility—appears not in these poems where he deliberately undertook the profession of poet, but rather either in those poems where he was overweeningly compelled to react to personal experience or in those poems where he wrote to celebrate an occasion. In neither case was there room for the intervention of formula. It is a satire of circumstance indeed, that for Hardy the wholly personal and the wholly objective could alone command his greatest powers; and it is in this sense that Eliot's remark that Hardy sometimes reached the sublime without ever having passed through the stage of good writing, is most accurate. The clear examples are such poems as those about the loss of the *Titanic*, with its extraordinary coiling imagery of the projected actual, by which the capacity for experience is stretched by the creation of experience; such poems as those on Leslie Stephen and Swinburne, each ending with a magnificently appropriate image, Stephen being joined to the Schreckhorn which he had scaled, and Swinburne joined with the waves—

> Him once their peer in sad improvisations,
> And deft as wind to cleave their frothy manes—

and again such poems as "Channel Firing" and "In Time of 'The Breaking of Nations,'" which need no comment; and finally in such poems as "An Ancient to Ancients" with its dignity and elegance making the strength of old age. But these poems are or ought to be too generally received to permit their being looked at as anything except isolated, like something in the Oxford Book of English Verse. Keeping their special merit in mind as a clue to what we do want, let us look at certain other poems, not yet isolated by familiarity, and perhaps not deserving to be because not as broadly useful, which achieve objectivity on the base of a deep personal reaction. If they can be made to show as part, and the essential, idiosyncratic part, of what Hardy's poetry has to give as value, then we can stop and have done, knowing what to exclude and what to keep close.

The poems chosen have all to do with death, and the first, "Last Words to a Dumb Friend," was occasioned by the death of a white cat and is one of two poems which may, or may not, refer to the same pet animal. The other poem, "The Roman Gravemounds," derives its effect from the collocation of Caesar's buried warriors and the cat about to be buried. Hardy had a perennial interest in Roman relics and used them frequently as furniture for his poems when some symbol of age, time passing, past, or come again, was wanted; and if in "The Roman Gravemounds" he had a definite design it was surely at once to heighten and to stabilize the man's sense of loss.

> "Here say you that Caesar's warriors lie?—
> But my little white cat was my only friend!
> Could she but live, might the record die
> Of Caesar, his legions, his aims, his end!"

But Hardy, oddly enough for him, apparently thought the effect strained or sentimental; for he adds, in the voice of the hypothetical observer of the burial, a superficial, commonsense moral which quite reduces and unclinches the dramatic value of the poem.

> Well, Rome's long rule here is oft and again
> A theme for the sages of history,
> And the small furred life was worth no one's pen;
> Yet its mourner's mood has a charm for me.

Granted the method—the hypothetical observer, the interposition of the stock intellectual consideration, and the consequent general indirectness of presentation—that was about all Hardy could do with the subject. By making it "objective" in the easy sense he made almost nothing of it; which is another way of putting our whole argument about the effect of formula in the crossed-fidelity lyrics.

The true charm of the mourner's mood, only imputed in "The Roman Gravemounds," is made actual in "Last Words to a Dumb Friend" through a quite different set of approaches, all direct, all personal, amounting to the creation or release of objective experience. Let us observe the stages of approach, not to explain the process but to expand our sense of participation in it. First there is the selectively detailed materialization of what it was that died: purrer of the spotless hue with the plumy tail, that would stand, arched, to meet the stroking hand. After the tenderness of immediate memory comes the first reaction: never to risk it again.

> Better bid his memory fade,
> Better blot each mark he made,
> Selfishly escape distress
> By contrived forgetfulness,
> Than preserve his prints to make
> Every morn and eve an ache.

Then come eight lines which envisage what must be done, and the impossibility of doing it, to blot the memory out. All this Hardy supplied, as it were, by a series of directly felt observations; and these, in their turn, released one of those deeply honest, creative visions of man in relation to death which summoned the full imagination in Hardy as nothing else could.

> Strange it is this speechless thing, . . .
> Should—by crossing at a breath
> Into safe and shielded death,
> By the merely taking hence
> Of his insignificance—
> Loom as largened to the sense,
> Shape as part, above man's will,
> Of the Imperturbable.

As a prisoner, flight debarred,
Exercising in a yard,
Still retain I, troubled, shaken,
Mean estate, by him forsaken;
And this home, which scarcely took
Impress from his little look,
By his faring to the Dim
Grows all eloquent of him.

Housemate, I can think you still
Bounding to the window-sill,
Over which I vaguely see
Your small mound beneath the tree,
Showing in the autumn shade
That you moulder where you played.

Andrew Marvell hardly did better; and the end rises like the whole of Yeats' "A Deep-sworn Vow." You can say, if you like, that all Hardy had to do was to put it down, which explains nothing and begs the question of poetic process which we want to get at. What should be emphasized is, that in putting it down, Hardy used no violence of intellect or predilection; the violence is inside, working out, like the violence of life or light. The burden of specific feeling in the first part of the poem set enough energy up to translate the thought in the second half to the condition of feeling; and the product of the two is the poetic emotion which we feel most strongly as the rhythm, not the pattern-rhythm of the lines, but the invoked rhythm, beating mutually in thought and feeling and syllable, of the whole poem.

Rhythm, in that sense, is the great enacting agent of actuality in poetry, and appears seldom, without regard to good will or application, and is fully operative only when certain other elements are present in combination, but by no means always materializes even then. Perhaps, for the poet, it is what comes when, in Eliot's language, he sees beneath both beauty and ugliness, "the boredom, the horror, and the glory"; what Eliot had in mind, too, when he said that he who has once been visited by the Muses is everafterwards haunted. However that may be, it involves the power of words to preserve—to create—a relation to experience, passionate quite beyond violence, intense beyond any tension. Hardy's poetry engaged that power now and again, but most purely when responding directly and personally to death or the dead. "Last Words to a Dumb Friend" is only a single example, chosen for the unfamiliar dignity Hardy brought to the subject. The twenty-one poems, written after the death of his first wife, which appear under the motto: *Veteris vestigia flammae*, give, as a unit, Hardy's most sustained invocation of that rhythm, so strong that all that was personal—the private drive, the private grief —is cut away and the impersonal is left bare, an old monument, mutilated or weathered as you like to call it, of that face which the personal only hides. Here, for example, is one of the shorter, called "The Walk."

> You did not walk with me
> Of late to the hill-top tree
>   By the gated ways,
>   As in earlier days;
>   You were weak and lame,
>   So you never came,
> And I went alone, and I did not mind,
> Not thinking of you as left behind.
>
>   I walked up there to-day
>   Just in the former way;
>   Surveyed around
>   The familiar ground

THOMAS HARDY

By myself again:
What difference, then?
Only that underlying sense
Of the look of a room on returning thence.

Like the others in the series, it is a poem almost without
style; it is style reduced to anonymity, reduced to riches:
in the context of the other twenty, precisely the riches
of rhythm.

As Theodore Spencer has remarked (in conversation,
but no less cogently for that) Hardy's personal rhythm is
the central problem in his poetry. Once it has been struck
out in the open, it is felt as ever present, not alone in his
thirty or forty finest poems but almost everywhere in
his work, felt as disturbance, a pinioning, or a liberation;
sometimes present as something just beyond vision, sometimes immanent, sometimes here; sometimes beaten
down, mutilated, obliterated by ideas, formulas, obsessions, but occasionally lifting, delivering into actuality,
the marks of life lived. If these notes have served any
useful purpose it is double: that by naming and examin-
ing the obstacles set up by a lifetime of devoted bad or
inadequate practice, we are better able both to value
what we exclude and to acknowledge—which is harder
than to value—the extraordinary poetry which was
produced despite and aside from the practice. Hardy
is the great example of a sensibility violated by ideas;
and perhaps the unique example, since Swift, of a sensibility great enough—locked enough in life—to survive
the violation.

The Later Poetry of W. B. Yeats

THE later poetry of William Butler Yeats is certainly great enough in its kind, and varied enough within its kind, to warrant a special approach, deliberately not the only approach, and deliberately not a complete approach. A body of great poety will awaken and exemplify different interests on different occasions, or even on the same occasions, as we may see in the contrasting and often contesting literatures about Dante and Shakespeare: even a relation to the poetry is not common to them all. I propose here to examine Yeats' later poetry with a special regard to his own approach to the making of it; and to explore a little what I conceive to be the dominant mode of his insight, the relations between it and the printed poems, and—a different thing—the relations between it and the readers of his poems.

The major facts I hope to illustrate are these: that Yeats has, if you accept his mode, a consistent extraordinary grasp of the reality of emotion, character, and aspiration; and that his chief resort and weapon for the grasping of that reality is magic; and that if we would make use of that reality for ourselves we must also make some use of the magic that inspirits it. What is important is that the nexus of reality and magic is not by paradox or sleight of hand, but is logical and represents, for Yeats in his poetry, a full use of intelligence. Magic performs for Yeats the same fructifying function that Christianity does for Eliot, or that ironic fatalism did for

Thomas Hardy; it makes a connection between the poem and its subject matter and provides an adequate mechanics of meaning and value. If it happens that we discard more of Hardy than we do of Yeats and more of Yeats than we do of Eliot, it is not because Christianity provides better machinery for the movement of poetry than fatalism or magic, but simply because Eliot is a more cautious craftsman. Besides, Eliot's poetry has not even comparatively worn long enough to show what parts are permanent and what merely temporary. The point here is that fatalism, Christianity, and magic are none of them disciplines to which many minds can consciously appeal today, as Hardy, Eliot, and Yeats do, for emotional strength and moral authority. The supernatural is simply not part of our mental furniture, and when we meet it in our reading we say: Here is débris to be swept away. But if we sweep it away without first making sure what it is, we are likely to lose the poetry as well as the débris. It is the very purpose of a supernaturally derived discipline, as used in poetry, to set the substance of natural life apart, to give it a form, a meaning, and a value which cannot be evaded. What is excessive and unwarranted in the discipline we indeed ought to dismiss; but that can be determined only when what is integrating and illuminating is known first. The discipline will in the end turn out to have had only a secondary importance for the reader; but its effect will remain active even when he no longer considers it. That is because for the poet the discipline, far from seeming secondary, had an extraordinary structural, seminal, and substantial importance to the degree that without it he could hardly have written at all.

Poetry does not flow from thin air but requires always

either a literal faith, an imaginative faith, or, as in Shake-speare, a mind full of many provisional faiths. The life we all live is not alone enough of a subject for the serious artist; it must be life with a leaning, life with a tendency to shape itself only in certain forms, to afford its most lucid revelations only in certain lights. If our final interest, either as poets or as readers, is in the reality declared when the forms have been removed and the lights taken away, yet we can never come to the reality at all without the first advantage of the form and lights. Without them we should *see* nothing but only glimpse something unstable. We glimpse the fleeting but do not see what it is that fleets.

So it was with Yeats; his early poems are fleeting, some of them beautiful and some that sicken, as you read them, to their own extinction. But as he acquired for himself a discipline, however unacceptable to the bulk of his readers, his poetry obtained an access to reality. So it is with most of our serious poets. It is almost the mark of the poet of genuine merit in our time—the poet who writes serious works with an intellectual aspect which are nonetheless poetry—that he performs his work in the light of an insight, a group of ideas, and a faith, with the discipline that flows from them, which taken together form a view of life most readers cannot share, and which, furthermore, most readers feel as repugnant, or sterile, or simply inconsequential.

All this is to say generally—and we shall say it particularly for Yeats later—that our culture is incomplete with regard to poetry; and the poet has to provide for himself in that quarter where authority and value are derived. It may be that no poet ever found a culture complete for his purpose; it was a welcome and arduous part of his business to make it so. Dante, we may say, completed for poetry the Christian culture of his time, which was itself the completion of centuries. But there was at hand for Dante, and as a rule in the great ages of poetry, a fundamental agreement or convention between the poet and his audience about the validity of the view of life of which the poet deepened the reality and spread the scope. There is no such agreement today. We find poets either using the small conventions of the individual life as if they were great conventions, or attempting to resurrect some great convention of the past, or, finally, attempting to discover the great convention that must lie, willy-nilly, hidden in the life about them. This is a labor, whichever form it takes, which leads as often to subterfuge, substitution, confusion, and failure, as to success; and it puts the abnormal burden upon the reader of determining what the beliefs of the poet are and how much to credit them before he can satisfy himself of the reality which those beliefs envisage. The alternative is to put poetry at a discount—which is what has happened.

This the poet cannot do who is aware of the possibilities of his trade: the possibilities of arresting, enacting, and committing to the language through his poems the expressed value of the life otherwise only lived or evaded. The poet so aware knows, in the phrasing of that prose-addict Henry James, both the sacred rage of writing and the muffled majesty of authorship; and knows, as Eliot knows, that once to have been visited by the muses is ever afterwards to be haunted. These are qualities that once apprehended may not be discounted without complete surrender, when the poet is no more than a haunt haunted. Yeats has never put his poetry at a discount. But he has made it easy for his readers to do so—as Eliot has in his way—because the price he has paid for it, the expense he has himself been to in getting it on paper, have been a price most readers simply do not know how to pay and an expense, in time and labor and willingness to understand, beyond any initial notion of adequate reward.

The price is the price of a fundamental and deliberate surrender to magic as the ultimate mode for the apprehension of reality. The expense is the double expense of, on the one hand, implementing magic with a consistent symbolism, and on the other hand, the greatly multiplied expense of restoring, through the *craft* of poetry, both the reality and its symbols to that plane where alone their experience becomes actual—the plane of the quickened senses and the concrete emotions. That is to say, the poet (and, as always, the reader) has to combine, to fuse inextricably into something like an organic unity the constructed or derived symbolism of his special insight with the symbolism animating the language itself. It is, on the poet's plane, the labor of bringing the representative forms of knowledge home to the experience which stirred them: the labor of keeping in mind *what* our knowledge is of: the labor of craft. With the poetry of Yeats this labor is, as I say, doubly hard, because the forms of knowledge, being magical, do not fit naturally with the forms of knowledge that ordinarily preoccupy us. But it is possible, and I hope to show it, that the difficulty is, in a sense, superficial and may be overcome with familiarity, and that the mode of magic itself, once familiar, will even seem rational for the purposes of poetry—although it will not thereby seem inevitable. Judged by its works in the representation of emotional reality—and that is all that can be asked in our context—magic and its burden of symbols may be a major tool of the imagination. A tool has often a double function; it performs feats for which it was designed, and it is heuristic, it discovers and performs new feats which could not have been anticipated without it, which it indeed seems to instigate for itself and in the most unlikely quarters. It is with magic as a tool in its heuristic aspect—as an agent for discovery—that I wish here directly to be concerned.

One of the finest, because one of the most appropriate to our time and place, of all Yeats' poems, is his "The Second Coming."

> Turning and turning in the widening gyre
> The falcon cannot hear the falconer;
> Things fall apart; the centre cannot hold;
> Mere anarchy is loosed upon the world,
> The blood-dimmed tide is loosed, and everywhere
> The ceremony of innocence is drowned;
> The best lack all conviction, while the worst
> Are full of passionate intensity.
>
> Surely some revelation is at hand;
> Surely the Second Coming is at hand.
> The Second Coming! Hardly are those words out
> When a vast image out of *Spiritus Mundi*
> Troubles my sight: somewhere in sands of the desert
> A shape with lion body and the head of a man,
> A gaze blank and pitiless as the sun,
> Is moving its slow thighs, while all about it
> Reel shadows of the indignant desert birds.
> The darkness drops again; but now I know
> That twenty centuries of stony sleep
> Were vexed to nightmare by a rocking cradle,
> And what rough beast, its hour come round at last,
> Slouches towards Bethlehem to be born?

There is about it, to any slowed reading, the immediate conviction of pertinent emotion; the lines are stirring, separately and in their smaller groups, and there is a sensible life in them that makes them seem to combine in the form of an emotion. We may say at once then, for what it is worth, that in writing his poem Yeats was able to choose words which to an appreciable extent were the right ones to reveal or represent the emotion which was its purpose. The words deliver the meaning which was put into them by the craft with which they were arranged, and that meaning is their own, not to be segregated or given another arrangement without diminution. Ultimately, something of this sort is all that can be said of this or any poem, and when it is said, the poem is known to be good in its own terms or bad because not in its own terms. But the reader seldom reaches an ultimate position about a poem; most poems fail, through craft or conception, to reach an ultimate or absolute position: parts of the craft remain machinery and parts of the conception remain in limbo. Or, as in this poem, close inspection will show something questionable about it. It is true that it can be read as it is, isolated from the rest of Yeats' work and isolated from the intellectual material which it expresses, and a good deal gotten out of it, too, merely by submitting to it. That is because the words are mainly common, both in their emotional and intellectual senses; and if we do not know precisely what the familiar words drag after them into the poem, still we know vaguely what the weight of it feels like; and that seems enough to make a poem at one level of response. Yet if an attempt is made at a more complete response, if we wish to discover the precise emotion which the words mount up to, we come into trouble and uncertainty at once. There is an air of explicitness to each of the separate fragments of the poem. Is it, in this line or that, serious? Has it a reference?—or is it a rhetorical effect, a result only of the persuasive over-tones of words?—or is it a combination, a mixture of reference and rhetoric?

Possibly the troubled attention will fasten first upon the italicized phrase in the twelfth line: *Spiritus Mundi;* and the question is whether the general, the readily available senses of the words are adequate to supply the specific sense wanted by the poem. Put another way, can the poet's own arbitrary meaning be made, merely by discovering it, to participate in and enrich what the "normal" meanings of the words in their limiting context provide? The critic can only supply the facts; the poem will in the end provide its own answer. Here there are certain facts that may be extracted from Yeats' prose writings which suggest something of what the words symbolize for him. In one of the notes to the limited edition of *Michael Robartes and the Dancer*, Yeats observes that his mind, like another's, has been from time to time obsessed by images which had no dis-coverable origin in his waking experience. Speculating as to their origin, he came to deny both the conscious and the unconscious memory as their probable seat, and finally invented a doctrine which traced the images to sources of supernatural character. I quote only that sentence which is relevant to the phrase in question "Those [images] that come in sleep are (1) from the state immediately preceding our birth; (2) from the *Spiritus Mundi*—that is to say, from a general storehouse of images which have ceased to be a property of any personality or spirit." It apparently follows, for Yeats, that images so derived have both an absolute meaning of their own and an operative force in determining meaning and predicting events in this world. In another place (the Introduction to "The Resurrection" in *Wheels and Butterflies*) he describes the image used in this poem, which he had seen many times, "always at my left side just out of the range of sight, a brazen winged beast that I associated with laughing, ecstatic destruction." Ecstasy, it should be added, comes for Yeats just before death, and at death comes the moment of revelation, when the soul is shown its kindred dead and it is possible to see the future.

Here we come directly upon that central part of Yeats' magical beliefs which it is one purpose of this poem emotionally to represent: the belief in what is called variously *Magnus Annus*, The Great Year, The Platonic Year, and sometimes in a slightly different symbolism, The Great Wheel. This belief, with respect to the history of epochs, is associated with the procession of the equinoxes, which bring, roughly every two thousand years, a Great Year of death and rebirth, and this belief, with respect to individuals, seems to be associated with the phases of the moon; although individuals may be influenced by the equinoxes and there may be a lunar interpretation of history. These beliefs have a scaffold of geometrical figures, gyres, cones, circles, etc., by the application of which exact interpretation is secured. Thus it is possible to predict, both in biography and history, and in time, both forwards and backwards the character, climax, collapse, and rebirth in antithetical form of human types and cultures. There is a subordinate but helpful belief that signs, warnings, even direct messages, are always given, from *Spiritus Mundi* or elsewhere, which the poet and the philosopher have only to see and hear. As it happens, the Christian era, being nearly two thousand years old, is due for extinction and replacement, in short for the Second Coming, which this poem heralds. In his note to its first publication (in *Michael Robartes and the Dancer*) Yeats expresses his belief as follows:

At the present moment the life gyre is sweeping outward, unlike that before the birth of Christ which was narrowing, and has almost reached its greatest expansion. The revelation which approaches will however take its character from the contrary movement of the interior gyre. All our scientific, democratic, fact-accumulating, hererogeneous civilisation belongs to the outward gyre and prepares not the continuance of itself but the revelation as in a lightning flash, though in a flash that will not strike only in one place, and will for a time be constantly repeated, of the civilisation that must slowly take its place.

So much for a major gloss upon the poem. Yeats combined, in the best verse he could manage, the beliefs which obsessed him with the image which he took to be a specific illustration of the beliefs. Minor and buttressing glosses are possible for many of the single words and phrases in the poem, some flowing from private doctrine and some from Yeats' direct sense of the world about him, and some from both at once. For example: The "ceremony of innocence" represents for Yeats one of the qualities that made life valuable under the dying aristocratic social tradition; and the meaning of the phrase in the poem requires no magic for completion but only a reading of other poems. The "falcon and the falconer" in the second line has, besides its obvious symbolism, a doctrinal reference. A falcon is a hawk, and a hawk is symbolic of the active or intellectual mind; the falconer is perhaps the soul itself or its uniting principle. There is also the apposition which Yeats has made several times that "Wisdom is a butterfly/And not a gloomy bird of prey." Whether the special symbolism has actually been incorporated in the poem, and in which form, or whether it is private débris merely, will take a generation of readers to decide. In the meantime it must be taken provisionally for whatever its ambiguity may seem to be worth. Literature is full of falcons, some that fly and some that lack immediacy and sit, archaic, on the poet's wrist; and it is not always illuminating to determine which is which. But when we come on such lines as

> The best lack all conviction, while the worst
> Are full of passionate intensity,

we stop short, first to realize the aptness of the statement to every plane of life in the world about us, and then to connect them with the remote body of the poem they illuminate. There is a dilemma of which the branches grow from one trunk but which cannot be solved; for these lines have, not two meanings, but two sources for the same meaning. There is the meaning that comes from the summary observation that this is how men are —and especially men of power—in the world we live in; it is knowledge that comes from knowledge of the "fury and the mire in human veins"; a meaning the contemplation of which has lately (April, 1934) led Yeats to offer himself to any government or party that, using force and marching men, will "promise not this or that measure but a discipline, a way of life." And there is in effect the same meaning, at least at the time the poem was written, which comes from a different source and should have, one would think, very different consequences in prospective party loyalties. Here the meaning has its source in the doctrines of the Great Year and the Phases of the Moon; whereby, to cut exegesis short, it is predicted as necessary that, at the time we have reached, the best minds, being subjective, should have lost all faith though desiring it, and the worst minds, being so nearly objective, have no need of faith and may be full of "passionate intensity" without the control of any faith or wisdom. Thus we have on the one side the mirror of observation and on the other side an imperative, magically derived, which come to the conclusion of form in identical words.

The question is, to repeat, whether the fact of this double control and source of meaning at a critical point defeats or strengthens the unity of the poem; and it is a question which forms itself again and again in the later poems, sometimes obviously but more often only by suggestion. If we take another poem on the same theme, written some years earlier, and before his wife's mediumship gave him the detail of his philosophy, we will find the question no easier to answer in its suggested than in its conspicuous form. There is an element in the poem called "The Magi" which we can feel the weight of but cannot altogether name, and of which we can only guess at the efficacy.

> Now as at all times I can see in the mind's eye,
> In their stiff, painted clothes, the pale unsatisfied ones
> Appear and disappear in the blue depths of the sky
> With all their ancient faces like rain-beaten stones,
> And all their helms of silver hovering side by side,
> And all their eyes still fixed, hoping to find once more,
> Being by Calvary's turbulence unsatisfied,
> The uncontrollable mystery on the bestial floor.

I mean the element which, were Yeats a Christian, we could accept as a species of Christian blasphemy or advanced heresy, but which since he is not a Christian we find it hard to accept at all: the element of emotional conviction springing from intellectual matters without rational source or structure. We ought to be able, for the poem's sake, to accept the conviction as an emotional possibility, much as we accept *Lear* or Dostoieffsky's *Idiot* as valid, because projected from represented experience. But Yeats' experience is not represented consistently on any one plane. He constantly indicates a supernatural validity for his images of which the authority cannot be reached. If we come nearer to accepting "The Magi" than "The Second Coming" it is partly because the familiar Christian paradigm is more clearly used, and, in the last two lines what Yeats constructs upon it is given a more immediate emotional form, and partly because, *per contra*, there is less demand made upon arbitrary intellectual belief. There is, too, the matter of scope; if we reduce the scope of "The Second Coming" to that of "The Magi" we shall find it much easier to accept; but we shall have lost much of the poem.

We ought now to have enough material to name the two radical defects of magic as a tool for poetry. One defect, which we have just been illustrating, is that it has no available edifice of reason reared upon it conventionally independent of its inspiration. There is little that the uninspired reader can naturally refer to for authority outside the poem, and if he does make a natural reference he is likely to turn out to be at least partly wrong. The poet is thus in the opposite predicament; he is under the constant necessity of erecting his beliefs into doctrines at the same time that he represents their emotional or dramatic equivalents. He is, in fact, in much the same position that Dante would have been had he had to construct his Christian doctrine while he was composing *The Divine Comedy:* an impossible labor. The Christian supernaturalism, the Christian magic (no less magical than that of Yeats), had the great advantage for Dante, and imaginatively for ourselves, of centuries of reason and criticism and elaboration: It was within reason a consistent whole; and its supernatural element had grown so consistent with experience as to seem supremely *natural*—as indeed it may again. Christianity has an objective form, whatever the mysteries at its heart and its termini, in which all the phenomena of human life may find place and meaning. Magic is none of these things for any large fraction of contemporary society. Magic has a tradition, but it is secret, not public. It has not only central and terminal mysteries but has also peripheral mysteries, which require not only the priest to celebrate but also the adept to manipulate. Magic has never been made "natural." The practical knowledge and power which its beliefs lead to can neither be generally shared nor overtly rationalized. It is in fact held to be dangerous to reveal openly the details of magical experience: they may be revealed, if at all, only in arbitrary symbols and equivocal statements. Thus we find Yeats, in his early and innocuous essay on magic, believing his life to have been imperiled for revealing too much. Again, the spirits or voices through whom magical knowledge is gained are often themselves equivocal and are sometimes deliberately confusing. Yeats was told to remember, "We will deceive you if we can," and on another occasion was forbidden to record anything that was said, only to be scolded later because he had failed to record every word. In short, it is of the essence of magical faith that the supernatural cannot be brought into the natural world except through symbol. The distinction between natural and supernatural is held to be substantial instead of verbal. Hence magic may neither be criticized nor institutionalized; nor can it ever reach a full expression of its own intention. This is perhaps the justification of Stephen Spender's remark that there is more magic in Eliot's "The Hollow Men" than in any poem of Yeats; because of Eliot's Christianity, his magic has a rational base as well as a supernatural source: it is the magic of an orthodox, authoritative faith. The dogmas of magic, we may say, are all heresies which cannot be expounded except each on its own authority as a fragmentary insight; and its unity can be only the momentary unity of association. Put another way, magic is in one respect in the state of Byzantine Christianity, when miracles were quotidian and the universal frame of experience, when life itself was held to be supernatural and reason was mainly a kind of willful sophistication.

Neither Yeats nor ourselves dwell in Byzantium. At a certain level, though not at all levels, we conceive life, and even its nonrational features, in rational terms. Certainly there is a rational bias and a rational structure in the poetry we mainly agree to hold great—though the content may be what it will; and it is the irrational bias and the confused structure that we are mainly concerned to disavow, to apologize or allow for. It was just to provide himself with the equivalent of a rational religious insight and a predictable rational structure for the rational imagination that in his book, *A Vision* (published, in 1925, in a limited edition only, and then withdrawn), he attempted to convert his magical experience into a systematic philosophy. "I wished," he writes in the Dedication to that work, "for a system of thought that would leave my imagination free to create as it chose and yet make all that it created, or could create, part of the one history, and that the soul's." That is, Yeats hoped by systematizing it to escape from the burden of confusion and abstraction which his magical experience had imposed upon him. "I can now," he declares in this same Dedication, "if I have the energy, find the simplicity I have sought in vain. I need no longer write poems like 'The Phases of the Moon' nor 'Ego Dominus Tuus,' nor spend barren years, as I have done three or four times, striving with abstractions that substitute themselves for the play that I had planned."

"Having inherited," as he says in one of his poems, "a vigorous mind," he could not help seeing, once he had got it all down, that his system was something to disgorge if he could. Its truth as experience would be all the stronger if its abstractions could be expunged. But it could not be disgorged; its thirty-five years of growth was an intimate part of his own growth, and its abstractions were all of a piece with his most objective experience. And perhaps we, as readers, can see that better from outside than Yeats could from within. I suspect that no amount of will could have rid him of his magical conception of the soul; it was by magic that he knew the soul; and the conception had been too closely associated with his profound sense of his race and personal ancestry. He has never been able to retract his system, only to take up different attitudes towards it. He has alternated between granting his speculations only the validity of poetic myth and planning to announce a new deity. In his vacillation—there is a poem by that title—the rational defect remains, and the reader must deal with it sometimes as an intrusion upon the poetry of indeterminate value and sometimes as itself the subject of dramatic reverie or lyric statement. At least once he tried to force the issue home, and in a section of *A Packet for Ezra Pound* called "Introduction to the Great Wheel" he meets the issue by transforming it, for the moment, into wholly poetic terms. Because it reveals a fundamental honesty and clarity of purpose in the midst of confusion and uncertainty the section is quoted entire.

Some will ask if I believe all that this book contains, and I will not know how to answer. Does the word belief, as they will use it, belong to our age, can I think of the world as there and I here judging it? I will never think any thoughts but these, or some modification or extension of these; when I write prose or verse they must be somewhere present though it may not be in the words; they must affect my judgment of friends and events; but then there are many symbolisms and none exactly resembles mine. What Leopardi in Ezra Pound's translation calls that 'concord' wherein 'the arcane spirit of the whole mankind turns hardy pilot'— how much better it would be without that word 'hardy' which slackens speed and adds nothing—persuades me that he has best imagined reality who has best imagined justice.

The rational defect, then, remains; the thought is not always in the words; and we must do with it as we can. There is another defect of Yeats' magical system which is especially apparent to the reader but which may not be apparent at all to Yeats. Magic promises precisely matters which it cannot perform—at least in poetry. It promises, as in "The Second Coming," exact prediction

of events in the natural world; and it promises again and
again, in different poems, exact revelations of the supernatural, and of this we have an example in what has to
many seemed a great poem, "All Souls' Night," which
had its first publication as an epilogue to *A Vision*. Near
the beginning of the poem we have the explicit declaration: "I have a marvelous thing to say"; and near the
end another: "I have mummy truths to tell." "Mummy
truths" is an admirable phrase, suggestive as it is of the
truths in which the dead are wrapped, ancient truths as
old as Egypt perhaps, whence mummies commonly
come, and truths, too, that may be unwound. But there,
with the suggestion, the truths stop short; there is, for
the reader, no unwinding, no revelation of the dead.
What Yeats actually does is to summon into the poem
various of his dead friends as "characters"—and this is the
greatness, and only this, of the poem: the summary,
excited, even exalted presentation of character. Perhaps
the rhetoric is the marvel and the evasion the truth. We
get an impact as from behind, from the speed and weight
of the words, and are left with an ominous or terrified
frame of mind, the revelation still to come. The revelation, the magic, was in Yeats' mind; hence the exaltation
in his language; but it was not and could not be given
in the words of the poem.

It may be that for Yeats there was a similar exaltation
and a similar self-deceit in certain other poems, but as
the promise of revelation was not made, the reader feels
no failure of fulfillment. Such poems as "Easter, 1916,"
"In Memory of Major Robert Gregory," and "Upon a
Dying Lady" may have buried in them a conviction of
invocation and revelation; but if so it is no concern of
ours: we are concerned only, as the case may be, with

the dramatic presentations of the Irish patriots and poets, Yeats' personal friends, and Aubrey Beardsley's dying sister, and with, in additon, for minor pleasure, the technical means—the spare and delicate language, the lucid images, and quickening rhymes—whereby the characters are presented as intensely felt. There is no problem in such poems but the problem of reaching, through a gradual access of intimacy, full appreciation; here the magic and everything else are in the words. It is the same, for bare emotion apart from character, in such poems as "A Deep-Sworn Vow," where the words accumulate by the simplest means an intolerable excitement, where the words are, called as they may be from whatever source, in an ultimate sense their own meaning.

> Others because you did not keep
> That deep-sworn vow have been friends of mine;
> Yet always when I look death in the face,
> When I clamber to the heights of sleep,
> Or when I grow excited with wine,
> Suddenly I meet your face.

Possibly all poetry should be read as this poem is read, and no poetry greatly valued that cannot be so read. Such is one ideal towards which reading tends; but to apply it as a standard of judgment we should first have to assume for the poetic intelligence absolute autonomy and self-perfection for all its works. Actually, autonomy and self-perfection are relative and depend upon a series of agreements or conventions between the poet and his readers, which alter continually, as to what must be represented by the fundamental power of language (itself a relatively stable convention) and what, on the other hand, may be adequately represented by mere reference, sign, symbol, or blue print indication. Poetry is so little autonomous from the technical point of view that the greater part of a given work must be conceived as the manipulation of conventions that the reader will, or will not, take for granted; these being crowned, or animated, emotionally transformed, by what the poet actually represents, original or not, through his mastery of poetic language. Success is provisional, seldom complete, and never permanently complete. The vitality or letter of a convention may perish although the form persists. *Romeo and Juliet* is less successful today than when produced because the conventions of honor, family authority, and blood-feud no longer animate and justify the action; and if the play survives it is partly because certain other conventions of human character do remain vital, but more because Shakespeare is the supreme master of representation through the reality of language alone. Similarly with Dante; with the cumulative disintegration, even for Catholics, of medieval Christianity as the ultimate convention of human life, the success of *The Divine Comedy* comes more and more to depend on the exhibition of character and the virtue of language alone—which may make it a greater, not a lesser poem. On the other hand, it often happens that a poet's ambition is such that, in order to get his work done at all, he must needs set up new conventions or radically modify old ones which fatally lack that benefit of form which can be conferred only by public recognition. The form which made his poems available was only gradually conferred upon the convention of evil in Baudelaire and, as we may see in translations with contrasting emphases, its limits are still subject to debate; in his case the more so because the life of his language depended more than usual on the viability of the convention.

Let us apply these notions, which ought so far to be commonplace, to the later work of Yeats, relating them especially to the predominant magical convention therein. When Yeats came of poetic age he found himself, as Blake had before him, and even Wadsworth, but to a worse extent, in a society whose conventions extended neither intellectual nor moral authority to poetry; he found himself in a rational but deliberately incomplete, because progressive, society. The *emotion* of thought, for poetry, was gone, along with the emotion of religion and the emotion of race—the three sources and the three aims of the great poetry of the past. Tyndall and Huxley are the villains, Yeats records in his Autobiographies, as Blake recorded Newton; there were other causes, but no matter, these names may serve as symbols. And the dominant aesthetics of the time were as rootless in the realm of poetic import and authority as the dominant conventions. Art for Art's sake was the cry, the Ivory Tower the retreat, and Walter Pater's luminous languor and weak Platonism the exposition. One could say anything but it would mean nothing. The poets and society both, for opposite reasons, expected the poet to produce either exotic and ornamental mysteries or lyrics of mood; the real world and its significance were reserved mainly to the newer sciences, though the novelists and the playwrights might poach if they could. For a time Yeats succumbed, as may be seen in his early work, even while he attempted to escape; and of his poetic generation he was the only one to survive and grow in stature. He came under the influence of the French Symbolists, who gave him the clue and the hint of an external structure but nothing much to put in it. He read, with a dictionary, Villiers de L'Isle-Adam's

Axel's Castle, and so came to be included in Edmund Wilson's book of that name—although not, as Wilson himself shows, altogether correctly. For he began in the late 'nineties, as it were upon his own account, to quench his thirst for reality by creating authority and significance and reference in the three fields where they were lacking. He worked into his poetry the substance of Irish mythology and Irish politics and gave them a symbolism, and he developed his experiences with Theosophy and Rosicrucianism into a body of conventions adequate, for him, to animate the concrete poetry of the soul that he wished to write. He did not do these things separately; the mythology, the politics, and the magic are conceived, through the personalites that reflected them, with an increasing unity of apprehension. Thus more than any poet of our time he has restored to poetry the actual emotions of race and religion and what we call abstract thought. Whether we follow him in any particular or not, the general poetic energy which he liberated is ours to use if we can. If the edifice that he constructed seems personal, it is because he had largely to build it for himself, and that makes it difficult to understand in detail except in reference to the peculiar unity which comes from their mere association in his life and work. Some of the mythology and much of the politics, being dramatized and turned into emotion, are part of our common possessions. But where the emphasis has been magical, whether successfully or not, the poems have been misunderstood, ignored, and the actual emotion in them which is relevant to us all decried and underestimated, merely because the magical mode of thinking is foreign to our own and when known at all is largely associated with quackery and fraud.

We do not make that mistake—which is the mistake of unwillingness—with Dante or the later Eliot, because, although the substance of their modes of thinking is equally foreign and magical, it has the advantage of a rational superstructure that persists and which we can convert to our own modes if we will. Yeats lacks, as we have said, the historical advantage and with it much else; and the conclusion cannot be avoided that this lack prevents his poetry from reaching the first magnitude. But there are two remedies we may apply, which will make up, not for the defect of magnitude, but for the defect of structure. We can read the magical philosophy in his verse *as if* it were converted into the contemporary psychology with which its doctrines have so much in common. We find little difficulty in seeing Freud's preconscious as a fertile myth and none at all in the general myth of extroverted and introverted personality; and these may be compared with, respectively, Yeats' myth of *Spiritus Mundi* and the Phases of the Moon: the intention and the scope of the meaning are identical. So much for a secular conversion. The other readily available remedy is this: to accept Yeats' magic literally as a machinery of meaning, to search out the prose parallels and reconstruct the symbols he uses on their own terms in order to come on the emotional reality, if it is there, actually in the poems—when the machinery may be dispensed with. This method has the prime advantage over secular conversion of keeping judgment in poetic terms, with the corresponding disadvantage that it requires more time and patience, more "willing suspension of disbelief," and a stiffer intellectual exercise all around. But exegesis is to be preferred to conversion on still another ground, which may seem repellent: that magic, in the sense that we all experience it, is nearer the represented emotions that concern us in poetry than psychology, as a generalized science, can ever be. We are all, without conscience, magicians in the dark.

But even the poems of darkness are read in the light. I cannot, of course, make a sure prognosis; because in applying either remedy the reader is, really, doctoring himself as much as Yeats. Only this much is sure: that the reader will come to see the substantial unity of Yeats' work, that it is the same mind stirring behind the poems on Crazy Jane and the Bishop, on Cuchulain, on Swift, the political poems, the biographical and the doctrinal—a mind that sees the fury and the mire and the passion of the dawn as contrary aspects of the real world. It is to be expected that many poems will fail in part and some entirely, and if the chief, magic will not be the only cause of failure. The source of a vision puts limits upon its expression which the poet cannot well help over-passing. "The limitation of his view," Yeats wrote of Blake, "was from the very intensity of his vision; he was a too-literal realist of imagination, as others are of nature"; and the remark applies to himself. But there will be enough left to make the labor of culling worth all its patience and time. Before concluding, I propose to spur the reader, or inadvertently dismay him, by presenting briefly a few examples of the sort of reconstructive labor he will have to do and the sort of imaginative assent he may have to attempt in order to enter or dismiss the body of the poems.

As this is a mere essay in emphasis, let us bear the emphasis in, by repeating, on different poems, the sort of commentary laid out above on "The Second Coming" and "The Magi," using this time "Byzantium" and "Sailing to Byzantium." Byzantium is for Yeats, so to speak, the heaven of the man's mind; there the mind or soul dwells in eternal or miraculous form; there all things are possible because all things are known to the soul. Byzantium has both a historical and an ideal form, and the historical is the exemplar, the dramatic witness, of the ideal. Byzantium represents both a dated epoch and a recurrent state of insight, when nature is magical, that is, at the beck of mind, and magic is natural—a practical rather than a theoretic art. If with these notions in mind we compare the two poems named we see that the first, called simply "Byzantium," is like certain cantos in the *Paradiso* the poetry of an intense and condensed declaration of doctrine; not emotion put into doctrine from outside, but doctrine presented as emotion. I quote the second stanza.

> Before me floats an image, man or shade,
> Shade more than man, more image than a shade;
> For Hades' bobbin bound in mummy-cloth
> May unwind the winding path;
> A mouth that has no moisture and no breath
> Breathless mouths may summon;
> I hail the superhuman;
> I call it death-in-life and life-in-death.

The second poem, "Sailing to Byzantium," rests upon the doctrine but is not a declaration of it. It is, rather, the doctrine in action, the doctrine actualized in a personal emotion resembling that of specific prayer. This is the emotion of the flesh where the other was the emotion of the bones. The distinction should not be too sharply drawn. It is not the bones of doctrine but the emotion of it that we should be aware of in reading the more dramatic poem: and the nearer they come to seeming two reflections of the same thing the better both poems will be. What must be avoided is a return to the poem of doctrine with a wrong estimation of its value gained by confusion of the two poems. Both poems are serious in their own kind, and the reality of each must be finally in its own words whatever clues the one supplies to the other. I quote the third stanza.

> O sages standing in God's holy fire
> As in the gold mosaic of a wall,
> Come from the holy fire, perne in a gyre,
> And be the singing-masters of my soul.
> Consume my heart away; sick with desire
> And fastened to a dying animal
> It knows not what it is; and gather me
> Into the artifice of eternity.

We must not, for example, accept "perne in a gyre" in this poem merely because it is part of the doctrine upon which the poem rests. Its magical reference may be too explicit for the poem to digest. It may be merely part of the poem's intellectual machinery, something that will *become* a dead commonplace once its peculiarity has worn out. Its meaning, that is, may turn out not to participate in the emotion of the poem: which is an emotion of aspiration. Similarly a note of aspiration would have been injurious to the stanza quoted from "Byzantium" above.

Looking at other poems as examples, the whole problem of exegesis may be put another way; which consists in joining two facts and observing their product. There is the fact that again and again in Yeats' prose, both in that which accompanies the poems and that which is independent of them, poems and fragments of poems are introduced at strategic points, now to finish off or clinch an argument by giving it as proved, and again merely to balance argument with witness from another plane. *A Vision* is punctuated by five poems. And there is the complementary fact that, when one has read the various autobiographies, introductions, and doctrinal notes and essays, one continually finds echoes, phrases, and developments from the prose in the poems. We have, as Wallace Stevens says, the prose that wears the poem's guise at last; and we have, too, the poems turning backwards, reilluminating or justifying the prose from the material of which they sprang. We have, to import the dichotomy which T. S. Eliot made for his own work, the prose writings discovering and buttressing the ideal, and we have the poems which express as much as can be actualized—given as concrete emotion—of what the prose discovered or envisaged. The dichotomy is not so sharp in Yeats as in Eliot. Yeats cannot, such is the unity of his apprehension, divide his interests. There is one mind employing two approaches in the labor of representation. The prose approach lets in much that the poetic approach excludes; it lets in the questionable, the uncertain, the hypothetic, and sometimes the incredible. The poetic approach, using the same material, retains, when it is successful, only what is manifest, the emotion that can be made actual in a form of words that need only to be understood, not argued. If props of argument and vestiges of idealization remain, they must be felt as qualifying, not arguing, the emotion. It should only be remembered and repeated that the poet invariably requires more machinery to secure *his* effects—the machinery of his whole life and thought—than the reader requires to secure what he takes as the *poem's* effects; and that, as readers differ, the poet cannot calculate what is necessary to the poem and what is not. There is always the débris to be cut away.

In such a fine poem as "A Prayer for My Son," for example, Yeats cut away most of the débris himself, and it is perhaps an injury to judgment provisionally to restore it. Yet to this reader at least the poem seems to richen when it is known from what special circumstance the poem was freed. As it stands we can accept the symbols which it conspicuously contains—the strong ghost, the devilish things, and the holy writings—as drawn from the general stock of literary conventions available to express the evil predicament in which children and all innocent beings obviously find themselves. Taken so, it is a poem of natural piety. But for Yeats the conventions were not merely literary but were practical expressions of the actual terms of the predicament, and his poem is a prayer of dread and supernatural piety. The experience which led to the poem is recounted in *A Packet for Ezra Pound.* When his son was still an infant Yeats was told through the mediumship of his wife that the Frustrators or evil spirits would henceforth "attack my health and that of my children, and one afternoon, knowing from the smell of burnt feathers that one of my children would be ill within three hours, I felt before I could recover self-control the mediaeval helpless horror of witchcraft." The child *was* ill. It is from this experience that the poem seems to have sprung, and the poem preserves all that was actual behind the private magical conventions Yeats used for himself. The point is that the reader has a richer poem if he can substitute the manipulative force of Yeats' specific conventions for the general literary conventions.

Belief or imaginative assent is no more difficult for either set. It is the emotion that counts.

That is one extreme to which the poems run—the extreme convention of personal thought. Another extreme is that exemplified in "A Prayer for My Daughter," where the animating conventions *are* literary and the piety *is* natural, and in the consideration of which it would be misleading to introduce the magical convention as more than a foil. As a foil it is nevertheless present; his magical philosophy, all the struggle and warfare of the intellect, is precisely what Yeats in this poem *puts out of mind*, in order to imagine his daughter living in innocence and beauty, custom and ceremony.

A third extreme is that found in the sonnet "Leda and the Swan," where there is an extraordinary sensual immediacy—the words meet and move like speaking lips—and a profound combination of the generally available or literary symbol and the hidden, magical symbol of the intellectual, philosophical, impersonal order. Certain longer poems and groups of poems, especially the series called "A Woman Young and Old," exhibit the extreme of combination as well or better; but I want the text on the page.

> A sudden blow: the great wings beating still
> Above the staggering girl, her thighs caressed
> By the dark webs, her nape caught in his bill,
> He holds her helpless breast upon his breast.
>
> How can those terrified vague fingers push
> The feathered glory from her loosening thighs?
> And how can body, laid in that white rush,
> But feel the strange heart beating where it lies?

W. B. YEATS

A shudder in the loins engenders there
The broken wall, the burning roof and tower
And Agamemnon dead.
                              Being so caught up,
So mastered by the brute blood of the air,
Did she put on his knowledge with his power
Before the indifferent beak could let her drop?

It should be observed that in recent years new images, some from the life of Swift, and some from the Greek mythology, have been spreading through Yeats' poems; and of Greek images he has used especially those of Œdipus and Leda, of Homer and Sophocles. But they are not used as we think the Greeks used them, nor as mere drama, but deliberately, after the magical tradition, both to represent and hide the myths Yeats has come on in his own mind. Thus "Leda and the Swan" can be read on at least three distinct levels of significance, none of which interferes with the others: the levels of dramatic fiction, of condensed insight into Greek mythology, and a third level of fiction and insight combined, as we said, to represent and hide a magical insight. This third level is our present concern. At this level the poem presents an interfusion among the normal terms of the poem two of Yeats' fundamental magical doctrines in emotional form. The doctrines are put by Yeats in the following form in his essay on magic: "That the borders of our mind are ever shifting, and that many minds can flow into one another, as it were, and create or reveal a single mind, a single energy. . . . That this great mind can be evoked by symbols." Copulation is the obvious nexus for spiritual as well as physical seed. There is also present I think some sense of Yeats' doctrine of Annunciation and the Great Year, the Annunciation, in this case, that produced Greek culture. It is a neat question for the reader, so far as this poem is concerned, whether the poetic emotion springs from the doctrine and seizes the myth for a safe home and hiding, or whether the doctrine is correlative to the emotion of the myth. In neither case does the magic matter as such; it has become poetry, and of extreme excellence in its order. To repeat the interrogatory formula with which we began the commentary on "The Second Coming," is the magical material in these poems incorporated in them by something like organic reference or is its presence merely rhetorical? The reader will answer one way or the other, as, to his rational imagination, to all the imaginative understanding he can bring to bear, it either seems to clutter the emotion and deaden the reality, or seems rather, as I believe, to heighten the emotional reality and thereby extend its reference to what we call the real world. Once the decison is made, the magic no longer exists; we have the poetry.

Other approaches to Yeats' poetry would have produced different emphases, and this approach, which has emphasized little but the magical structure of Yeats' poetic emotions, and has made that emphasis with an ulterior purpose: to show that magic may be a feature of a rational imagination. This approach should be combined with others, or should have others combined with it, for perspective and reduction. No feature of a body of poetry can be as important as it seems in discussion. Above all, then, this approach through the magical emphasis should be combined with the approach of plain reading—which is long reading and hard reading—plain reading of the words, that they may sink in and do as much of their own work as they can. One more thing:

When we call man a rational animal we mean that reason is his great myth. Reason is plastic and takes to any form provided. The rational imagination in poetry, as elsewhere, can absorb magic as a provisional method of evocative and heuristic thinking, but it cannot be based upon it. In poetry, and largely elsewhere, imagination is based upon the reality of words and the emotion of their joining. Yeats' magic, then, like every other feature of his experience, is rational as it reaches words; otherwise it is his privation, and ours, because it was the rational defect of our society that drove him to it.

Emily Dickinson

Notes on Prejudice and Fact

THE disarray of Emily Dickinson's poems is the great obvious fact about them as they multiply from volume to volume—I will not say from edition to edition, for they have never been edited—just as a kind of repetitious fragmentariness is the characterizing fact of her sensibility. No poet of anything like her accomplishment has ever imposed on the reader such varied and continuous critical labor; and on few poets beyond the first bloat of reputation has so little work been done. Few poets have benefited generally, and suffered specifically, from such a handsome or fulsome set of prejudices, which, as they are expressed, seem to remove the need for any actual reading at all.

The barriers to critical labor are well known, and some of them are insuperable. No text will be certain so long as the vaults at Amherst remain closed. Without benefit of comparative scholarship it is impossible to determine whether a given item is a finished poem, an early version of a poem, a note for a poem, a part of a poem, or a prose exclamation. Worse, it is impossible to know whether what appear to be crotchets in the poems as printed are correctly copied. The poet's handwriting was obscure, loose, and run-over; hence it is plain that unskilled copyists cannot be relied on in matters of punctuation, line structure, and the terminal letters of words. It is plainer still, if suspicion be in case, that many examples of merely irritating bad grammar—mistakes that merely hinder the reader—may well represent systematic bad guessing by the copyist. Perhaps it is not plain, but it is plausible, to imagine that a full and open view of the manuscripts would show the poet far less fragmentary and repetitious than the published work makes her seem. Most poets have a desk full of beginnings, a barrel of fragments and anything up to an attic full of notes. The manner of notation, if it were known, might make a beginning at the establishment of a canon. With the obvious fragments cut out, or put in an appendix, a clean, self-characterizing, responsive, and responding body of poetry, with limits and a fate and a quaking sensibility, might then be made to show itself.

Then is not now. This essay cannot enact a prophecy. This disarray of fragments, this mob of verses, this din of many motions, cannot be made to show itself in its own best order—as the strong parade we hoped it really was. This essay proposes, in lieu of adumbrating a complete criticism, first to examine a set of prejudices which are available as approaches to Emily Dickinson, and then to count—and perhaps account for—a few staring facts: obvious, animating, defacing facts about the verses as they now appear. If the essay has a good eye for the constitution of poetic facts, the affair of counting will be adventurous, a part of the great adventure of sensibility which consists, one sometimes thinks, in an arduous fealty to facts. If the fealty is sound, perhaps the vestiges of a complete criticism will be there too, or at least a bias, a prejudice, in that direction.

For it takes a strong and active prejudice to see facts at all, as any revolutionist will tell you. And just as the body must have a strong prejudice, which is its wisdom, about the nature of time in order to wake up exactly *before* the alarm goes off—an affair of counting, if ever —so the sensibility must have a pretty firm anterior conviction about the nature of poetry in order to wake up to a given body of poetry at all. We suddenly realize that we have, or have *not*—which in a very neat way comes to the same thing—counted some of these facts before. We know where we are in terms of where we thought we were, at home, lost, or shaking: which is when the alarm goes off. To depend on prejudice for the nature of time or poetry may seem a little willful and adventitiously mysterious. But it is a method that allows for mistakes, and in the present condition of Emily Dickinson's poetry, it is imperative to allow for continuous error, both in the facts and in their counting—in the prejudices by which we get at them.

Most prejudices are frivolous to the real interests concerned, which is why they are so often made to appear as facts instead of mere keys to facts. That Emily Dickinson is a great poet, "with the possible exception of Sappho, the greatest woman poet of all time," or the author of poetry "perhaps the finest by a woman in the English language," or that in one of the volumes of her verse "there are no dregs, no single drop can be spared," —these are variations upon an essentially frivolous prejudice. Only the last variation is dangerous, because by asserting perfection it makes the poet an idol and removes her from the possibility of experience. On the whole, statements of this order are seldom taken seriously, but are felt as polite salutations and farewells. The trouble is that it is hard to persuade oneself to read work towards which one has accomplished gestures so polite. If not a drop can be spared, let us not risk spilling any; let us say, rather, here is great poetry—we know what *that* is like! A chalice, a lily, a sea-change. Old memories are mulled. We have the equivalent of emotion. And equivalents, like substitutes, though not so good as what you asked for, are often, for sensibilities never exercised enough to have been starved, a full meal.

It would be unfair, though, to leave the prejudice of Emily Dickinson's magnitude so naked. Politeness may conceal a legitimate wish that dare not put itself in bald speech. I am convinced that Conrad Aiken, in referring to Emily Dickinson's poetry as "perhaps the finest by a woman in the English language," had the legitimate wish to condition the reader with a very good fundamental prejudice—which we shall come to—about Emily Dickinson to the effect that there was something exciting or vital or amusing in her work. It is a kind of flag-waving; it reminds you of what you ought to be able to feel. Most readers of poetry are flag-wavers, and in order to get them to be more, you have to begin by waving a flag. I cannot imagine Mr. Aiken, or any other reader, addressing a Dickinson poem as "perhaps the finest by a woman in the English language." That is only how he addresses other people, hoping that they will thus be prejudiced into responding to the poem as he actually does, in terms of the words and the motions of the words which make it up: which are the terms (not the thing itself) of magnitude. I too would like to begin and end with the idea that in some such sense Emily Dickinson is sometimes a great poet.

There is a more dangerous but no less frivolous type of prejudice in the following sentence. "Her revolt was absolute; she abandoned rhyme altogether when she chose, and even assonance, writing in meter alone, like a Greek." There is a Spanish proverb that if God does not bless you with children, the devil will send you nieces. As a literary critic, if not as a niece, Mme. Bianchi, who is responsible for the sentence quoted, is thoroughly diabolic; as idolaters are by rule. The idea is to make you feel that the slips and roughnesses, the truncated lines, false rhymes, the inconsistencies of every description which mar the majority of Emily Dickinson's poems are examples of a revolutionary master-craftsman. Only the idol is served here; no greater disservice could be done to the poetry the reader reads than to believe with however great sincerity that its blemishes have any closer relation than contrast to its beauty. Emily Dickinson never knew anything about the craft of verse well enough to exemplify it, let alone revolt from it. If, where you are autonomous as in the *practice* of verse, you revolt first, you only revolve in a vacuum; and you will end as Emily Dickinson did in many of her failures by producing chaotic verses which have no bearing on the proper chaos of their subject—the life where precisely, as Emily Dickinson well enough knew, you are not autonomous but utterly dependent and interlocked.

As for Mme. Bianchi's specific terms: if the ear and arithmetic of this essay are right, Emily Dickinson did not abandon rhyme so much as she failed to get that far —her lines strike *as if* they intended to end in rhyme; and her assonances seem frequently incomplete substitutes, for rhyme and not assonances at all. She did not write in meter alone; her meters were most often exiguous or overrun proximations of common English meter —or again they met the pattern of meter in syllabification miter-perfect without meeting the enlivening movement of meter. And as for writing like a Greek it would be more nearly correct, metrically, to say that she wrote like an Italian with recurring pairs of stressed syllables. I do not refer here to the successful meters in Emily Dickinson, but only to the variously deficient meters.

But Mme. Bianchi is not half so dangerous in idealizing her aunt's technical inadequacy as absolute, as Ludwig Lewisohn is in magnifying her intellectual and mystical force—a composition of magnitudes not commonly come by outside Dante. "She can be," says Mr. Lewisohn, "of a compactness of expression and fullness of meaning not less than Goethean in Goethe's epigrammatic mood . . . She can soar like the intense mystical poets of the seventeenth century." This is the method of instilling prejudice by means of the unexpanded comparison. We are assumed to have the American poet in front of us and to know what she is; then our knowledge of her is heightened by a comparison with Goethe's epigrams, which are probably not in front of us except by reputation. As we think, we suddenly realize that the cognate qualities in Emily Dickinson are not with us either. They are precisely as far off as Goethe. Mr. Lewisohn has compared abstracted qualities for a concrete effect: the effect, I take it, of vivid moral insight; but he has not *made* the comparison. He has not shown us what it is in either poet that he is talking about. If he expanded and did show us, he might prove right; I do not at the moment say he is wrong—although I suspect an intolerable identification: the target of insight for the two poets could hardly have been the same. What I want to emphasize is merely this: Mr. Lewisohn is actually only saying that Emily Dickinson's poetry possesses moral insight. What he pretends to do is to put her insight on the level of the supreme type of moral insight —by mentioning Goethe's name. He would have done better to distinguish the *difference* between the achieved qualities in the epigrams of the two poets—the difference between insight as wisdom, say, and insight as vision.

Mr. Lewisohn's other comparison, with the intense mystical poets of the seventeenth century, is equally unexpanded and equally misleading. He does not say which poets nor in what respects; and what we actually get out of his comparison is the idea that Emily Dickinson was intensely mystical in an exciting and inexpensive way. The spread of such a prejudice may multiply readers, but it fosters bad reading. Poetic mysticism, as the term is loosely used, is a kind of virus that gets about through the medium of the printed page, and its chief effect is to provide a matchless substitute for the discipline of attention in incapable minds. By making ultimate apprehension of God—or matter—free in words, it relieves the poet of the necessity to make his words first apprehend the *manifestation*—what is actually felt—in this world; and it relieves the reader of the obligation to apprehend anything at all when everything may always be apprehended at once. To exercise this sort of prejudice on a really interesting poet is to carry politeness too far—and far beyond, as it happens, Emily Dickinson's poems' own idea of their operative reach and willed intention. I quote, as facts worth counting in this connection, the following lines and phrases: they illuminate Mr. Lewisohn's prejudice by reducing it to the actual scope of the poems.

> The missing All prevented me
> From missing minor things . . .

Almost we wish the end
Were further off—too great it seems
So near the Whole to stand . . .

Was the Pine at my window a "Fellow"
Of the Royal Infinity?
Apprehensions are God's introductions
Extended inscrutably.

These lines are, I think, characteristic of the general "mystical" attitude in the poems. It is not mysticism itself. It is an attitude composed partly of the English Hymnal, partly of instinctive protestant transcendentalism, partly of instinctively apprehended Puritan theology, and partly of human sensibility bred with experience to the point of insight. There is besides an element of composition at work, which is the most important of all the distinguishable elements, and which makes the lines quoted, at least in their contexts, into poetry.

Admittedly this language is as loose as Mr. Lewisohn's, and as open to reduction; but I, too, am dealing with initial prejudice. My prejudice is that Emily Dickinson is a mid-nineteenth century New England Christian poet. Christianity moved her, and experience moved through her poems upon the machinery of Christianity, which is a machinery for the worship of God in all his works, and, among other things, for the redemption, which is to say the completion, of the soul. Christianity in action, especially in poetry, often looks to the outsider like an exercise in mysticism; and that is perhaps the mistake Mr. Lewisohn makes—just as so many have made a similar mistake about Gerard Manley Hopkins, or, for that matter, about Herbert and Vaughan. All these poets approached the mystery of God which is unity, but they approached it in human terms; they did what every Christian must; but they never seized or lost themselves in the unity of God as St. Francis and St. Theresa seemed to do—or as the great cathedrals and the great Church music, to the lay imagination, indubitably did. Put another way, there is nothing in the poems of Hopkins or Emily Dickinson which passes the willing understanding; if their poems sometimes confront the supersensible—and they mostly do not—it is always on the plane of the rational imagination, never in the incomprehensible terms of the mystical act. The mystery is there, but like the mystery of physical death the relation of the poetry to it is heuristic—an affair of discovery of which the very excitement, promise, and terror are that it never takes place, yet may, indeed momently, must.

Those who persist in calling this relationship mystical underestimate the scope of rational imagination working in language and in the face of mystery. That scope is exhausted only in the instance; the mystery is never exhausted merely by being expressed; and the mystery, as a fact, is always the same. When Shakespeare, who never troubled directly about God, mastered the emotion of jealousy in *Othello*, he was precisely as rational or precisely as "mystical" in his approach to mystery— and the same mystery, the mystery of the actual—as Emily Dickinson was in her deliberate approach to God in terms of nature and death. What differs is the machinery, or sometimes the formula, of approach.

Here we come on a different type of prejudice, in its own way as general and as beyond the point if taken too solemnly as those we have been discussing, but with an air of specificity about it which is disarming. This is the prejudice about the poet in relation to his time, where the poet is taken as a fatal event in cultural history. The time produced the poet, we say, and the poet crowned the time—crowned it with its own meaning. If we go far enough on this line, the time, or the age, tends to disappear in the meaning—as for many of us early Greece disappears in Homer; which is only a way of bringing the time up to date, of telescoping all the coördinates rashly into the one image of meaning. Mr. Allen Tate has in an admirable essay (in his *Reactionary Essays*) performed this labor upon Emily Dickinson, with the further labor that when he has got his image all made he proceeds to sort out its component parts. It is hard to separate what Mr. Tate found in Emily Dickinson as traces or inklings from what he brought with him on his own account; which is all in his favor if you like what he says, as I do, and if the combination illuminates and enlivens Emily Dickinson, as I believe it does. Mr. Tate as a critic has the kind of rightness that goes with insight, and not at all the kind of wrongness that goes with sincerity—which is perhaps how we should characterize Mr. Lewisohn.

At any rate, Mr. Tate builds up a pretty good historical prejudice and makes it available in the guise of insight. Emily Dickinson came, he says, exactly at the dying crisis of Puritan New England culture—not at the moment of death, but at the moment—it was years long —when the matrix began to be felt as broken. Spiritual meaning and psychic stability were no longer the unconscious look and deep gesture worn and rehearsed lifelong; they required the agony of doubt and the trial of deliberate expression in specifically, wilfully objective form. Faith was sophisticated, freed, and terrified—but still lived; imagination had suddenly to do all the work of embodying faith formerly done by habit, and to embody it with the old machinery so far as it could be used. There was no other machinery available. Thus the burden of poetry was put upon the New England version of the Christian sensibility.

It is arguable that Greek tragedy came at the analogous moment in Athenian history, when the gods were seen as imaginative instead of magical myths. The advantage for the poet is in both instances double and pays in poetry for the burden. There is the advantage of the existing machinery of meaning in the specific culture, which is still able to carry any weight and which is universally understood; and there is the advantage of a new and personal plasticity in the meanings themselves. Faith, in the agonized hands of the individual, becomes an imaginative experiment of which all the elements are open to new and even blasphemous combinations, and which is subject to the addition of new insights. It is no longer enough to repeat prayers and to rehearse Mass or its protestant equivalent; indeed the institutional part of culture is the first to show itself as dead; faith becomes to the secularized imagination of Emily Dickinson "the Experiment of our Lord!"—which it could never have seemed, on the same foundation, half a century earlier. The great advantage for a poet to come at a time of disintegrating culture is, then, to sum up, just this: the actuality of what we are and what we believe is suddenly seen to be nearly meaningless as habit, and must, to be adequately known, be translated to the terms and modes of the imagination. Nothing can be taken for granted but the machinery, which is there, all available, and which indeed cannot help being taken for granted. These are the conditions of belief—though not the only conditions—which may produce great poetry: the conditions of spiritual necessity and mechanical freedom. It is worth adding, for proportion, that the opposite conditions—spiritual freedom (a unity of belief and discipline) and mechanical necessity—produced such a great poet as Dante; and, again, it is quite possible that Shakespeare may have been produced at the nexus of quite a different set of conditions which had more to do with the state of language than with the state of belief. Here we are concerned with the occurrence of Emily Dickinson at the precise time when it became plain that Puritan Christianity was no longer the vital force in New England culture and before any other force had recognizably relieved the slack. If we are inclined to see a causal connection it is only as a more vivid and dramatic way of seeing the association it may really and only have been.

Now I do not want to let it appear that Mr. Tate would assent to my treatment of his idea; he has his own treatment, which is certainly not so highfalutin as mine; and besides, I am not sure how far I can assent to my own remarks without a feeling that I am merely succumbing to the temptation of a bright idea, which like the idea of chance explains less and less the more you look into it. Let us take the idea provisionally, and more provisionally for me than for Mr. Tate. So taken, it indicates a source, and with the source a tragic strength, for the fund and flow of Emily Dickinson's meaning. As the Massachusetts theocracy failed, became, say, more humane and individualized, its profoundly dramatic nature—all that it had left—became sharper and plainer, until in the imagination of Hawthorne and Melville and Emily Dickinson it took in, or implied, pretty near the whole of human experience. Then it died. It fed the imagination; then it died; and at the same time that particular form of the New England imagination reached its small surfeit and died too.

In the last sentence lies buried, but not in the least dead, the fundamental prejudice we have been looking for all the time: the prejudice contained in the idea of imagination being fed and dying, or for that matter living or doing anything whatever—that is to say, a prejudice about the nature of poetry itself as the chief mode of imagination. Poetry is composed of words and whenever we put anything into poetry—such as meaning or music; whenever poetry is affected by anything —such as the pattern of a culture or the structure of a stanza; whenever anything at all happens in poetry it happens in the medium of words. It is also near enough the truth to say that whenever we take anything out of poetry, either to use it or to see just what it is, we have to take it out in the words—and then put it right back before it gets lost or useless. The greatness of Emily Dickinson is not—to review our select list of prejudices —going to be found in anybody's idea of greatness, or of Goethe, or intensity, or mysticism, or historical fatality. It is going to be found in the words she used and in the way she put them together; which we will observe, if we bother to discriminate our observations, as a series of facts about words. What is behind the words or beyond them, we cannot know as facts, as any discussion amply demonstrates. Our knowledge of implication and inkling, quite as much as our knowledge of bald sound and singing sense, will be governed solely by what we can recognize, and perhaps by a good deal that we cannot recognize, of the poetic relations of the words—that is to say, by what they make of each other. This rule, or this prejudice, applies, which is why it is mentioned at all, exactly as strongly to our method of determining the influence of a culture or a church or a philosophy, alive, dead, or dying, upon the body of Emily Dickinson's poetry. We will see what the influence did to the words, and more important, what the words did to the influence.

So far as poetry goes, then, the influence of intellectual or other abstracted considerations can be measured only as it effects the choice and arrangement of words—as it richens or impoverishes the texture of the imaginative vehicle of the poetry. The puritan theory of renunciation, for example, will be not at all the same thing in a hortatory tract, no matter how eloquent and just, as in a poem of Emily Dickinson, which might well have drawn from the tract, however loose or fragmentary the poem may be. Imagination, if it works at all, works at the level of actualized experience. Here is the example, pat to the purpose, and to other purposes as well.

> Renunciation
> Is a piercing virtue,
> The letting go
> A presence for an expectation—
> Not now.

There is no forensic here, nor eloquence, nor justness; it is a bare statement amounting to vision—vision being a kind of observation of the ideal. It has nothing to do with wisdom, there is no thinking in it; and there is no ordinary observation in it—in the sense that there is no relation between an observer and a thing observed. The lines do not prove themselves, or anything else; they make a statement. Yet it is not a naïve statement—it is not directly itself—however much it may seem to be. It rises rather out of a whole way of life—the protestant, puritan way, felt suddenly at what can be called nothing less than a supremely sophisticated level. The feeling is in the sophistication. As a religious or philosophical statement it is probably vain and tragic and an example of self-arrogation; certainly it is without humility. Perhaps I am not competent to judge, being in a worse predicament than the poet, but it is possible to say that this is the sort of thing that happens to a religious notion when one's awareness of it becomes personal and without authority, when one is driven to imagine—in words or otherwise—the situation actually felt.

We do not examine these lines with a view to calling them great poetry but in order to present a series of facts as to how they derive their being and to afford a clue to the facts about a whole species of Dickinson poems—those that deal with the renunciation of love, the death of the beloved, and the heavenly reward. The machinery of meaning remains roughly the same throughout the group; what differs is the degree or amount of experience actualized in the verse. The machinery and the experience are perhaps inseparable, or at any rate are in their varying proportions equally necessary to the production of the kind of poetry Emily Dickinson wrote. When the balance is lost, when the fusion is not made, or when resort is had to feeling alone or to machinery insufficiently felt, something less than good poetry appears. We have either a poem without mooring or a poem without buoyancy.

Let us provisionally inquire what it is in the words that makes poetry of the statement about renunciation. Let us treat the machinery, not as what we may or may not know it to be intellectually, but as an example of words in operation; and let us look at the image—what is imagined—as the emergent fact of the words in operation, indeed, as the operation itself. That is how our best reading takes poetry in its stride; here we arrest the stride or make slow motion of it. The words are all simple words, parts of our stock vocabulary. Only one, *renunciation*, belongs to a special department of experience or contains in itself the focus of a particular attitude, a department and an attitude we condition ourselves to keep mostly in abeyance. We know what renunciation is; we know it turns up as heroism or hypocrisy or sentimentality; and we do as little as possible about it. Only one word, *piercing*, is directly physical; something that if it happens cannot be ignored but always shocks us into reaction. It is the shock of this word that transforms the phrase from a mere grammatical tautology into a metaphorical tautology which establishes as well as asserts identity. Some function of the word *pierce* precipitates a living intrinsic relation between renunciation and virtue; it is what makes the phrase incandesce. The two adjectives in the last line of the following quatrain exhibit a similar incandescent function.

> Rehearsal to ourselves
> Of a withdrawn delight
> Affords a bliss like murder,
> Omnipotent, acute.

It is the adjectives that transform the verbal and mutually irrelevant association of delight and murder into a self-completing metaphor. But, to return to our other quotation, the word *pierce* enlivens not only the first phrase but the whole statement about renunciation; it is the stress or shock of it that is carried forward into and makes specific the general notion—physical but vague—of letting go; and letting go, in its turn, perhaps by its participial form, works back upon the first phrase. The piercing quality of renunciation is precisely, but not altogether, that it is a continuing process, takes time, it may be infinite time, before the renounced presence transpires in expectation in the "Not now." It is—if we may provisionally risk saying so— the physical elements in the word *pierce* and the participial phrase *letting go* that, by acting upon them, make the other words available to feeling, and it is the word *renunciation* that, so enlightened, focuses the feeling as actuality. That operation is almost enough to make the statement poetry; we have only pseudo-names for whatever else it is that it takes. There is no advantage here of meter or rhyme. There is instead the speech-tone of authority, a directness in the manner of the words which has nothing to do with their meaning, and the speech-quality of speed, an inner speed of the syllables like the inner velocity of an atom, which has nothing directly to do with the outward relations of the words. These qualities are characteristic of verse that is felt as actual; at least we say that these qualities exist in verse that exacts the sense of precise feeling in the reader. Perhaps it is simpler to say that there is an excitement in the language beyond the excitement of any meaning we can communicate through any medium different from that of the poem itself: the excitement of being. It is gained, that excitement, by the exercise of the fundamental technique of language as a mode of finding objective form for even the most abstract feelings. A further, and I hope not absurd, simplification is to say that the poet whose work showed these qualities had an aptitude for language; and if that is so, then all we have been saying merely illustrates how much that is complicated and beyond conscious control the word *aptitude* may sometimes simplify.

So be it. Emily Dickinson had an aptitude for language, and in the passage we have examined she needed nothing else to induce her verses to reach their appropriate objective level; for the aptitude included every necessary mechanical relation both to her age and to the general craft of verse. Although the same aptitude persists superficially through the rest of the poem, the persistence is only superficial and not substantial. The rest of the poem is not transformed, as the quoted stanza was, into something felt as actual in which the parts work upon themselves mutually. We can say either that the aptitude was not carried far enough *per se*— the poet did not pay enough attention to the words; or we can say that the conceiving imagination was not strong enough to carry the material through; or we can say that the poet was not sufficiently master of the compositional devices of external form—form as the organizing agent—to give the work crisis and consistency. The first statement is true anyway; the second is probably true; and the third is true in relation to the other two. Perhaps the three statements are merely different emphases of the same idea: the idea we took up a little while ago of the imagination being insufficiently fed into the words of the poem. Either the machinery of the poem was inadequate to objectify its purpose, or the motive of the poem, as it emerged, was inadequate to activate the machinery. The alternatives are not mutually exclusive; a combined view is possible. It is at least plausible to consider that if there is a state of culture which produces or precipitates a body of poetry, then there may also be a state of language—a general level of poetic habit—which is necessary to give that body of poetry relative perfection, and that, further, if there is failure in one quarter, no matter which, it is a likely sign of failure in the other, if not at the same point then round the nearest corner. The trouble is that the condition of language at a given time is just as hard to determine as the condition of a culture. We guess at something wrong or swear that everything was right, and are not sure which case produced the better poetry.

We can say, amiably enough, that the verse-language of mid-nineteenth century America was relatively nerveless, unsupple, flat in pattern, had very little absorptive power and showed no self-luxuriating power whatever. The mounting vitality that shows itself as formal experiment and the matured vitality that shows itself as the masterly penetration of accepted form (say Kyd followed by the mature Shakespeare) were equally absent. The great estate of poetry as an available condition of language lay flat in a kind of desiccated hibernation, and the clue to resurrection was unknown. It is not for nothing that our poets never mastered form in language. Poe and Longfellow accepted the desiccation, contributing a personal music which perhaps redeemed but never transfigured their talents. Whitman and Emily

Dickinson, with more genius, or as we have been saying with more favorable cultural situations, were unable to accept the desiccation and drove forward on the élan of their natural aptitudes for language, resorting regardless to whatever props, scaffolds, obsessive symbols, or intellectual mechanisms came to hand, but neither of them ever finding satisfactory form—and neither, apparently, ever consciously missing it. The great bulk of the verse of each appears to have been written on the sustaining pretense that everything was always possible. To see boundless good on the horizon, to see it without the limiting discipline of the conviction of evil, is in poetry as in politics the great stultifier of action.

Hence the great, repetitious wastes in both poets. With no criterion of achievement without there could be no criterion of completion within. Success was by accident, by the mere momentum of sensibility. Failure was by rule, although the rule was unknown, and often doubtless thought of in the shameless guise of simple self-expression. The practice of craft came to little more than so many exercises in self-expression. Thus something over two-thirds of Emily Dickinson's nine hundred odd printed poems are exercises, and no more, some in the direction of poetry, and some not. The object is usually in view, though some of the poems are but exercises in pursuit of an unknown object, but the means of attainment are variously absent, used in error, or ill-chosen. The only weapon constantly in use is, to repeat once more, the natural aptitude for language; and it is hardly surprising to find that that weapon, used alone and against great odds, should occasionally produce an air of frantic strain instead of strength, of conspicious oddity instead of indubitable rightness.

Let us take for a first example a reasonably serious poem on one of the dominant Dickinson themes, the obituary theme of the great dead—a theme to which Hawthorne and Henry James were equally addicted—and determine if we can where its failure lies.

> More life went out, when He went,
> Than ordinary breath,
> Lit with a finer phosphor
> Requiring in the quench
>
> A power of renownéd cold—
> The climate of the grave
> A temperature just adequate
> So anthracite to live.
>
> For some an ampler zero,
> A frost more needle keen
> Is necessary to reduce
> The Ethiop within.
>
> Others extinguish easier—
> A gnat's minutest fan
> Sufficient to obliterate
> A tract of citizen.

The first thing to notice—a thing characteristic of exercises—is that the order or plot of the elements of the poem is not that of a complete poem; the movement of the parts is downwards and towards a disintegration of the effect wanted. A good poem so constitutes its parts as at once to contain them and to deliver or release by the psychological force of their sequence the full effect only when the poem is done. Here the last quatrain is obviously wrongly placed; it comes like an afterthought, put in to explain why the third stanza was good. It should have preceded the third stanza, and perhaps with the third stanza—both of course in revised form—might have come at the very beginning, or perhaps in suspension between the first and second stanzas. Such suggestions throw the poem into disorder; actually the disorder is already there. It is not the mere arrangement of stanzas that is at fault; the units in disorder are deeper in the material, perhaps in the compositional elements of the conception, perhaps in the executive elements of the image-words used to afford circulation to the poem, perhaps elsewhere in the devices not used but wanted. The point for emphasis is that it is hard to believe that a conscientious poet could have failed to see that no amount of correction and polish could raise this exercise to the condition of a mature poem. The material is all there—the inspiration and the language; what it requires is a thorough revision—a reseeing calculated to compose in objective form the immediacy and singleness of effect which the poet no doubt herself felt.

Perhaps we may say—though the poem is not near so bad an example as many—that the uncomposed disorder is accepted by the poet because the poem was itself written automatically. To the sensitive hand and expectant ear words will arrange themselves, however gotten hold of, and seem to breed by mere contact. The brood is the meaning we catch up to. Is not this really automatic writing *tout court?* Most of the Dickinson poems seems to have been initially as near automatic writing as may be. The bulk remained automatic, subject to correction and multiplication of detail. Others, which reach intrinsic being, have been patterned, inscaped, injected one way or another with the élan or elixir of the poet's dominant attitudes. The poem presently examined remains too much in the automatic choir; the élan is there, which is why we examine it at all, but without the additional advantage of craft it fails to carry everything before it.

The second stanza of the poem is either an example of automatic writing unrelieved, or is an example of bad editing, or both. Its only meaning is in the frantic strain towards meaning—a strain so frantic that all responsibility towards the shapes and primary significance of words was ignored. "A temperature just adequate/So anthracite to live" even if it were intelligible, which it is not, would be beyond bearing awkward to read. It is not bad grammar alone that works ill; words sometimes make their own grammar good on the principle of ineluctable association—when the association forces the words into meaning. Here we have fiat meaning. The word *anthracite* is the crux of the trouble. Anthracite is coal, is hard, is black, gives heat, and has a rushing crisp sound; it has a connection with carbuncle and with a fly-borne disease of which one symptom resembles a carbuncle; it is stratified in the earth, is formed of organic matter as a consequence of enormous pressure through geologic time; etc., etc. One or several of these senses may contribute to the poem; but because the context does not denominate it, it does not appear which. My own guess is that Emily Dickinson wanted the effect of something hard and cold and perhaps black and took *anthracite* off the edge of her vocabulary largely because she liked the sound. This is another way of saying that *anthracite* is an irresponsible product of her aptitude for language.

The word *phosphor* in the third line of the first stanza

is a responsible example of the same aptitude. It is moreover a habitual symbol word rather than a sudden flight; it is part of her regular machinery for concentrating meaning in a partly willful, partly natural symbol. Phosphor or phosphorus—in various forms of the word—is used by Emily Dickinson at least twelve times to represent, from the like characteristic of the metal, the self-illumining and perhaps self-consuming quality of the soul. The "renownéd cold," "ampler zero," and "frost more needle keen," are also habitual images used to represent the coming or transition of death as effected seasonably in nature and, by analogue, in man. Examples of these or associated words so used run to the hundreds. The "gnat" in the fourth stanza with his "minutest fan" (of cold air?) is another example of a portmanteau image always ready to use to turn on the microcosmic view. In the word *Ethiop* in the third stanza we have a mixture of a similar general term—this time drawn from the outside and unknown world—and a special significance released and warranted by the poem. Ethiops live in tropical Africa; and we have here a kind of synecdoche which makes the Ethiop himself so full of heat that it would take great cold to quench it. That the contrary would be the case does not affect the actuality of the image, but makes it more intriguing and give it an odd, accidental character. The misconception does, however, bring out the flavor of a wrong image along with the shadow of the right one; and it is a question whether the flavor will not last longer in the memory than the shadow. Another nice question is involved in the effect of the *order* of the verbs used to represent the point of death: *quench, reduce, extinguish, obliterate.* The question is, are not these verbs pretty nearly interchangeable?. Would not any other verb of destructive action do just as well? In short, is there any word in this poem which either fits or contributes to the association at all exactly? I think not—with the single exception of "phosphor."

The burden of these observations on words will I hope have made itself plain; it is exactly the burden of the observations on the form of the whole poem. The poem is an exercise whichever way you take it: an approach to the organization of its material but by no means a complete organization. It is almost a rehearsal —a doing over of something not done—and a variation of stock intellectual elements in an effort to accomplish an adventure in feeling. The reader can determine for himself—if he can swallow both the anthracite and the gnat—how concrete and actual the adventure was made.

Perhaps determination will be assisted by a few considerations on Emily Dickinson's vocabulary as a whole and how it splits up under inspection into different parts which are employed for different functions, and which operate *from*, as it were, different levels of sensibility. It is not a large vocabulary compared to Whitman's, nor rich like Melville's, nor perspicuous like Henry James', nor robust like Mark Twain's. Nor is it a homogeneous vocabulary; its unity is specious for the instance rather than organic for the whole of her work. Its constant elements are mostly found, like most of the poems, in arrangements, not in compositions. The pattern of association is kaleidoscopic and extraneous far more frequently than it is crystalline and inwardly compelled. What it is, is a small, rigidly compartmented vocabulary of general and conventional groups of terms, plus a moderately capacious vocabulary of homely, acute, directly felt words from which the whole actualizing strength of her verse is drawn. The extraordinary thing is how much of the general and conventional vocabulary got activated by the homely word. In the fragment about renunciation, "piercing" and "letting go" are examples. The depressing thing is how much of the conventional vocabulary was not activated by the homely word but distracted by the homely word strained odd.

Let us list a few of the conventional types that turn up most often and most conspicuously. The most conspicuous of all is the vocabulary of romance royalty, fairy-tale kings, queens and courts, and the general language of chivalry. Emily Dickinson was as fond as Shakespeare of words like *imperial, sovereign, dominion,* and the whole collection of terms for rank and degree. Probably she got them more from Scott and the Bible and the Hymnal than from Shakespeare. There is none of Shakespeare's specific and motivating sense of kings and princes as the focus of society, and none of his rhetoric of power; there is nothing tragic in Emily Dickinson's royal vocabulary. On the other hand, there is a great deal of vague and general assumption that royalty is a good thing and that escape into the goodness of it is available to everyone: like the colorful escape into romance and fairy tale. Besides this general assumption, and more important, there is continuous resort to the trope of heavenly coronation for the individual and a continuous ascription of imperial titles and a chivalric, almost heraldic, code to God and the angels, to flowers and bees. This vocabulary, taken as a whole, provides a mixed formula which rehearsed like a ritual or just a verbal exercise sometimes discovers a poem and sometimes does not. I extract one stanza as example.

THE EXPENSE OF GREATNESS

He put a belt around my life,—
I heard the buckle snap,
And turned away, imperial,
My lifetime folding up
Deliberate as a duke would do
A kingdom's title-deed,—
Henceforth a dedicated sort,
A member of the cloud.

Other vocabularies include words taken from sewing and the kinds of cloth used in women's clothes—*stitch, seam, needle, dimity, serge, silk, satin, brocade,* etc.; legal words—*tenant, rent, litigant, title,* etc.; the names of jewels—*diamond, ruby, pearl, opal, amethyst, beryl,* and *amber;* words taken from the Civil War—*bayonet,* various images of musket and cannon fire, and of the soldier's heroism; words taken from sea-borne commerce —*port, harbor,* various kinds of ships and the parts of ships; the names of distant places—especially of mountains and volcanoes; and, not to exhaust but merely to stop the list, words taken from the transcendental theology of her time. It should be noted that only the first, second, and possibly the last of these groups named or activated anything she found in her daily life; but they had, like the vocabulary of royalty, everything to do with the stretching of her daily fancy, and they made a constant provision, a constant rough filling and occupation, for what did actually concern her—her prevision of death and her insight into the spiritual life. This is another way of saying that in what is quantitatively the great part of her work Emily Dickinson did not put the life of meaning into her words; she leaned on the formulas of words in the hope that the formulas would fully express what she felt privately—sometimes the emotion of escape and sometimes the conviction of assent—in her own self-centered experience. This is partly the mode of prayer, partly the mode of nonce-popular romance (which must always be repeated) and partly the mode of the pathetic fallacy applied to form—the fiat mode of expression which asserts that the need is equivalent to the object, that if you need words to mean something then they will necessarily mean it. But it is not except by accident the mode of the rational or actualizing imagination. The extraordinary thing in Emily Dickinson is, to repeat, that fragmentary accidents occur so often, and the terrible thing is that they need not have been accidents at all. The net result may be put as a loss of consistent or sustained magnitude equal to the impulse. We have a verse in great body that is part terror, part vision, part insight and observation, which must yet mostly be construed as a kind of *vers de société* of the soul—not in form or finish but in achievement.

This is to say that control was superficial—in the use, not the hearts, of words. We saw an example in the word *anthracite* a little above. Let us present two more examples and stop. We have the word *plush* in different poems as follows. "One would as soon assault a plush or violate a star . . . Time's consummate plush . . . A dog's belated feet like intermittent plush . . . We step like plush, we stand like snow . . . Sentences of plush." The word is on the verge of bursting with wrong meaning, and on account of the bursting, the stress with which the poet employed it, we are all prepared to accept it, and indeed do accept it, when suddenly we realize the wrongness, that "plush" was not what was meant at all, but was a substitute for it. The word has been distorted but not transformed on the page; which is to say it is not in substantial control. Yet it is impossible not to believe that to Emily Dickinson's ear it meant what it said and what could not otherwise be said.

The use of the word *purple* is another example of a word's getting out of control through the poet's failure to maintain an objective feeling of responsibility towards language. We have, in different poems, a "purple host" meaning "soldiers"; "purple territories," associated with salvation in terms of "Pizarro's shores"; "purple" meaning "dawn"; a "purple finger" probably meaning "shadow"; a purple raveling of cloud at sunset; ships of purple on seas of daffodil; the sun quenching in purple; a purple brook; purple traffic; a peacock's purple train; purple none can avoid—meaning death; no suitable purple to put on the hills; a purple tar wrecked in peace; the purple well of eternity; the purple or royal state of a corpse; the Purple of Ages; a sowing of purple seed which is inexplicable; the purple of the summer; the purple wheel of faith; day's petticoat of purple; etc., etc. Taken cumulatively, this is neither a distortion nor a transformation of sense; it is very near an obliteration of everything but a favorite sound, meaning something desirable, universal, distant, and immediate. I choose the word as an example not because it is particularly bad—it is not; it is relatively harmless—but because it is typical and happens to be easy to follow in unexpanded quotation. It is thoroughly representative of Emily Dickinson's habit of so employing certain favorite words that their discriminated meanings tend to melt into the single sentiment of self-expression. We can feel the sentiment but we have lost the meaning. The willing reader can see for himself the analogous process taking place—with slightly different final flavors—in word after word: for example in the words *dateless*, *pattern*, *compass*, *circumference*, *ecstasy*, *immortality*, *white*, *ruby*, *crescent*, *peninsula*, and *spice*. The meanings become the conventions of meanings, the asserted agreement that meaning is there. That is the end towards which Emily Dickinson worked, willy nilly, in her words. If you can accept the assertion for the sake of the knack—not the craft—with which it is made you will be able to read much more of her work than if you insist on actual work done.

But there were, to repeat and to conclude, three saving accidents at work in the body of Emily Dickinson's work sufficient to redeem in fact a good many poems to the state of their original intention. There was the accident of cultural crisis, the skeptical faith and desperately experimental mood, which both released and drove the poet's sensibility to express the crisis personally. There was the accident that the poet had so great an aptitude for language that it could seldom be completely lost in the conventional formulas towards which her meditating mind ran. And there was the third accident that the merest self-expression, or the merest statement of recognition or discrimination or vision, may sometimes also be, by the rule of unanimity and a common tongue, its best objective expression.

When two or more of the accidents occur simultaneously a poem or a fragment of a poem may be contrived. Sometimes the thing is done directly—with the compactness which Mr. Lewisohn compared to that of Goethe, but which had better be called the compactness of that which is unexpanded and depends for context entirely upon its free implications.

> Presentiment is that long shadow on the lawn
> Indicative that suns go down;
> The notice to the startled grass
> That darkness is about to pass.

If the reader compares this poem with Marvell's "To His Coy Mistress," he will see what can be gotten out of the same theme when fully expanded. The difference is of magnitude; the magnitude depends on craft; the Dickinson poem stops, Marvell's is completed. What happens when the poem does not stop may be shown in the following example of technical and moral confusion.

> I got so I could hear his name
> Without—
> Tremendous gain!
> That stop-sensation in my soul,
> And thunder in the room.
>
> I got so I could walk across
> That angle in the floor
> Where he turned—so—and I turned how—
> And all our sinew tore.
>
> I got so I could stir the box
> In which his letters grew—
> Without that forcing in my breath
> As staples driven through.
>
> Could dimly recollect a Grace—
> I think they called it "God,"
> Renowned to ease extremity
> When formula had failed—

And shape my hands petition's way—
Tho' ignorant of word
That Ordination utters—
My business with the cloud.

If any Power behind it be
Not subject to despair,
To care in some remoter way
For so minute affair
As misery—
Itself too vast for interrupting more,
Supremer than—
Superior to—

Nothing is more remarkable than the variety of inconsistency this effort displays. The first three stanzas are
at one level of sensibility and of language and are as
good verse as Emily Dickinson ever wrote. The next
two stanzas are on a different and fatigued level of sensibility, are bad verse and flat language, and have only
a serial connection with the first three. The last stanza,
if it is a stanza, is on a still different level of sensibility
and not on a recognizable level of language at all: the
level of desperate inarticulateness to which no complete
response can be articulated in return. One knows from
the strength of the first three stanzas what might have
been meant to come after and one feels like writing the
poem oneself—the basest of all critical temptations. We
feel that Emily Dickinson let herself go. The accidents
that provided her ability here made a contrivance which
was not a poem but a private mixture of first-rate verse,
bad verse, and something that is not verse at all. Yet—
and this is the point—this contrivance represents in
epitome the whole of her work; and whatever judgment

you bring upon the epitome you will, I think, be compelled to bring upon the whole.

No judgment is so persuasive as when it is disguised as a statement of facts. I think it is a fact that the failure and success of Emily Dickinson's poetry were uniformly accidental largely because of the private and eccentric nature of her relation to the business of poetry. She was neither a professional poet nor an amateur; she was a private poet who wrote indefatigably as some women cook or knit. Her gift for words and the cultural predicament of her time drove her to poetry instead of antimacassars. Neither her personal education nor the habit of her society as she knew it ever gave her the least inkling that poetry is a rational and objective art and most so when the theme is self-expression. She came, as Mr. Tate says, at the right time for one kind of poetry: the poetry of sophisticated, eccentric vision. That is what makes her good—in a few poems and many passages representatively great. But she never undertook the great profession of controlling the means of objective expression. That is why the bulk of her verse is not representative but mere fragmentary indicative notation. The pity of it is that the document her whole work makes shows nothing so much as that she had the themes, the insight, the observation, and the capacity for honesty, which had she only known how—or only known why—would have made the major instead of the minor fraction of her verse genuine poetry. But her dying society had no tradition by which to teach her the one lesson she did not know by instinct.

The Craft of Herman Melville:
A Putative Statement

THIS essay proposes to approach Herman Melville altogether gingerly and from behind the safe bulwark of his assured position—whatever that is—in American literature,—whatever *that* may be. The tacit assumption will be all along that Melville is a sufficiently great writer in a sufficiently interesting literature to make the sidelong look, the biased comment, and even a little boring-from-within, each valuable in itself, if perhaps only as characterising an inadequate response on the part of one reader. We need, of course, a preliminary assertion to get us under way; and the last thing we want is anything in the direction of reducing Melville's greatness to sub-human terms. What we want is an assertion that, pursued, will elucidate one aspect of the work actually performed, irrespective of its greatness.

If we assert that Melville was an imaginative artist in the realm of fiction, then it is legitimate to think of him as he was concerned with the craft of fiction in his two most interesting works, *Moby Dick* and *Pierre*. As a further limitation, let us think of the craft principally under two heads: dramatic form with its inspiriting conventions, and the treatment of language itself as a medium. Other matters may come in by the way, and further matters may suggest themselves in conclusion; but the mode of discovery will be everywhere at bottom in the consideration of the tools by which Melville himself secured his effects: the tools of craft.

It is of preliminary interest that Melville never influenced the direction of the art of fiction, though in *Pierre* he evidenced the direction, and it is astonishing, when you consider the magnitude of his sensibility, that he never affected the modes of apprehension, the sensibilities, of even the ablest of his admirers. He added nothing to the novel as a form, and his work nowhere showed conspicuous mastery of the formal devices of fiction which he used. Unlike most great writers of fiction, he left nothing to those who followed him except the general stimulus of high and devoted purpose and the occasional particular spur of an image or a rhythm. It is not that he is inimitable but that there was nothing formally organised enough in his work to imitate or modify or perfect. It is easy enough to say on this score that Melville was a sport, and unique, and perhaps that is the right thing to say; but it would be more useful if we were able to say that Melville's lack of influence at least partly arose from a series of technical defects in persuasive craft—from an inefficient relation between the writer and the formal elements of his medium. None of us would want to recommend his wares along the lines of Melville's strategy. To adumbrate such a statement is a part of this essay's purpose.

Of secondary, but deeply contributory interest is the fact that though a young man still as writers go, Melville wrote nothing of major significance in the forty years he lived after writing *Pierre*. (I mean that only a lesser case could be made out for *The Confidence Man* and *Billy Budd* than for *Pierre*, not that the later books were uninteresting; they could not fail of interest as forced through Melville's sensibility.) It was not that his mind rotted or that insight faltered. It was not, I think, that the poor reception of *Pierre*, nor the long aggravation of his private life, dried his desire as a novelist. It was, I think, partly bad luck—the luck of the age, if you like—though it was no worse than Dante's luck and not so bad as Villon's, as Melville himself knew; and it was partly that his work discovered for itself, if we may say so, and in the very process of writing, that it was not meant to be fiction. Melville was only a story teller betimes, for illustrative or apologetic or evangelical purposes, and when the *writing* of *Pierre* proved that the material of illustration had been exhausted in *Moby Dick*—which is one way of noting the break-down of *Pierre* as a story—there was no longer any need to tell a story. His means determined, as they always do, not the ends in view, but the ends achieved; and Melville had never predominantly relied upon the means of the novelist, had never attempted to use more than the overt form of the novel, until he attempted to compose *Pierre*.

What is really interesting, and what this essay intends to make most use of in this corner, is the light that *Pierre*, technically considered as a novel, casts upon the means, quite different from the means of fiction, which Melville actually employed both in *Moby Dick* and *Pierre* itself. For these books with their great effects, if they were not written out of the means of the novelist, were written out of great means of some other mode or modes of the imagination. It will most likely appear that there is an operative connection between Melville's lack of influence upon following writers and his forty years of comparative silence; and it is, again, a connection, as moral as may be, that can best be seen as a technical consideration. Similarly, the problem of the inarticulateness of *Hamlet* is better accounted for technically than philosophically. We shall see, or try to see, what modes determined what ends—but always provisionally within the modes of the rational imagination.

There is, again on this train, a dubious kind of consideration which in the very doubtfulness of its nature exerts its great attraction. In our literature we are accustomed to the question precisely because it gets itself asked at every turn. It is a coroner's question: what devilish thing did his age do to Melville? What malevolence was there in the current of American life that struck from the heights of possibility writer after writer, even those most satisfied with the American scene?—for the Longfellows, the Whittiers, the Holmeses were as fatally struck as Hawthorne and Melville and Mark Twain. But does an age act? Is not an age itself a long action, an unfolding, a display, a history, with limits set by the discernment and capacity of the observer, never by Clio herself? And is not every age an enemy of every artist it cannot directly use, an enemy not out of antipathy but of inner necessity? An age moves; it is momentum felt. An artist expresses an arrested version of movement, expresses it at the level of actuality. But this is pushing consequence intolerably. We are all enemies of our age the moment we begin to tamper with it, whether we arrest it to take its picture, hasten it towards its end in the guise of leadership, or just consciously live in it our own lives. Consciousness is the agent, not the age.

It is the whole consciousness, not its mere miniscule conscience, that makes us cowards. Hence in all large doings we are adept at removing compassion from our experience by at once inserting it in the formula of a dead convention; and so are often enabled to skip consciousness, along with conscience, altogether. How otherwise could we attend the Christian service of Holy Communion, quite aside from the matter of faith and for the "poetry" in it merely, without terror and dismay and the conviction of inadequacy. How could we attend *King Lear* on the stage if we did not commonly channelise our attention upon the obscuring details of the performance, letting the actual play work in us, if at all, unawares? This is precisely what the artist cannot substantially do if his work is to live; and this is precisely what society compels him to seem to do if his work is to succeed in the open,—that is, be widely persuasive upon the consciousness of the great audience most artists aim at. Upon his skill and luck in performing this equivocal act depends all that part of an artist's achievement which rests on a firm relation with his age.

Here we have a crux in the deliberately maintained, wilfully heightened consciousness of the artist. It is the crux in which we see that the conceptual faculty of consciousness is honesty if we can manage it, but that the executive faculty of consciousness must be hypocrisy. I do not wish to strain or seem far-fetched, but I believe this to be a technical matter in so far as we think of the arts—whatever it may be in religion or politics, which are not always condemned to actuality but can often play free havoc with the ideal. What it comes to in practice is that the artist must dramatise his theme, his vision, his observation, his "mere" story, in terms of existing conventions however adverse those conventions may seem to his intentions, or however hollow or vain they ring when struck. The deadest convention was meant for life—to take its place; and if by putting life into it the artist does not always change it for the better, he at least shows it for what it is. Instinctive artists commonly resort to the nearest conventions susceptible of dramas. Consider the negro spirituals or the anonymous architecture of the twelfth century. Highly individualised artists have done the same. There is Dante who mastered the conventions of Tomistic Christianity to represent the actuality—far from Tomistic—of fourteenth century Italy; and there is Henry James who resorted to the "social" conventions so well that many people for long believed he was taken in by them, when his predominant concern was to dramatise the actual good and evil of his time in terms of the conventions through which he most saw good and evil operating.

The point here is, for us, that Melville either refused or was unable to resort to the available conventions of his time as if they were real; he either preferred or was compelled to resort to most of the conventions he used for dramatic purposes not only as if they were unreal but also as if they were artificial. Artificial they surely were to the kind of philosopher Melville was—though they would not have seemed unreal to Montaigne or Plato; but to the dramatist of any description they would have glowed with the possibility of every reality. As for Melville's case we have his own words, put in extremity, for his attitude towards all conventions of the mind.

For the more and the more that he wrote, and the deeper and deeper that he dived, Pierre saw the everlasting elusiveness of Truth; the universal lurking insincerity of even the greatest and purest written thoughts. Like knavish cards, the leaves of all great books were covertly packed. He was but packing one set the more; and that a very poor and jaded set and pack indeed.

Here we see the ineptitude, for the artist, of moral preoccupation with what ought to be as compared with the equally moral obsession with what is. As thought, we can leave Melville's text alone, and insist merely that as an artist Melville misunderstood the import of his own words. The "universal lurking insincerity" he spoke of, is just the most fascinating aspect of the face of dramatic truth; and the conviction of it should liberate the artist's honesty among his material generally, as the preposterous fables of *Lear, Othello,* and the *Merchant of Venice* particularly liberated the profound honesty of Shakespeare, or as the *smallness* of life in Emma Bovary's town liberated Flaubert's honesty. Melville apparently felt that his insight condemned him to a species of dishonesty. Feeling the necessity—feeling the condemned state as unreprievable—he proceeded to employ conventions of character and form in which he obviously and almost avowedly did not believe. Had he been a convicted and not a condemned novelist he would have felt his insight of insincerity on the same level that he felt the convention in the following lines, in which he never detected the insincerity at all.

It is a thing most sorrowful, nay shocking, to expose the fall of valor in the soul. Men may seem detestable as joint stock-companies and nations; knaves, fools, and murderers there may be; men may have mean and meagre faces; but man, in the ideal, is so noble and so sparkling, such a grand and glowing creature, that over any ignominious blemish in him all his fellows should run to throw their costliest robes. That immaculate manliness we feel within ourselves, so far within us, that it remains intact though all the outer character seem gone; bleeds with the keenest anguish at the undraped spectacle of a valor-ruined man. Nor can piety itself, at such a shameful sight, completely stifle her upbraidings against the permitting stars.

At his best—his best as a novelist of character and aspiration—this sentiment controlled Melville's perception of dramatic fate. Had he felt the immaculate manliness as Henry James, say, felt his perception of the Sacred Fount, as a germinal, copulative, and plastic principle in every human relation, and also as the very prod and forward stress towards form, then his sentiment would not only have opened up inexhaustible subject-matter, but would also have required of him that in his execution every resource, every trick, every mediate insincerity, either of craft or of social pattern, be used for the utmost there was in them. That would have been to work on the representative, the dramatic level. What he did, as we shall see more particularly below, was to work on the putative level. His work constantly *said* what it was doing or going to do, and then, as a rule, stopped short.

As it happens, Melville's is not a putative smallness but a putative immensity, and he puts it with such eloquence that the mere statement produces a lasting tone in the general atmosphere. He was without knowing it in the habit of succumbing to the greatest insincerity of all, the intoxicating insincerity of cadence and rhythm and apt image, or, to put it on another plane, the insincerity of surrendering to the force of a single insight, which sometimes amounts to a kind of self-violation. Who can measure for example the effect of the preparatory statements about Ahab upon our actual reception of him when he appears? For instance, in chapter XVI there is a paragraph about the greatness of some whaling men rising from a combination of Quaker blood and the perils of the sea. "Nor will it at all detract from him, dramatically regarded, if either by birth or other circumstances, he have what seems a half wilful, over-ruling morbidness at the bottom of his nature. For all men tragically great are made so through a certain morbidness. Be sure of this, O young ambition, all mortal greatness is but disease." . . . This is but one of the many preparatory, almost minatory statements that Melville made about Ahab. Many directly named him; many more, like this one, were purely indirect and putative in character. Ahab is not mentioned, but the reader who remembers the passage will know that it was he who was meant all the same; and if the reader does remember it may well occur to him that Melville meant his sentences about greatness and disease to spread throughout the novel. They were planted of a purpose, whether by instinct or intention, to prefigure in the general atmosphere the specific nature of the burden Ahab wore.

The interesting thing is that Melville preferred to make his statement, in which one version of the whole theme of the book is expressed, not only baldly in isolation, but out of place and rootlessly; which is how the reader will ultimately remember it. It worked, indeed; but it worked outside the story. A dramatist would have been compelled to find the sentiment of these sentences in a situation, an action, and they could have been used only as the situation called for them and the action carried them along; and a novelist when he can should follow the example of the dramatist. Melville, as we have said, preferred the non-dramatic mode. To put it sharply, he did not write of characters in action; he employed the shells of stock characters, heightened or resounding only by the eloquence of the author's voice, to witness, illustrate, decorate, and often as it happened to impede and stultify an idea in motion. This is, if you like, the mode of allegory—the highest form of the putative imagination, in which things are *said* but need not be *shown* to be other than they seem, and thus hardly require to *be* much of anything. But successful allegory—*La Vita Nuova* and *Pilgrim's Progress*—requires the preliminary possession of a complete and stable body of belief appropriate to the theme in hand. Melville was not so equipped; neither was Hawthorne; neither was anyone in nineteenth century America or since. That is why Melville's allegorical devices and patterns had to act *as if* they were agents in a novel; and that is why we are compelled to judge Melville at his most allegorical yet formally as a novelist.

Perhaps the point needs labouring. Many critics—many students of Melville—have done a good deal to make an allegorical interpretation of *Moby Dick*, and I am sure they are right and accurate in the form of what they say. Melville certainly had allegorical intentions. My argument—again it is technical—is that the elaboration of these intentions was among the causes that prevented him from the achievement of enacting composition and the creation of viable characters. He mistook allegory in *Moby Dick* as a sufficient enlivening agent for the form of the novel. Actually it was a chief defective element which, due to the peculiarly confused, inconsistent and incomplete state of belief he was in, he could not possibly have used to good advantage. In the craft of writing, in any form of expression, artificial allegory, like willed mysticism (of which Melville showed a trace), is a direct and easy mode only in that it puts so much in by intention as to leave nearly everything out in execution. Bad allegory, even to the allegorist, comes very soon to seem not worth doing; which is why charades and political parties break down. Melville's allegory in *Moby Dick* broke down again and again and with each resumption got more and more verbal, and more and more at the mercy of the encroaching event it was meant to transcend. It was an element in the putative mode in which, lofty as it was, Melville himself could not long deeply believe.

We have so far been concerned mostly with what Melville did not do as a practitioner in the novel and with certain possible causes which, technically, prevented him from doing what he wanted to do. Let us now examine particular instances of what he did do under the two heads first mentioned: dramatic form with its inspiriting conventions, and the treatment of language itself as medium. If anything so far said has made its point it will be in the degree that it certifies and illuminates what follows—in the degree, that is, that it makes it seem natural and just and necessary to find so much fault in a genius so great.

The dramatic form of a novel is what holds it together, makes it move, gives it a centre and establishes a direction; and it includes the agency of perception, the consciousness set up in the book upon which, or through which, the story is registered. Dramatic form cannot in practice be wholly isolated from other formal elements; form is the way things go together in their medium—and the medium itself, here language, may properly be considered the major element of form; but we may think of different ways in which things go together in a given work, and strangely, the labour of abstraction and violation will seem to deepen our intimacy with the substance of the work and, more valuable, to heighten our sense of how that substance is controlled. The sense of control is perhaps the highest form of apprehension; it is understanding without immersion.

The question we have here to ask then is how did Melville go about controlling his two novels, *Moby Dick* and *Pierre?* The general, strictly true, and mainly irrelevant answer would be: haphazardly—that is, through an attitude which varied from the arrogance of extreme carelessness to the humility of complete attention. It is not that he attended only to what seriously interested him, for he was as careless of what he thought important as of what he thought trivial, but that apparently he had no sure rule as to what required management and what would take care of itself. His rule was vagary, where consequential necessities did not determine otherwise. And even there, Melville's eye was not good; he did not always see that if you took one series of steps your choice of further directions was narrowed, and that you could not step in two directions at once without risk of crippling yourself. It is perhaps his intellectual consistency, which he felt putatively omniform, that made him incorrigibly inconsistent in the technical quarter. For example, in *Moby Dick*, after setting up a single consciousness to get inside of, he shifted from that consciousness at will without sense of inconsistency, and therefore, which is the important thing, without making any effort to warrant the shifts and make them credible. Ignorance could not have excused him, because he had the example of Hawthorne, who was adept at shifting his compositional centres without disturbing his gravity, plumb in front of him. Not ignorance, but ineptitude and failure to discriminate. For the contrary example, I can think of only three occasions of importance in *Pierre*, if we except the digressions of the author himself in his own voice, where the consciousness of the hero is not left the presumed sole register of the story. Of these occasions, two are unnecessary to the story, and the third, where in the very end the perceiving centre is turned over to the turnkey in the prison, funks its job. Yet in *Pierre* the theme cried out, one would think, for as many and as well chosen centres of consciousness as possible, all to be focussed on Pierre himself, the distraught and ambiguous, otherwise not measurable: the principle being that the abnormal can only be seen as viable, as really moving in response to the normal world, if seen through normal eyes.

Meanwhile we have approached a little nearer the composition of the two novels. Melville was right, granting the theme of *Moby Dick*, in choosing Ishmael the novice, to represent a story in which he had only a presumed and minor but omnipresent part; he was only wrong where he breached his choice without covering up. Ishmael, not otherwise ever named, is as mysterious as Ahab, but he is credible because he tells us not what he is but what he sees and what he sees other people see. The mere interposition of a participating consciousness between the story and its readers, once it has been made logical by tying the consciousness to the story, is a prime device of composition: it limits, compacts, and therefore controls what can be told and how. The only error Melville made is that he failed to distinguish between what Ishmael saw and what the author saw on his own account. If an author is to use digressions, which are confusing but legitimate by tradition, he ought to follow Fielding and put them in inter-chapters, and especially where the narrative is technically in the first person. Otherwise, as with Ishmael, the narrator will seem to know too much at a given time for the story's good; it will tend to tell itself all at once, and the necessary modicum of stupidity in the operative consciousness will be blighted by excess intelligence. As Ahab said to the carpenter who handed him a lantern: "Thrusted light is worse than presented pistols." Ishmael of course is Melville's alter ego, which explains why so much is imputed to him, but does not condone the excess.

On the whole the mode of Ishmael is a success exactly where the mode of *Pierre* (another alter ego of Melville) is wrong. Ishmael is looking on, and able to see; Pierre is in the centre of his predicament, and lost in the action. Ishmael represents speech; Pierre represents rhetoric. Ishmael reports the abnormal, driven and demonic Ahab, either through his own normal sensibility or through the reported sensibilities of the mates and the crew. Pierre is seen principally without the intervening glass and focus of any sensibility whatever—so that he falls apart into a mere voice whenever he speaks, whereas the voice of Ahab, equally eloquent and rhetorical past belief, rings true in ears that have actually heard it.

It should be noted, curiously, that Ishmael is the only character in the book not "characterised" by Melville; he is merely situated in the centre, explained a little, and let speak his part of recording angel. The curiosity is that all the other characters except Ahab and Queequeg near the beginning (the night at the inn), although given

set characterisations as they appear, are far less viable and
are far less *present* in the book than Ishmael. The reason
may be that the other characters are only pulled out at
intervals and are usually given stock jobs to do, set
speeches to make, whereas Ishmael, sacking his creative
memory, is occupied all the time. Which suggests two
or three things: that character requires the sense of continuous action to show continuously, that the mates and
crew were not *in* the book substantially but that their
real use was to divide up the representation of the image
of Ahab. There is nothing illegitimate about such characters, but to be successful and maintain interest they
must be given enough to do to seem everywhere natural,
and never obviously used, as here, *only* to make the
wheels go round. One suspects, therefore, that Ahab
comes out a great figure more because of the eloquence
of the author's putative conception of him, and Ishmael's
feeling for him, than from any representational aids on
the part of the crew. The result is a great figure, not a
great character. Ahab is as solitary in the book as he
was in his cabin.

Pierre was in his way as compositionally isolated as
Ahab; he was so situated, and so equipped as a consciousness, that he recorded his own isolation to the point of
solipsism. If Pierre was real, as he was asserted to be,
then nothing else properly in the novel was real except
in terms of his perception or through the direct and un-
warrantable intervention of the author. That is the risk
attached to making the protagonist record the action in
which he participates to the exclusion of other agents
and while the action is going on. Melville instinctively
tried to get round the difficulty by resorting to a series
of dramatic scenes in which Pierre was chief interlocu-

tor. The device was the right one—or one of the right ones—but it failed to work for a number of reasons, of which the chief was that Melville had no talent for making his dramatic scenes objective except by aid of external and unrelated force—as in *Moby Dick* he was able to resort to the ordinary exigences of life on a whaling ship. In *Pierre* the White Whale was entirely in the protagonist's own inadequate perception of it; and the real weight of the book—what it was really about: tragedy by unconsidered virtue—was left for the author's digressions and soliloquys to carry as it could; which is to say that the book had no compositional centre at all.

Something of the same sort may also be true of *Moby Dick*. Is it not possible to say that Ishmael, the narrator, provides only a false centre? Is it not true that a great part of the story's theme escapes him, is not recorded through his sensibility, either alone or in connection with others? Then the real centre would lie where? It would lie variously, I think, in the suspense attached to the character of Ahab and the half imputed, half demonstrated peril of the White Whale—the cold, live evil that is momently present. If we think of the book in that way, we may say that its compositional form is a long, constantly interrupted but as constantly maintained suspense, using as nexi or transitions the recurring verbal signs of Melville's allegory, Ahab's character, and the business of whaling. The business of whaling, including both the essays on anatomy and those on butchery, takes the most space and provides the most interest. All the reader has to do is to *feel* whaling as interest and he will recognise it as a compositional device mounting to the force of drama. Indeed we speak of the drama of whaling, or of cotton, or of gold without substantial injustice to the language; and I cannot for the life of me see why the drama of whaling should not be as efficient an agent of interest, if well felt, as the drama of who fired the second shot; and with Melville there is the additional advantage that the business of whaling points to the ever-lasting assassin instead of the casual and no doubt remorseful murderer. Interest is the thing of prime importance as any artist and any audience will tell you. If it takes up time and prepares for life, it does not matter how it is secured and does not fatally matter if it is overdone or vulgar in its appeal as it is in *Moby Dick*.

But is the real interest in the whaling or in the firing of the shot? Is it not always partly in the presentation, the feeling of detail and design, and partly in the image towards which the design points? Melville was lucky in *Oomoo* and *Typee*, to a less degree in *Mardi* and *White Jacket*, and most of all in *Moby Dick*; he was lucky or it was his genius that he had material in perfect factual control with which to take up time and point towards an image—in *Moby Dick* a profound and obsessive image of life. As it happened, it was in each case the material of a special and vanishing experience, dramatic enough in its own right to require very little fictionising —very little actualising—to exert the invaluable hold of natural interest over the average reader. If to interest, you add eloquence, you have all the essentials of the great novel below the first order. Many readers will be deceived and think the provision greater than it is. I have discovered a number of readers who on being asked reported enjoyment of a great story in a book of which Henry James would have said that it told no story to speak of; which indeed it does not.

In *Pierre* we are in a different box; a box quite empty

of special material of objective interest to do for compositional strength otherwise lacking. There is no sea, or ship, or whale, or unique tradition of behaviour, no unusual daily life—most precious of all—to give atmosphere, and weight and movement to carry the book towards the image of its chosen end. Melville was required to depend more than ever before upon the actual technique of the craft, and nothing much else, to make the book hang together. What is most illuminating is most pitiful. The glaring weaknesses of *Pierre* show up the hidden weaknesses of *Moby Dick*, and each set of weaknesses shows the other as essential—at least in the critical context in which we here provisionally place both books.

That one novel may criticise another is a commonplace when we think of different authors, as when we say that the novels of Henry James form a criticism of the novels of Flaubert and Turgenev, or that, in a way, the *Comedie Humaine* is a critique of the Waverly Novels. I think it is equally true that a consideration of the failures of a single author will often form the severest criticism of his successes, and a consideration of his successes may relatively improve our estimation of his failures. A great author is of one substance and often of one theme, and the relation between his various creations is bound to be reciprocal, even mutual; each is the other in a different form. So with *Pierre* and *Moby Dick*. If we wish to take up thinking of the two novels together in this way—which is the purpose of this essay—the alert consciousness will be struck with the repetition of the vices of *Pierre* in *Moby Dick*, or struck the other way round with the fact that the tragedy of *Pierre* fails to come off as well as *Moby Dick* only because the later book lacked the demonstrable extraneous interest of whaling. The efforts at plot in the two books are as lame; narrative runs as often offside. Dramatic motive on the subordinate level is as weakly put; Starbuck's tentative rebellion against Ahab and the threatened revenge of Glendinning Stanly and Frederick Tartan upon Pierre are equally unconvincing. The dialogue is as by turns limp and stiff and flowery in one book as the other. The delineations of character are almost interchangeable examples of wooden caricature. And so on. More important, the force and nobility of conception, the profundity of theme, were as great in either book—not from the dramatic execution but in spite of it, in the simple strength of the putative statement, and in the digressions Melville made from the drama in front of him, which he could not manage, into apologues or sermons, which he superbly could.

The strength of the putative statement is only simple when thought of abstractly and as appealing to the intellect—to the putative element in appreciation: as if we read lyric poetry solely for the schematic paraphrase we make of it in popular discussion, or as if, in contemplating war, we thought only of political causes or in terms of the quartermaster's technique alone. What we want is to see what is the source of putative strength and how deeply its appeal is asserted; and in that pursuit we shall find ourselves instantly, I think, in the realm of language itself. Words, and their intimate arrangements, must be the ultimate as well as the immediate source of every effect in the written or spoken arts. Words bring meaning to birth and themselves contained the meaning as an imminent possibility before the pangs of junction. To the individual artist the use of words is an adventure in discovery; the imagination is heuristic among the words it manipulates. The reality you labour desperately or luckily to put into your words—and you may put it in consciously like Coleridge or by instinct as in the great ballads or from piety and passion like the translators of the Bible—you will actually have found there, deeply ready and innately formed to give objective being and specific idiom to what you knew and did not know that you knew. The excitement is past belief; as we know from the many myths of heavenly inspiration. And the routine of discovery is past teaching and past prediction; as we know from the vast reaches of writing, precious and viable to their authors, wholly without the conviction of being. Yet the adventure into the reality of words has a technique after the fact in the sense that we can distinguish its successful versions from those that failed, can measure provisionally the kinds and intensities of reality secured and attempted, and can even roughly guess at the conditions of convention and belief necessary for its emergence.

Melville is an excellent example for such an assay. We have only to relate the conception of the reality of language just adumbrated to the notion of the putative statement to see whence the strength of the latter comes; and we have only to relate the conception of language to its modifying context of conventions in order to understand the successes and at least excuse the many shortcomings and over-leapings of Melville's attempts at the paramount and indefeasible reality that great words show. For Melville habitually used words greatly.

Let us take first an example not at all putative and with as little supporting context of convention as possible: an example of words composed entirely of feelings and the statement of sensuous facts, plus of course the usual situating and correlative elements which are the real syntax of imaginative language.

To a landsman, no whale, nor any sign of a herring, would have been visible at that moment; nothing but a troubled bit of greenish white water, and thin scattered puffs of vapor hovering over it, and suffusingly blowing off to lee-ward, like the confused scud from white rolling billows. The air around suddenly vibrated and tingled, as it were, like the air over intensely heated plates of iron. Beneath this atmospheric waving and curling, and partially beneath a thin layer of water, also, the whales were swimming. Seen in advance of all the other indications, the puffs of vapor they spouted, seemed their forerunning couriers and detached flying outriders.

This is the bottom level of good writing, whether in prose or verse; and a style which was able to maintain the qualities of accurate objective feeling which it exemplifies at other levels and for other purposes could not help being a great style. The words have feelers of their own, and the author contributes nothing to the emotion they call forth except the final phrasing, which adds nothing but finish to the paragraph. It is an example of words doing their own work; and let no one think it is not imaginative work, or does not come to an emotion, because the mode is that of close description, and neither directly expressive nor enacting. Let us compare it, with achieved emotion in mind, with a deliberately "emotional" description taken from the chapter called Enceladus in *Pierre*.

Cunningly masked hitherto, by the green tapestry of the interlacing leaves, a terrific towering palisade of dark mossy massiness confronted you; and, trickling with unevaporable moisture, distilled upon you from its beetling brow slow thunder-showers of water-drops, chill as the last dews of death. . . . All round and round, the grim scarred rocks rallied and re-rallied themselves; shot up, protruded, stretched, swelled, and eagerly reached forth; on every side bristlingly radiated with hideous repellingness. . . . 'Mid this spectacle of wide and wanton spoil, insular noises of falling rocks would boomingly explode upon the silence and fright all the echoes, which ran shrieking in and out among the caves, as wailing women and children in some assaulted town.

This is, if I may insist on the term, putative description. It asserts itself to be description and passes for description until it is looked into, when you see that it is primarily the *assertion* of an emotional relation to landscape, and through effects of which landscape is incapable. Its force depends on the looseness, vagueness, and tumultuousness of the motion of the words. As a matter of fact the words are so chosen and arranged that they cannot contribute any material of emotion beyond that which may be contained in a stock exclamation. The primary point of our comparison is that the second passage dilutes and wastes an emotion assumed to have existed prior to its expression, whereas the first passage built up and united the elements of an emotion which exists only and actually in the words employed. The first passage discovers its meaning in words, the second never reached the condition of meaning. The first passage reminds you of Gerard Hopkins, the second of Ann Radcliffe; a contrast which brings up the secondary point of our comparison.

The spirit of the gothic novel ran frothily through the popular literature of America in the first half of the nineteenth century, ending possibly with its own travesty in *The Black Crook*. Melville, faced with the bad necessity, as it must have seemed to him, of popularising the material of *Pierre* and *Moby Dick*, adopted outright the gothic convention of language with all its archaisms and rhetorical inflations. The effect in the two books was similar in fact though not quite the same in effect. Some of the soliloquies in *Moby Dick* seem more like tantrums than poetry, but they were the tantrums of a great imagination fed with mastered material. In *Pierre*, without any fund of nourishing material, the dialogues, soliloquies, and meditations get lost in the flatulence of words.

Now, the gothic convention is not insusceptible of reality in itself, as we see in Beckford and Peacock and Brontë—perhaps in Poe and occasionally in Hawthorne —but it requires on the part of the author unconditional assent to it as a convention. This assent Melville could not give; he used it, so far as I can see, as a solemn fraud and hoped for the best. In *Moby Dick* the fraud passed preliminary muster because the lofty "unreal" terror that rode the *Pequod* made it seem at least plausible, even in its greatest extravagance, as a vehicle of response. And there is the further defence, often made, that the worst excesses of language and sentiment are excusable because of the poetry they are supposed to hold. To which the answer is that the poetry would have been better without the excess; when Melville dropped the mode and wrote in language comparable to the passage first quoted above, as in Ahab's last soliloquy, better poetry was actually produced. But no one, so far as I know, unless it be Foster Damon who writes *con amore* of anything both American and gothic, has defended the excesses of *Pierre*, of which the passage quoted above is a tame example.

It may be said in passing that what is often called the

Elizabethan influence in Melville's prose might more accurately be called the gothic influence heightened by the greatness of Melville's intentions. If I may have the notation for what it is worth, I suspect that in "the three boats swung over the sea like three samphire baskets over high cliffs," while the samphire baskets undoubtedly came from *King Lear*, still they had got well spattered with gothic mire on the long journey. Again, the sister-brother crux in *Pierre*, while it may be found in John Ford has a very different reality of expression from that in Ford's verse.

The menancings in thy eyes are dear delights to me; I grow up with thy own glorious stature; and in thee, my brother, I see God's indignant ambassador to me, saying—Up, up, Isabel, and take no terms from the common world, but do thou make terms to it, and grind thy fierce rights out of it! Thy catching nobleness unsexes me, my brother; and now I know that in her most exalted moment, then woman no more feels the twin-born softness of her breasts, but feels chain-armour palpitating there!

These lines, spoken by Isabel in response to similar declarations on the part of Pierre on the occasion of their second conversation, could not have been matched in Ford, but they could be matched a hundred times in the popular gothics. As for the minor effects of Elizabethan influence, where it has been said, by Mumford among others, that Melville's prose is Websterian—and perhaps it sometimes is—yet it far more often supplies us with Marlovian tropes. For every phrase such as "the cheeks of his soul collapsed in him," there are a dozen on the tone of the following: "With a frigate's anchors for my bridle-bits and fasces of harpoons for spurs, would I could mount that whale and leap the topmast skies . . .!"

This is the Marlowe of Tamerlane, and the unregenerate Marlowe letting himself go, not the Marlowe remodelled and compacted of *Faustus* and *The Jew*. Occasionally there is such a triumphant meeting of rhetoric and insight as the passage which contains the famous phrases: "To trail the genealogies of these high mortal miseries, carries us at last among the sourceless primogenitures of the gods,"—a passage more mindful of the *Urn Burial* than of anything in *The Duchess of Malfi*, but which is mindful most of Melville himself.

If it was the gothic excess that gave occasional opportunity for magnificent flashes, we should be grateful to it that much: it is at least a delight by the way; but it far more often produced passages like the speech of Isabel, which are perhaps collector's items, but not delights. Besides, what is most and finally illuminating, when Melville really had something to say, and was not making a novel, he resorted to another mode, which was perhaps the major expressive mode of his day, the mode of the liberal Emersonian sermon, the moral apologue on the broad Christian basis. There Melville's natural aptitude lay; when he preaches he is released, and only then, of all weak specifications. That the sermon was to say the best of it an artificial mode in fiction mattered nothing, and emphasises the fact that Melville was only a novelist betimes. He made only the loosest efforts to tie his sermons into his novels, and was quite content if he could see that his novels illustrated his sermons and was reasonably content if they did not; or so the books would show. He preached without scruple, and with full authority, because he felt in full command of the mode he used: he believed in its convention of structure and its deeper convention of its relation to society with all his heart. Father Mapple's sermon on Jonah and Plotinus Phinlimmon's lecture—it is really a sermon—on Chronometricals and Horologicals are the two sustained examples of self-complete form in his work. The doctrine might not have appealed to Channing or Parker, but the form, the execution, the litheness and vigour and verve, the homely aptnesses, the startling comparisons, the lucidity of presentation of hard insights, the dramatic and pictorial quality of the illustrations, and above all the richness of impact and the weighted speed of the words, would have appealed as near perfection.

The curiosity—and Melville looked at is all curiosity—that needs emphasis here is that the vices of his style either disappeared or transpired only as virtues when he shifted his mode to the sermon, and this without any addition of insight or eloquence, but simply, I believe, because he had found a mode which suited the bent of his themes, which allowed the putative statement to reach its full glory without further backing, which made room for rhetoric and demanded digression, and which did not trouble him, so great was his faith in it, with its universal lurking insincerity. Consider the following lines, which form the counter sermon to Phinlimmon's lecture in *Pierre*.

All profound things, and emotions of things are preceded and attended by Silence. What a silence is that with which the pale bride precedes the responsive *I will*, to the priest's solemn question, *Wilt thou have this man for thy husband?* In silence, too, the wedded hands are clasped. Yea, in silence the child Christ was born into the world. Silence is the general consecration of the universe. Silence is the invisible laying on of the Divine Pontiff's hands upon the world. Silence is at once the most harmless and the

HERMAN MELVILLE

most awful thing in all nature. It speaks of the Reserved
Forces of Fate. Silence is the only Voice of our God.

Nor is this so august Silence confined to things simply
touching or grand. Like the air, Silence permeates all
things, and produces its magical power, as well during that
peculiar mood which prevails at a solitary traveller's first
setting forth on a journey, as at the unimaginable time when
before the world was, Silence brooded on the face of the
waters.

The author of these paragraphs was at home in his
words and completely mastered by them; and he had
reached in that language, what Pierre never reached, the
"sense of uncapitulatable security, which is only the
possession of the furthest advanced and profoundest
souls."

In our present context there seems little more to say.
The consideration of Melville as a novelist should have
shown, at least in the superficial aspects which this brief
essay has been able to touch, that it was precisely the
practice of that craft that put his books, and himself, at
a loss, and left him silent, stultified, and, before the great
face of possibility, impotent for forty years of mature
life. I trust that it will have been shown as at least
plausible that Melville suffered the exorbitant penalty of
his great failure, not as a result of the injuries inflicted
upon him by his age, but because of his radical inability
to master a technique—that of the novel—radically foreign to his sensibility. The accidents of his career, the
worse accidents of his needs, brought him to a wrong
choice. Yet had he made a right choice, the accident of
his state of beliefs might well have silenced him altogether. Judging by the reception of his two serious
books, he would have been anathema as a preacher and
unpublishable as an essayist. We should be grateful

for his ill luck in only a lesser sense than we are for Dante's, or we should have lost the only great imagination in the middle period of the American nineteenth century: a putative statement to which all readers must assent.

A Note on Yvor Winters

WHAT is most valuable about Yvor Winters as a critic is just what is most valuable about him as a poet: his power of controlled discernment of matters usually only observed fragmentarily, by the way, willy-nilly, with the merely roving eye. His observations carry the impact of a sensibility which not only observed but modified the fact at hand; and we feel the impact as weight, as momentum, as authority. The weight is of focussed knowledge, the momentum that of a mind which has chosen—by an ethic of the imagination—its direction, and the authority is the authority of tone: the tone of conviction that cannot be gainsaid without being undone. The weight and momentum, as we feel them, give our sense of value—of the reality and exigence of what is said. The tone of authority, however, variously emphasises, impedes, or irritates—for it appears in the guise of explicit assertions of fact and affords the reader sensations—our sense of the validity of the judgments it is meant to buttress. This is another way of saying that Mr. Winters does not apparently find enough authority within his sensibility—in the very tone of experience itself—and is compelled to resort to constructions of the mind outside the data of experience, either because they ought to be given or because they are consonant with the emotion of what has been given. When it happens that these constructions are not disparate from those of his audience, they are successful, though not thereby valid in themselves; and emphasise the point of what he actually brings to view. When, on the other hand, the constructions are seen conspicuously to be imported, the audience tends to feel, for the most part with injustice, that their invalidity vitiates the whole operative force of the sensibility. Men everywhere are unwilling to trust, to confide, either in the work their own minds do or in that which they see actually performed by the minds of others, though that is all they have in either case finally to depend on. They are driven rather to accept or dismiss, to foster or destroy, the little work actually done in terms of work not done at all, but merely imputed. At least, this is so of every imaginative field; of religion, of politics, of philosophy, and of literary criticism.

Mr. Winters is one of these men, but only conspicuously so because his set of intellectual constructions are not superficially in keeping with those abroad in our time, and only dangerously so because his constructions occasionally permit him to issue in judgments which would be untenable without them. His elevation of Jones Very above Emerson, Bridges and Sturge Moore above Yeats, Williams above Pound and Eliot, and Edith Wharton above Henry James, taken together with the applications of his construction of the fallacy of expressive form, furnish examples both of what is dangerous and what is conspicuous. They make an artificial barrier—himself he might call it the framework—which obscures but does not touch the work he has actually performed. It is the purpose of this Note, if not to remove, then to show how transparent and artificial that barrier is.

If only Mr. Winters had been dead twenty odd centuries like Plato and Aristotle, or three generations like

Arnold and Pater, the task would be easy and grateful;
for it would amount to little more than remarking that
most of the principles of thought turn out to be foibles
of manner and crotchets of personality: touchstones that
get in the way of the facts if taken seriously, but illuminating enough if taken, as they mostly are, as contributory facets of fact. But Mr. Winters is alive and
uncommonly kicking; and to deprive him, by mere
fiat, of his principles and his prejudices, would be so
much to anticipate history as to seem amputation. Like
everybody else he thinks he needs the assurance of his
principles to reassure his prejudices; just as the reader,
doubtless, would be terribly deprived on his part, for
in a critic where principle and prejudice were minimised
it would be necessary to read every word with attention,
as in a poem or any table of values.

Which is precisely the burden which Mr. Winters'
real work unremittingly imposes. His intimacy with the
matter-and-form of poetry and imaginative prose, when
it exists at all, is genuine and complete and stirring; it is
also infectious. The reader who ignores the obstacle
race of irrelevant formulation and incompatible comparison and returns straight to the matter-and-form considered will find Mr. Winters has given him, in just
payment for attention, an access of intimacy both accurate and viable in detail: an advantage of position from
which the whole labour of principle seems wilful, if
expedient, waste.

The expedience we will come to, and end on; here let
us represent the intimacy, and let us do so in the form
of a tribute. No reader willing to see what Mr. Winters plainly demonstrates in his studies of the experimental school of American poetry (in *Primitivism and*

Decadence chiefly, but also in uncollected reviews, particularly of Crane and Williams) will be able to avoid the conviction that the incompleteness, confusion, and ultimate emptiness of that poetry *as a school* are radical, and due to a wrong objective, namely: poetry without subject-matter. No critic has done more to deflate, in detail, specifically, under your nose and in your mouth, the final value of poetry, however otherwise valuable, which fails to declare its subject. No critic has done more both to restore both a sense for the need of objective substance and to indicate the modes by which it may be secured if it is there to secure. (No one, obviously, can set springes for woodcock that can't fly.) Again, (in the same book and the same reviews), Mr. Winters has done a great deal towards developing a usable set of notions about metre; whether they are the right notions or the only notions, and whether Mr. Winters' applications of them are always correct, matters relatively little; they are usable in a field wide enough to include Pound, Williams, Tate, Eliot, Yeats, Marianne Moore, Crane—anybody you will. Metre, like substance, had tended to disappear from consideration, which is to say had passed beyond control, and therefore did its work badly; rather running away with than sustaining, or on the other hand rather imprisoning than supplying motive-power to the efforts of developing sensibility, whether compositional or appreciative. Metre still tends to disappear, just as subject-matter still tends to fail to eventuate; the fallacy which Mr. Winters calls expressive form is still with us; but the congeries of critical opinion and the habits of poetic practice have been enough modified in the last ten years to make the following summary statement of the metrical virtues generally acceptable.

Neither deliberate privation of medium nor wilful defect of sensibility is esteemed for cultivation. Mr. Winters' metrical virtues therefore involve the virtues of sensibility. For metre: "coherence of movement, variety of movement, and fine perceptivity . . . in a system in which every detail is accounted for. Every syllable must be recognizeably in or out of place; . . . in brief, the full sound-value of every syllable must be willed for a particular end, and must be precise in the attainment of that end. . . . Traditional metre . . . tends to exploit the full possibilities of language; experimental metre . . . is incomplete. . . . Experimental conventions in general tend to abandon comprehensible motive, to resort to unguided feeling; similarly experimental metre loses the rational frame which alone gives its variations the precision of true perception." Anyone who grew up, as I did, between 1920 and 1930, will appreciate the change in poetic weather which these fragmentary quotations indicate, and will regret, as I do, that the change was not sooner felt. I believe that Mr. Winters is as responsible as anybody that the change has been felt at all.

Mr. Winters' background point of view, and the same faculty of controlled discernment of illuminating fact, which produced the valuable aspects of his essays on modern poetry, are also responsible for the seven studies in American obscurantism which he calls *Maule's Curse:* the curse that required of Hawthorne, Cooper, Melville, Dickinson, Poe, Emerson and Very, Henry James, and the culture which they express, that they drink or shed their own blood: the curse of inadequacy, on the expressive level, of life lived. It seems to me that every fact and almost all the interpretive or explanatory observations brought forward in these studies are both pertinent and useful. No one who reads the section on Poe will be content to accept him indifferently thereafter, and no one who reads the quotations from Cooper will risk dismissing him indifferently, though I doubt that in either case many readers will share Mr. Winters' extremes of opinion. Similarly, the remarks on James will well limit appreciation, as those on Melville will deepen it of those writers. The essays on Hawthorne and on Dickinson seem to me to achieve more, though they intended no more, than the others, possibly because of a greater native sympathy in the critic; they may be taken as tolerably complete versions of their subjects, but without any effect of substitution—the reader is driven back, guided and controlled with the sympathy of right preparation, to experience what is offered and to miss only what is not there. The essay on Jones Very and Emerson, by contrast, at least to me, is at its critical point an act of substitution: the substitution of a superficial attack upon Emerson (an attack, I mean, which strikes nowhere near the centre of Emerson, his extraordinary and fertile sensibility, but only upon the incoherence of its periphery) in order to elevate the absolutism, the rigid mysticism, of Jones Very: a substitution performed in lieu of critical observation in the interests of Mr. Winters' own intellectual predilections. It is good to have Jones Very; and there is no harm in Mr. Winters employing his prejudice in the discovery; but it is a very dangerous kind of criticism which judges one writer advantageously by applying *merely* prejudice, as appears here, to another writer. The danger is the vitiation of the very standards the prejudice is meant to support.

A closer illustration may be seen in the comparison of James and Mrs. Wharton to the disadvantage of James;

closer, because no sooner does Mr. Winters make his comparison than he comes, with justice, to deny that after all, Mrs. Wharton's orderly competence—my summary of what Mr. Winters attributes to her—is anywhere equal to "the vast crowd of unforgettable human beings whom" James created. Here Mr. Winters was compelled by his experience of it to return—despite its diffuseness, its mad concentration upon detail, its confusion at crucial points of morals with manners, it lapses from the advantage of plot—to what James actually everywhere exposed, an inviolable and inexhaustible sensibility. That return is the obligation of the critic as it is the necessity, for survival, of the writer. The point about Mr. Winters is that he returns often enough so that we can afford to dismiss him where he does not: we lose little to gain much.

What we lose, if I may reverse the language of religion, we tend to find in a different, less annoying, more appropriate place. For example, in this nexus, if we apply the weight of Mrs. Wharton to the mass of Henry James and see just where it bears—see just how Mr. Winters did actually apply it—it modifies without diminishing our sense of the mass of James. We know better what *James* is; which is the object of criticism. Something similar is true of the relation between Very and Emerson, Moore and Yeats, Bridges or Mrs. Daryush and Eliot or Pound. It is only by a kind of mechanical inadvertence almost universal in intellectual operations that Mr. Winters himself would have us see more; or, to use a more familiar (though hiddenly more complex) term, it is only a difference in the *operation* of taste that comes between us. Which explains the justice of Mr. Winters' charge that Poe had no taste to operate, and that

Emily Dickinson could not control the operation of hers.

To make these observations is not, I think, to injure the frame of Mr. Winters' thought; certainly it does not vitiate the moral insight upon which the frame rests; it merely reduces thought taken as principle back to the condition of thought taken as value, as discrimination, as an order, among other orders, of discernment, which is the condition or level where it is most useful in the reading or composition of literature, or for that matter, of religion or philosophy or politics. Here we come to the point of expedience where we began. Without the expedience of his principles—the logic of his taste—and without the exaggerations and irrelevances to which they led him, Mr. Winters could probably have gotten nowhere with the aspects of American poetry and fiction which absorbed his instinctive attention. It may even have been his principles which let him see what he sees. For his subject was confusion, confusion of mode, subject, source, and flux; and the best, or at any rate the quickest way to clarify a confusion is by imposing, as you think, an order upon it which you have derived elsewhere, whether from the general orthodoxy or from your special heresy of the orthodox—your version of the superrational. Actually, of course, you do no such thing, except so far as you fall into error; actually you find, discern, the order which already exists in the confusion before you and of which you form, by sheer egocentricity, the integrating part. Order is the objective form of what you know, and reaches its highest value as familiarity, its lowest as boredom, conscious or not. In between lie the operative reaches of error, heresy, shock, and irritation: the confusion that fills or the speculative leap that crosses the gaps in discernment.

Orthodoxy, which is the order of orders and absorbs them, is not for the individual. It is honest, as well as prudent, in setting up an order to leave room for disorder, which is merely the order you have not yet discerned. The difficulty is great and usually insuperable, such is the pride, and the fear beneath the pride, of intellect. But if you fail, others who come after you will do it for you, seeing, as they will with enough effort, that your order is but the condition of the disorder they, and you, both find.

It is my contention that Mr. Winters knows all this is practice, and that if you will permit yourself to know what he knows you will be able both to ignore and to profit by the mere provisional form of his argument. It is the sensibility, in the end, that absorbs, and manifests like light, the notion of order.

For what it is worth, as a sort of postscription to this whole context, is not the following couplet the sensibility declaring order rather than the intellect inviting anarchy?

Allez!   Steriles ritournelles!
La vie est vraie et criminelle!

Notes on the Novel: 1936

THE twenty novels and two collections of short stories divide with convenient ease into approximately five classes, and it is with regard to those classes rather than to any order of merit that I have arranged the order of treatment given below. Their respective rank as works of the imagination will arrange itself, if at all. Some, indeed, are not works of imagination at all—are either mere communications about living or a presentation of an informative or argumentative burden; others only use the imaginative faculty by implication. Our great concern will be with the two classes where an attempt is made at an imaginative ordering or actualization of experience within the terms of art. The other classes will be dismissed as cleanly as possible with definition and recommendation, not because their interest or use is less, but because they show little material for literary criticism to fasten on.

The Son of Marietta, by Johan Fabricius. Boston: Little Brown and Co. $3.00. *The Jew of Rome*, by Lion Feuchtwanger. New York: The Viking Press. $2.50. *The Stars Look Down*, by A. J. Cronin. Boston: Little, Brown and Co. $2.50. *The Sound Wagon*, by T. S. Stribling. New York: Doubleday, Doran and Co. $2.50. *It Can't Happen Here*, by Sinclair Lewis. New York: Doubleday, Doran and Co. $2.50. *The World With a Fence*, by Marian Sims. Philadelphia: J. B. Lippincott and Co. $2.00. *After a Hundred Years*, by Ruth Eleanor McKee. New York: Doubleday, Doran and Co. $2.50. *The Hurricane*, by Charles Nord-

Of the class furthest removed from specific criticism, we have three examples: *The Son of Marietta*, by Johan Fabricius, which is a full-blown historical romance, with picaresque trappings, of undifferentiated and unqualified action and spontaneous adventure in the Italian eighteenth century; *The Jew of Rome*, by Lion Feuchtwanger, which is part of the author's dramatized history of the Jews, realistic in historical perspective and circumstance, but communicating a historical pattern—here with philosophical subpatterns—rather than expressing or constructing the emotion of experience; and *The Stars Look Down*, by A. J. Cronin, which is a narrative of two families in the coal-mining north of England from the turn of the century to the rise of the National Gov-

---

hoff and James Norman Hall. Boston: Little, Brown and Co. $2.50. *Banjo on My Knee*, by Harry Hamilton. Indianapolis: The Bobbs-Merrill Co. $2.00. *Green Hills of Africa*, by Ernest Hemingway. New York: Charles Scribner's Sons. $2.75. *Perish in their Pride*, by Henry de Montherlant. New York: Alfred A. Knopf. $2.50. *Stoker Bush*, by James Hanley. New York: The Macmillan Co. $2.50. *Mr. Aristotle*, by Ignazio Silone. New York: Robert M. McBride and Co. $2.00. *Butcher Bird*, by Reuben Davis. Boston: Little, Brown and Co. $2.50. *Innocent Summer*, by Frances Frost. New York: Farrar and Rinehart. $2.50. *Men and Brethren*, by James Gould Cozzens. New York: Harcourt, Brace and Co. $2.50. *King Coffin*, by Conrad Aiken. New York: Charles Scribner's Sons. $2.50. *From Death to Morning*, by Thomas Wolfe. New York: Charles Scribner's Sons. $2.50. *Flamethrowers*, by Gordon Friesen. Caldwell, Idaho: The Caxton Printers, Ltd. $3.50. *The Foxes*, by R. P. Harriss. Boston: The Houghton Mifflin Co. $2.50. *The Root and the Flower*, by L. H. Myers. New York: Harcourt, Brace and Co. $3.00. *The Last Puritan*, by George Santayana. New York: Charles Scribner's Sons. $2.75.

ernment, where again the perspective is dramatic as it exemplifies history in particular lives rather than as it focuses experience in the felt lives of individuals. What these three works have in common is the informative interest—whether social or historical—of the material. Each of its type is excellent, and *The Jew of Rome* approaches mastery; none of them offers openings to the critic of imaginative form. In this class the limit of form is reached in the arrangement of information as related to viable characters, and that form, by long-standing convention, depends upon the interest of the material alone.

Of a second class, which is a little nearer to literary form in the sense that its examples attempt to persuade us of something—but by force rather than imagination, by argument rather than qualification—we have two pairs. T. S. Stribling's *The Sound Wagon* persuades us by a one-sided account, garnished by fact, humor, caricature, and ferocity, of the fundamental corruption of American politics under the twin control of the corporations and the racketeers; and Sinclair Lewis' *It Can't Happen Here* persuades the American Liberal that he must rise to action from his long dilemma of quiescence in order to destroy, before it occurs, the fascist terror which Mr. Lewis envisages with hateful care. The lessons of both authors are worth learning, because vivid, pertinent, and eloquently taught; but in learning the lessons nothing is added to our understanding of human character or of the basic American scene through which the lessons must react. My second pair perhaps make a subclass of their own, but as they exhibit a fundamentally similar attitude towards the use of the novel, showing, in effect, abstractions of character in relation to a society abstractly conceived, the advantage of comparison by natural parallelism is gained by considering them here. Both *The World with a Fence*, by Marian Sims, and *After a Hundred Years*, by Ruth Eleanor McKee, show their characters in the attempt to find a *formula* for self-realization, and both authors identify without proving their characters as superior people—which is the height of abstraction. Hence an egocentric snobbery provides the point of view and chooses the incidents. Both books have the speed—and the wastes sped over—of what does not stop to feel, but they lack the momentum of that sensibility which never stops feeling. The language used in all four books—and here is their common ground in sensibility—is that which indicates or communicates attitudes: never the language that produces and controls attitudes. The difference between the two pair is in intellectual stature, not in depth of actualizing imagination.

A third class, which reaches the condition of literature by exemplifying its basis or rudiment in narrative, is shown here by Messrs. Nordhoff and Hall's *The Hurricane* and by Harry Hamilton's *Banjo on My Knee*, the first excellent for the rising pitch of its excitement and the external vividness of its descriptive narrative, and the second welcome for light reading because amusing and bizarre and quotidian. But there seems to me no point in the many reviews that make *The Hurricane* a masterpiece outside its own limit. What effectually prevents it from being great literature is that the terrible events related happen less to the personages in the book than safely in the reader's mind; narrative in the first person can never do more without the imposed medium of a great poetic style. It is better to take *The Hurricane* for what it is, a yarn, a first-rate story any one might tell. That it keeps the limit of its class is for it rather than against it: its emphasis is laid on the event and not on the feeling of it, which, however, is the reverse of the emphasis of great literature.

We come now to the two classes where the reverse emphasis is meant to be dominant, whether by implication or presentation. One group is composed of books by those writers whose creative faculty is the post-War, barbarous, or nonrational imagination bent upon securing the impact of event and action as felt aesthetically for themselves, and whose technique is largely limited to rendering every effect and every value in its immediate aspect. The second group includes books by all those writers, presided upon by the rational imagination, who bring, or attempt to bring, the ultimate values of experience through varying perspectives of form and order to the felt condition of the actual rather than the merely immediate. As the first method is a short cut, in intention, to the ends of the second, and indeed a criticism of it, we shall examine the first group first, and briefly.

Mr. Hemingway and M. de Montherlant present two extremes of the type. *Green Hills of Africa* is a vivid, cleanly written account of hunting big game in Africa. Only the careful provision of a participating consciousness and the persuasiveness with which its theme of the active life is enacted raise it from the condition of a rambling yarn and make it, despite its autobiographical material, both a composed fiction and a gospel of action. If it is a pointless fiction and blind gospel it is because, by the simple distortion of the medicine of hardship into a sacrament of salvation, the action it celebrates absorbs point and extinguishes light. *Perish in Their Pride* is M. de Montherlant's version of the stupidity of inane inaction from which Mr. Hemingway's positive action pro-

vides the illusion of escape. I cannot see but what the
ensuing darkness is the same, whether it be taken as a
mercy or an ecstasy. But that is not the right emphasis
to place upon *Perish in Their Pride* as a work of fiction.
What is important is that M. de Montherlant leads
his three decayed Frenchmen, his rotting aristocrats,
through the ravages of stupidity and inanity to the terminal point of death for one, notably the youngest,
without ever allowing any of them to make or even to
feel an adequate response to the life around them. The
author is a victim of the apathetic fallacy, and it is as he
applies it to the sensibilities of his characters that they
become repulsive collections of fetishes rather than horrible and pathetic as their analogues are in Dostoieffsky.

Stoker Bush, by James Hanley, has an advantage over
both Mr. Hemingway and M. de Montherlant in resorting to a formal plot—a rounded sequence of adultery,
discovery, and retribution; but he loses most of his advantage by the inarticulate medium in which his particu-
lars are presented. The positive contribution of the
plot, aside from the valuable tying-in of its suspense, is
that it makes what is merely local color in his colleagues
seem more nearly, as the painters say, color in light and
air: unity and consistency of atmosphere. Between the
extremes of action and inanity, Mr. Hanley's book is exciting, veracious, and intensely apprehended in terms of
the bare materials of emotion, but it fails to come off, I
think, because only the atmosphere and not the values
of his people are focused by the plot. It is worth noting
that all three authors resort at critical junctures to the
releasing device of the lyric outburst, Mr. Hemingway
in a beautiful prayer to his wife, M. de Montherlant in
his metaphor of wild geese and dying at the death of his

protagonist, and Mr. Hanley in a sudden, free, and confused description of a storm and wreck at sea—all three passages being wholly inconsistent in mode and tone with the technical structure of their respective books.

Ignazio Silone in his collection of stories, *Mr. Aristotle*, makes no such defection. His portraits of peasant stupidity and violence and superstition, whether under the impact of the fascist terror or not, have a roundness of feeling and fullness of emotional implication all the more powerful because secured with the economy of bare statement. His peasants may be stupid in all they have to offer on the surface, but their stupidity has an air of participation in, at a deep, blind level of consciousness, all the feeling and understanding of their own meaning which a more articulate sensibility could avow for them. As Kenneth Burke once observed of Erskine Caldwell, Signor Silone indicates so well what he has left out—the humanity, the sentiment—that the reader knows exactly what to put in. These indications, these small lacunae, perhaps constitute an implied form in themselves, and as near a positive or rational form as authors may come who refuse to posit a full intelligence at the heart of sensibility.

There is more, of course, to say of each of these authors, more to demonstrate the unfailing responsibility of each at the periphery of his work, and more to explain the necessary defect of irresponsibility at the center; and it is an injustice to explain one without demonstrating the other. There is an element in every sensibility for which the periphery of things is often enough, which is a prudent and an aesthetic element as well as self-deluding and inconsolable. Let us say rashly, omitting all the rest, that where the only principle of control is peripheral, then, at the center—both of the works provided and of the reader's response to them—private and uncontrolled, unrealised emotions will creep in, and the value of your implications, if you have them, will be out of kilter. That is like life, confused; but a rational art is meant to improve it with the conscious illusion of form.

In turning now to our last group, we have in Reuben Davis' first novel, *Butcher Bird*, a natural transition from the nonrational to the rational imagination. We have a powerful but forced plot as in *Stoker Bush*, we have a superficial stupidity covering an animal intelligence as in *Mr. Aristotle*, and we have a good deal of apathetic or callous brutality as in *Green Hills of Africa* and *Perish in Their Pride*. But the differences are as marked as the resemblances. The plot lifts and gives the forward stress of life in suspense to the characters so that they contribute as well as suffer the action. The stupidity of surface is made to reveal, and not merely to imply, the suffusing animal intelligence beneath, and the device of exhibition is the irrefutable one of the spoken, idiomatic phrase, which in a novel accomplishes what gesture does on the stage. And the apathetic brutality is superficial, given for excitement and contrast, and does not drive the story: it is local colour in the good sense. Which is to say that every element is subordinate and contributes to the rational intelligence—in this case the omniscient author's—that presides upon the whole. The result is that Mr. Davis' negro share-croppers and their tale of love and labor, murder and fraud, will and sacrifice, are what is called *authentic*, presented as felt in every relevant aspect. Their actions are felt as rising out of their lives and their feelings are the equivalent of the action. But I should praise Mr. Davis too much and be unjust to the authors with whom I am comparing him if I did not add two qualifying facts: *Butcher Bird* is successful but slight, and the slightness, but not the success, depends on a too facile use of the stock conventions of the novel. The success is in the only promise worth noting, a measure of achievement. Magnitude, that is hoped for, comes only with a completely realized technique, and what matures in a rational imagination is exactly that technique.

Of Miss Frost's *Innocent Summer* what is at once plain is that it is built, like *The Waves* of Virginia Woolf, on the serial presentation of the parallel consciousnesses of half a dozen children aged five to fifteen. The parallels are meant to multiply at the same time that they focus. The product is the related action of the different children both as they perceive it themselves and as, from a detached and more nearly omniscient vantage, the reader sees it in wider implication. What is focused, seen magnified or made small, is the theme: the solid of emotion which is the novel's response to the growing up of these children in terms of the natural, if critically chosen, events of a single summer.

The device of the innocent sensibility as a freshener of experience and a purifier of judgment is a sound and, when adequately adhered to, a liberating device for any novelist. We have examples in James, Dostoieffsky, Gide, and Mann, and with a variety that might make adequacy seem prospectively omniform. Miss Frost's example shows that it is not; there is a limit to what the innocent sensibility will bear in itself and a cognate limit to what the reader will bear from it. The limit is indefinable, but it may be felt as transgressed when the *terms* in which the innocent sensibility is shown are richened or stretched beyond the powers of the sensibility itself. It is a matter of credibility and of the technique for securing it. Miss Frost's children are sometimes incredible, not for what they see and feel and know, but because the language of their minds, the terms of their knowledge, shows them as knowing too much *what* they know. The poetry of seeing, which ought to be the reader's, is too often substituted for the poetry of what is seen. The charm of the child's mind, at least in fiction, is that it knows and at the same time does not know. That is, the force of naïveté is always the force of experience taken as its own meaning, and this is true equally whether the experience is sensual, of a death, or intellectual, of an idea. Put positively, for the novelist, the rule of the innocent sensibility is this: it is capable of receiving and responding to any experience whatever, and the novelist may present it with as much experience as he can find perceptive terms for; but it is incapable, in the degree that it *is* innocent, of perceptive terms for the typical, the general, the stale, or the in-any-way sophisticated, because—and this is its greatest advantage as a mirror—to it the stalest experience will not only seem fresh but will *be* fresh, and to present it otherwise is not to present it at all.

If Miss Frost fails sometimes in constant freshness and falls into the stale and incredibile, it is only partly because she transgresses the limits of what the innocent sensibility will render as credible. There is also the inherent difficulty of employing at the same time the contrasting modes of the innocent sensibility and the stream of consciousness, a combination which requires a great technical mastery to effect. Miss Frost writes with authority but not with mastery; but her comparative failure comes primarily from the only spring of ultimate success: a sensibility possessed by the forward stress towards persuasive form. That her failure is technical only shows how much she has to fail from. Meanwhile *Innocent Summer* is superior in every realm of value to work which merely passes as competent.

It is not superior to the competence which characterizes James Gould Cozzens' *Men and Brethen;* a competence which includes a prudent mastery, and of which nothing could be asked except, superrogatively, a greater magnitude. Although we can say that Miss Frost fails in the management of a great theme through the immaturity of her formal technique, we cannot say anything of the sort about Mr. Cozzens' book. His management is excellent and his theme far from small: the theme of what life does to a man who has already matured in a special way, here an episcopal clergyman limited by the special strength and weakness of the intelligence that brought him into the Church. As Miss Frost employs the innocent sensibility Mr. Cozzens employs what is no less the device of the informed sensibility; and as Miss Frost presents her pure souls with the shock of life in a Vermont village and made a summer's picture, Mr. Cozzens presents the Reverent Ernest Cudlipp with the shock of the terrible business of the Church in this world, and makes, I think, a day's destruction of it. No novelist could ask more for theme and situation and circumambient natural interest; and, with so much given to begin on, few novelists could do more than Mr. Cozzens in the way of excitement, compactness, and the achieved air of momentum. Where the book falls short is not, in any ordinary sense, in its technique; as an essay in rational art it is everywhere in control of itself and establishes its own relative proportions and balances. Its concessions to melodrama—the coincidence, the packing of events into a single day which might have been expected to occur in a term of years—are heightened and made good by the sophisticated intelligence of Cudlipp and by the invoked power of the Church. Furthermore, the sensibility of the book itself, as distinguished from Cudlipp's sensibility, is remarkably civilized—equable and self-consistent—yet a prevailing witness of other lives, other sensibilities, to make up a whole.

And it is this civilized, this ironic, sensibility that sets the tone and contributes the novel's final nub of meaning; it is this that gives the equivocal answer to the question implied in the title: "Men and brethen, what shall we do?" and suggests analogues for any transposition the reader cares to make. Hence, when Cudlipp resorts to the lesser evil by procuring an abortion to save a marriage and a family, or when, in the end, he fails his friend Carl by resorting to the higher good, which happened to be his own wordly good, we have the same predicament exposed. Which drove him, in either case, his own weakness or the essential strength *and* weakness of his faith? The answer, in a novel, has no need to pass the equivocal, which is the realm of felt value—of life as lived by those aware of it; but it needs to reach that realm and be felt there, and felt by the person concerned. Cudlipp is not raised to that eminence; he is exposed to his predicament but is not made to feel enough of it; and that is the radical lack of the book, the dissatisfaction no reader who envisages it can supply. I think, granting Mr. Cozzens the will, the sensibility, and the craft, that the remedy is yet technical after all. Cudlipp is an example of the normal in his métier, and his predicament is normal; but for that normality to be driven home it must be shown as eminent, as towering, and, perhaps, as obsessive; and there is nothing on earth to show it so, finally, but the persuasive power of language, language made equal in actuality to the feelings involved. In the novel, in the art of words, every economy and every expense of structure and conception is validated, if at all, in the particular words that render them. I think, then, that if towards the end of his book Mr. Cozzens took more care of the words for Mr. Cudlipp's feelings, Mr. Cudlipp might turn out to be eminent after all.

If Mr. Cozzens' *Men and Brethen* is a case of the normal that fails of nothing but eminence, Conrad Aiken's *King Coffin* gives the opposite example: an eminent case of the abnormal where the failure, if there is one, is the very mark of success: which is to say that the book is a *tour de force* of the abnormal parading as the normal but nowhere subject to any normal appreciation except the reader's. What we have for the abnormality is the adventure of a man with an overweening need to commit himself, identify himself, realize himself absolutely, and who can only do so by killing a stranger. As his own vision of the decision, the choice, and the pursuit is unfolded, there is a hovering, a heightening, a shrinking; and when the act is performed it becomes, rightly, suicide. When you look into the abyss the abyss rises within you. That is the theme and the story; and the quality of the elaboration depends upon the fact that everything is seen directly through the consciousness of the protagonist, which is an abnormal, a diseased, an insane consciousness, scrupulous and proud of its own abnormality. We have the abnormal seen as an eminent case of the normal; and the effect is strengthened by making the normal view, as the protagonist catches it in his secret reading of his neighbor's diary, preposterous, irrelevant, intrusive, and horrible, an object of suspicion and mounting fear. Thus Henry James' rule for the rendering of evil is reversed; instead of giving us a normal perception of evil—except in the hints in the diary—Mr. Aiken gives us an abnormal perception of the normal. But at the same time James' rule is proved equal to the demands of the *tour de force* as well as to the demands of the straight novel; the object as well as the rule is here reversed; for the success of Mr. Aiken's story depends exactly up the degree in which the abnormal does strike, *for the moment*, with the ring and value of what we take to be the normal, and vice versa.

How to value such a work will remain a problem only to those who are devotees of the fine game of literary precedence. Admitting that it belongs in a special compartment, one ought to be able to take it for what it is—the imaginative exercise of a dramatic possibility based upon the conventional melodrama of modern psychology, in short a legimate, because persuasive, *tour de force*. But as many will refuse so simple a salute, I want to make one or two further distinctions. It should be insisted that the book itself is sane and everywhere alert to the responsibilities of the rational artist, and it is only by the seductive slight of art that the reader is made to feel otherwise. The value of that sanity and the scope of that rational responsibility may be felt most obviously in connection with works which are helpless, at bottom, because without their governance: *e.g.*, Thomas Wolfe's *From Death to Morning* and Gordon Friesen's *Flamethrowers*, both ailing over-growths of superabundant sensibility.

Both these authors take their material from experience felt at hysterical intensity, and as their works develop, the hysteria replaces and obscures instead of mirroring and controlling the experience. The subjects of both are the stupid, the distraught, the oppressed; and Mr. Wolfe with his greater talent and better knowledge merely expresses those qualities at their own level with more lyrical fervor than Mr. Friesen can muster. Mr. Friesen is a worse, because a more barbarous, Wolfe: both are equally guilty of the heresy of expressive form: the belief, held to exaggeration, that life best expresses itself in art by duplicating its own confusion in the trans-ferred form of the *spectator's* emotion. Write what you see, whatever it is, and say what you feel or ought to feel, and the thing will make itself a work of art. That most writing on this rule, not wholly turgid, is auto-biographical, is the first clue to its insufficiency. The fundamental insufficiency, however, is in the lack of sanity in the presiding form and the absence of a rational point of view. Returning, for our point, to Mr. Aiken's book: its hero, Jasper Ammen, might be as stupid, dis-traught, and oppressed as any creature of Mr. Wolfe or Mr. Friesen, and as a matter of fact, on his own *intel-lectual* level, he is. Form, we might say, is the only sanity—the only principle of balanced response—possible to art: as lyric form will make the right nonsense into poetry; and to force your material—which is to say to condense, to elaborate, to foreshorten and give perspec-tive and direction—into your chosen form so as to ex-press it primarily by actualizing it—that is the minimum of your rational responsibility. You may do more if you wish; your work may come to an ideal vision like Santayana's *Last Puritan* or *Gulliver's Travels;* but if you do less, you will not have written a responsible fiction; you will have expressed, not your subject, but yourself and more or less waste matter of emotion besides.

We do not need to resort to the special example of Mr. Aiken's *tour de force* for sane form; there is another, no less special, example from which the same counsel flows. This is *The Foxes,* by R. P. Harriss, which is on the surface the straightforward, zesty tale of the life of a fox in the fox-hunting Carolinas, with human interludes of trapping, hunting, rat-killing, cock-fighting, drinking, and botanizing at convenient intervals. Following no set rule of structure or point of view, resorting to the pathetic fallacy (with the foxes), the hardboiled or apathetic fallacy (securing emotion by being unemotional about brutality), and occasional rhapsodic enthusiasm for detail (as in the naming of the dogs), the book nevertheless escapes the character of serial sketches and conspires to produce a fictional center, a sensibility of its own, within itself and among its parts. It has a unity which is organic and which acts half by implication and half by the charm through which it is alone visible, but which, once perceived, acts back upon the whole of the book, illuminating and refining the duplicity of its purpose.

I do not know how this effect is secured any more than I can exactly define its under-purpose. Perhaps the chief means are a constant loving treatment of detail and action, the unifying force of an attentive personality, and the resulting fresh persuasiveness of the language. Perhaps the ulterior purpose so illuminated is only pictorial: that the reader may come away with all the moving elements of a picture of the whole terrain, human and animal and topographical, sinking back into a new wild, a wild stigmatized and pathetic because feral, all second growth and nothing primeval. The purpose may be more, or less, and may show different perspectives for different readers. Whatever it is, it is secured by the clean economy of the selected material and by the controlled intensity with which it is presented. The book is a mirror and its life is in the image shown there. The weakness of Mr. Harriss, if he has one, is, like Mr. Aiken's, negative rather than, like Mr. Wolfe's, positive and overwhelming. In the sense that it requires a special surrender, a special delimitation, of expectation, *The Foxes* is, like *King Coffin*, a *tour de force*: it is an example, perhaps, of unusual material made to parade as eminent, a fact which makes it, as it is, successful minor art, excelling but slight.

At another extreme, both of intention and sensibility —and the art of the novel is prodigious in the number and quality of the extremes it provides—there is L. H. Myers' trilogy, *The Root and the Flower*. Addressed avowedly to readers in the modern predicament, it states its theme of the moral sensibility on the spiritual plane, and the twin theme of character-discrimination on the social plane—in terms conscientiously removed as far as possible from the social, economic, political, and religious predicament of his audience. The action takes place in sixteenth-century India and its movement is governed by various intrigues concerning the succession to the throne of Akbar, the great emperor, with the intention that the significance of the work will be all the more clearly felt in the Western twentieth century because divorced from false issues and local spiritual vulgarity.

I do not think that the device works except against its purpose, and its use raises one of the great problems of the novel: the use of external action and the form it ought to take. It is in this case easier to recognize the nub of discussion because the action fails. The clear result of Mr. Myers' device is that his action counts chiefly as a frame. What happens, what is done, what eventuates, matters only as it helps us to envisage, to see as of concrete origin, what the characters think and feel and say apart from the action that may or may not have inspired them. I do not think Mr. Myers realizes the burden he has chosen for his prose to carry: which is the burden of making a great proportion of his words *tell* in and for themselves as separable, quotable, self-complete items of expression. Put the other way round, Mr. Myers is nowhere able to resort to the great advantages of plot, which are roundness in appearance, solidity of impact, the illusion of objectivity, and—here the greatest advantage—the releasing or precipitating force of psychological form. This last is emphatically the great advantage of plot in works like *The Root and the Flower* which mean to mirror or represent the ultimate conflicts of the spirit in relation both to God and the world; and the advantage consists in this, that the words released or precipitated by the crises of the plot will, however ordinary in themselves, gather from the plot an extraordinary or maximum force of meaning which will in turn suffuse and heighten qualities of meaning differently arrived at—*e.g.*, "The rest is silence."

It is the *system* of the *Divine Comedy* as it is the melodrama in *Hamlet* which precipitates and actualizes the great lines and passages we keep for value. Plot is the idiom, the special qualifying twist of action, and the writer who does not use it to the maximum tolerable degree fails to use the one dependable objective principle of composition. Mr. Myers in this case, in my judgment, has made that failure; his book has plot, but only for convenience in arranging movement and to provide the ornament of intrigue; it is all subplot and no major plot. Without a plot he depends for composition and forward stress upon the momentum of his theme, and for suspense and crisis upon the elaboration of debate. Which is to say that he depends upon the presentation of detail only thematically related, upon what, in short, is academically called *style*. The result is—to choose a few aspects from many—that the characters are superbly characterized, but never presented; their conflicts are profoundly envisaged, but seldom felt or understood; their debates and meditations are ably summarized and beautifully quoted, but seldom dramatized. The whole work seems somehow at the remove of comment, a chorus of apothegm. It is a novel everywhere acutely and nobly *about* its theme without ever becoming its representative equivalent. I do not say that if Mr. Myers had resorted to a fundamental invigorating and predicting plot, he would necessarily have achieved a deeper intention. Plot offers privations some cannot endure. I say only that plot would have offered a dependable opportunity to dramatize and enact, here not offered nor otherwise won.

But plot may not be the only mode of major composition. If plot is the idiom of action, the very articulation of the felt form of movement, surely there may be occasional perspectives where the plot needs no conscious formulation, so deep-seated and habitual may our consciousness of it be. *The Magic Mountain* is an eminent example of major composition without benefit of a major plot, where we have, topping all subplots, both the simple sequence of a life and the organic process of a disease contributing a sense of form altogether adequate to the greatest burden Mann could put upon it.

If I bring up a great novel here it is not to belittle *The Root and the Flower*, but to make room for George Santayana's *The Last Puritan*, which if it has a form at all—form in the sense of prevailing, animating structure —has form by the juncture in its center of a life-sequence not even complete and the felt organic process of an incomplete but profound imaginative insight—here called *puritanism*. It is only by conceiving the form on such a pattern and by construing the subject or narrative as flowing from it and depending upon it that we can consider the book rightly as a novel. We had otherwise better call it a "Soliloquy on America," containing dialogues, apologues, descriptions, and commentaries. Certainly if we look for any of the contributory achievements and graces of the ordinary novel, we shall be disappointed with what we find. The characters are not well drawn in their externals, are thin in their blood, and are wholly inadequate in the expression of the stock personal emotions. The narrative lacks sweep, and events do not sustain each other on the wing. Where most novelists would have worked a scene for all it was worth, Mr. Santayana either dodges it altogether or stops it short with a sermon, a meditation, or a note. On the supporting side, the transitions are for the most part merely gaps, the atmosphere is never completely localized and is usually given in terms of comparisons, judgments, and evaluations. Of the devices not integral to the theme of a novel but necessary to keep it rolling, those Mr. Santayana chooses are not well oiled and silent as good wheels should be, but creak awkwardly as they do in real life.

Mr. Santayana, in short, is not a novelist, not one of the craft; yet he has written a novel. *The Last Puritan*—to come to the point—succeeds to the status of a novel by building upon its substantial form in two directions. It composes a memoir of American life through its complementary intellectual portraits of Peter and Oliver Alden, and these portraits, in turn, are made the double focus to image the type of American society—the final stiff strawflower of New England Puritanism—which produced them. The radical weakness of each character is identical: the weakness of the puritan heritage in its final form, its incapacity to actualize life without decimating it. Each character realizes that weakness in himself, and that realization gives them their tragic strength and perspective. Each is an extreme of the type and knows the agony of extreme self-consciousness. Each has "a moral nature burdened and over-strung, and a critical faculty fearless but helplessly subjective." It is the scruple of the subjective conscience that decimates the life it realizes; hence Peter, the father, in attempting to be unscrupulous, in attempting vice, luxury, and waste, only finds his scruple weary but no less active, and his achieved waste fatal; and hence too, the son Peter, taking the other path, knowing his scruple false, follows it the more intensely, doing everywhere the duty he despises, and in the end "wanders off again into the mist, empty-handed and puzzled-headed," morally self-slain.

Such is the intellectual direction the book takes, and

its success in that direction is enough to make a profound critical appreciation of its chosen version of American life. What makes it a novel, a major example of imaginative dramatization, is its success in treating the same material in the opposite direction: the direction of poetic expression. Every important character in the book is given speech of inspired clairvoyance with which to crown and satisy the needs of his being. The circumstance and the need are of the character, the inspiration is that of the book's material acting upon itself, but the clairvoyance springs from the language of moral philosophy raised to the level of absolute or dramatic poetry. That is the great technical feat of the book and the measure of its imaginative performance. The idiom, the fresh and indestructible sign of imagined characters, is here not in action nor in the felt quality of experience directly; it is, by the illusion of clairvoyance, translated or absorbed into the idiom of dramatic, re-creative philosophy: which is an absolute idiom of poetry. An excellent example for reference, because self-complete, is Mr. Darnley's sermon at the unexpected sight of his son, Jim, and Peter Alden coming into church.

It may be noted, finally, that in giving an objective, independent form to the inspirations of his characters, in most cases far beyond their practical capacities of expression, Mr. Santayana merely restores to the novel an ancient prerogative of poetry. "I have made you all speak the lingo natural to myself," he writes, "as Homer made all his heroes talk in Ionian hexameters. Fiction is poetry, poetry is inspiration, and every word should come from the poet's heart, not out of the mouths of other people . . . Even in the simplest of us passion and temperament have a rich potential rhetoric that never finds utterance; and all the resources of a poet's language are requisite to convey not what his personages would have been likely to say, but what they were really feeling."

The Composition in Nine Poets: 1937

NONE of the poets here represented, except Euripides behind his English guise, is a master of composition, and only two, not counting the Greek, show evidence of even aiming at composition, namely Conrad Aiken and Wallace Stevens. None of these poets, again excepting Mr. Aiken and Mr. Stevens, makes a genuine attempt to use in his poems the maximum resource of poetic language consonant with his particular talent. These statements, here initially assumed as true, ought at the close of this discussion to have shown themselves as the governing facts of judgment and the conditioning facts of appreciation. What is not at least approximately composed cannot act with unity upon the responding sensibility, and what fails to reach its appropriate limit in words so far fails to establish its character as an idiom of the imagination, and so further confuses the details of response. The fate of poetry is in the character of its composition, and a body of poetry that does not reach the condition of idiom does not reach the dignity of fate.

Arranged in the order of this discussion: *Gaily the Troubadour*, by Arthur Guiterman. New York: E. P. Dutton & Co. $2.00. *More Poems*, by A. E. Housman. New York: Alfred A. Knopf. $2.00. *Poems of People*, by Edgar Lee Masters. New York: D. Appleton-Century Co. $2.50. *The People, Yes*, by Carl Sandburg. New York: Harcourt, Brace

THE EXPENSE OF GREATNESS

These remarks, in one version or another, ought to be the commonplaces upon which criticism is built; not touchstones—which more often have to do with intention or aspiration than with accomplishment; not cornerstones even—which have much more to do with the act of consecration, or exhilaration, than with what is consecrated, and have nothing at all to do with the obstinate source of exhilaration; but foundation stones, simply, the stalwarts that bear every weight like so much air and lean only upon each other, leaning not for strength but for balance and resilience and spring. Certainly, if we do take them for commonplaces, if we do look for composition in the conceiving imagination and for the twist and shape of idiom in the executive imagination of the poems before us, we shall know what, in what measure, to accept as living poetry and what to dismiss as merely occasional, or personal, or vain before the possibility.

The possibility is always great, though the performance may often be such that no sight is caught of it: it is beyond the closed and closing horizon in which the poet makes his verse. This is the circumstance with Mr. Arthur Guiterman. Mr. Guiterman is a writer of light verse, and as such, I take it, he means to be frivolous

---

and Co. $2.50. *The Assassins*, by Frederic Prokosch. New York: Harper and Brothers. $2.00. *Selected Poems*, by Witter Bynner. Edited by Robert Hunt with a Critical Preface by Paul Horgan. New York: Alfred A. Knopf. $2.50. *The Alcestis of Euripides*, an English Version by Dudley Fitts and Robert Fitzgerald. New York: Harcourt, Brace and Co. $1.25. *Owl's Clover*, by Wallace Stevens. New York: Alcestis Press (Limited edition). $10.00. *Ideas of Order*, by Wallace Stevens. New York: Alfred A. Knopf. $2.00. *Time in the Rock*, by Conrad Aiken. New York: Charles Scribner's Sons. $2.50.

and mordant, superficial and acute, sophisticated without snobbery, satirical without bad manners, spontaneous and finished. In the best light verse the outward moorings of composition come all provided in the verse forms as traditionally used and instinctively modified—as we see in Rochester and Herrick. There remains, however, an indefeasible need for serious composition in the conceiving mind of the poet. To maintain gaiety at a definite level of taste is as difficult and requires as much composed unity of approach and as mature an attitude towards the material as is required to maintain fury or disgust. Light verse may be as bad as bad tragedy. Taste, being educable, varies with the generations; and poor schooling produces fatuous self-confidence that the réchauffé, in light verse as in the hash of life, will show organic warmth. It is extraordinary how stodgy cold is the wit of the average light poet underneath. Mr. Guiterman seldom misses the average on this score, and when he does it is because he escapes, for a line or so, his more dominant defect of lazy or facile language. Gaiety, and especially gaiety in finished form, is the last thing to be caught in a formula of facility, and the formula is the last thing Mr. Guiterman's language leaves behind.

The misapplication of Mr. Guiterman's title—*Gaily, the Troubadour*—furnishes another clue to the story. The troubadours wrote perhaps the most complexly and intimately controlled verse of the western world; their lightness of touch and melody of line were made possible partly by that control and partly by their completely serious, if limited, view of the life they wrote of. If their poetry was an intricate game, it was always a game that had life in it—the life of their whole society. The same thing is true, to a lesser degree, of such men as

Greene and Herrick, of Rochester, of the dramatic prose of Congreve, and of the best of Prior and Gay. It is not true of Mr. Guiterman; his verse is not a game with life in it—as, for example, the game of Gogarty's verse has life in it. Being without control, intricate or otherwise, it has least in common with life precisely at its gayest, and most in those dull reaches where the only possible response is the flip, the smart, the cute. That is a large domain and deserves its documentation, but only in the daily columns.

The counterpart, in this list, to Mr. Guiterman is A. E. Housman. Housman was not a writer of light verse, but a desperately solemn purveyor of a single adolescent emotion. He wrote, as he said, when he felt ill, and he wrote, as if by consequence, almost entirely of death, and almost entirely of one sort of death, the blotting death which has no relation to life. The advantage of this sort of death is that, if you apply it, it cancels the obligations and conditions that lead to the desire for it. It is a very practical sort of death, and very popular with the adolescent sensibility of any age; it is both your alternative and your revenge, and being complete does not seem to suggest any weakling desire for escape. It is a very strong negative, this death; its only positive element is its otherness; it is the other place, the other thing, and you can go on morally applying it all your life long with unimpeachable authority, which was what Housman did. But for people who want a positive death Housman's notion seems not only inadequate but offside, lacking any composition with the life which makes it possible, and having very little composition with the vital predicament which makes it emotionally plausible. Not despair but a disorderly kind of inactive desperation which some call Quietism—a clutter of private horror—perennially makes the notion consoling: it is so available, so free of experience, and so meaningless by construction. Hence the wide distribution of Housman's versions—which showed a singular want of variety for all the years involved in their repetition; he made practical poetry for all those who willy-nilly survived an impracticable need—an audience potentially universal. And hence Housman's reputation as a great, and perfect, minor poet. Hence, too, Ezra Pound's verses, first printed in 1911, called "Housman's Message to Mankind" of which I quote the first stanza.

> O woe, woe,
> People are born and die,
> We also shall be dead pretty soon,
> Therefore let us act as if we were dead already.

And if it be argued that Housman, being dead, ought not to be ill spoken of, the answer is that Housman himself, speaking of little else, never spoke well of death. He had not the equipment for speech nor the maturity of being that ripens the urge to speech into objective form as the sloppy flatness in the following stanza shows (from number XLII of *More Poems*, which is evidently, by the Preface, a late poem).

> Strange, strange to think his blood is cold
>   And mine flows easy on;
> And that straight look, that heart of gold,
>   That grace, that manhood gone.

A poet's treatment of death is one test of his magnitude and perhaps the best test of his maturity. To complete the test of Housman in these respects we have only to remind ourselves of other and positive conceptions of death: in Dante and Leopardi, in Baudelaire and even in Victor Hugo, in Shakespeare and Donne—or, if we wish for foils in prose, in Thomas Mann and Sigmund Freud. The point needs no laboring; there is the Cross which sets death as background and perspective for all human life. Death maturely meditated gives life moorings; death enacted in imagination and worked intimately, as Shakespeare worked it, into the processes of living, gives life bearings and a course, however mysterious. The image of death is an image of all expense and of all becoming, and the image, too, of all terror and dismay, both of what is known and of what cannot be known. Whatever Housman may have known or felt, he disciplined out of his verse all but the easiest and least valid form of death: the invoked death, that can never be known. It was not a matter of submitting to the limitations of his sensibility and so stretching them to the utmost, but a matter of deliberately imposing a narrow discipline in the interests of what can only be called an escape from a full response to experience.

Thus Housman was not a great minor poet in terms of his conceiving imagination. He did not even attempt to compose anything but the least possibility of his dominant idea with the life it was meant to express. Neither was he a great minor poet in the lesser sense of possessing extraordinary control of his medium without reference to its burden. The medium of poetry is language, and the sign of achievement is the persistent emergence of fresh and vital idiom. Housman's language is full of archaism, stock phrasings, correct attitudes, metronomic meters, dulled rhymes, and all the baggage of dead idiom. All that retrieves him from disuse is his personal intensity and the universal popularity—as it strikes a universal weakness—of his theme. Taking him seriously, as he meant to be taken, we have only to compare the best of Housman with Hamlet's most famous soliloquy, or for that matter with Gray's "Elegy," to feel that substantially Housman had as little control over his material as Mr. Guiterman and that his response to life is no less flip. You cannot be a classicist without a classical theme, and you cannot write perfect verse in dead language however pat your cadence falls. You cannot take out of words more than you find there, and it takes the utmost imagination to find much.

Mr. Masters' *Poems of People* is more ambitious and more slovenly than anything in Housman. Mr. Masters attempts, here and in his other books, a broad impasto panorama of American history and character. But he has forgotten or never learned the first lesson of craft or morals: that our means determine, if not our willed purpose, certainly our achieved ends. Mr. Masters writes largely without any poetic means at all, on a level of thought which is mere unselective notation, at a level of language which is mere indifferent communication. Hence, as poetry, his poems largely do not achieve the ends expected of them. His words make merely the initial ruins of undeclared possibilities. As extended, ornate anecdotes many of the poems are successful, pointed or poignant, tart or exemplary, and would be more so if they were not so often slowed and mired in bad verse. But anecdotes at best can never be more than imputed poems—they are hints, specific données for the poet to make actual. Mr. Masters finds his données broadcast; rightly his provision is everywhere and omniform; he is, if you like, all genuine aspiration and quick response; but, no doubt in his hurry, he does nothing to digest his provision into poetry. The reader gets waste and roughage, copious, warm, and bulky, but not good victuals.

Let me specify Mr. Masters' defects more closely; they are the common stultifying denominators of most productions meant to be taken as serious narrative or dramatic verse. Mr. Masters knows all about how people outwardly behave and he knows what it feels like to behave outwardly, but he does not know how to transform outward behavior into words—whether of description or of speech—so that the mould of represented action is the moving and visible sign, the very form of experience, of the inward being that acts. The wellspring of character does not flow. Actions are not joined, but filled in, are not ordained and certified by the representative and uniting devices of the art of language, but merely occur as they can. Hence Mr. Masters' crises and his generalizations have only the authority of isolated cries and casual epigrams, and cannot have more, because the material they illustrate, in its merely specious array, did not and could not produce them. The ends of intention cannot transpire without the means of achievement. The first means of poetry—of making life actual in the art of language—is always a means, and such have been various, of putting your elements together so that they seem mutually to interact and work together to compose a new whole; which is to say, again, that the first necessity is an approach to a principle of composition. Most of the other means are means of making your elements move; they are the operating devices of the synergizing process of poetry. Many of these devices are so intimately a part of the movement of language that they are difficult to segregate for discussion:

e.g., those devices of order and cadence whereby a particular sense of a word or phrase is enhanced without injury to other possible senses. Other devices are obvious and easy to bring into discussion by the handle of a standard feature—as the characteristic duplication or echo of sound is the handle for the complex instrument we call rhyme. I do not think that Mr. Masters has ever, unless by accident, taken rhyme by anything but the handle. No man would consciously produce so many jolting, jarring, isolated reproductions of similar sound as Mr. Masters does if he had any idea of the advantages rhyme may be made to show. It is not isolated words that rhyme but sounds that occupy position in a line, and there is no advantageous effect of rhyme if the lines are malformed in order to ensure position. Mr. Masters, I take it, is employing rhyme in the following stanzas from "Tom Barron" chiefly to keep things going, to mark intervals of space and time.

> Was it because he married Sadie Mack?
> Was it because she bore him children two?
> Was it that mother, daughter grew
> Spiders behind his back,
>
> Which spun conspiracies and bit his breast
> When he was sleeping, feeding, or full of smiles
> Sucking his blood? Was it these wiles
> That all his labors messed?

The malformation of line consequent upon the rhymes reduces a serious rhetorical question—one of the major heightening devices of the craft—to the condition of doggerel, and the rhymes themselves impede the movement and blur the intervals of the meter. There is hardly more to say of Mr. Masters as a poet. The publication of these stanzas and of the hundreds more no better and many worse brings down its own particular punishment. Yet there is this. Mr. Masters blames the misery and failure in which many of his characters end on what he calls the American Scene. Perhaps it is a major failure of American society—considering the indubitable fundamental talent in the best of Mr. Masters' work—that it requires so little of its poets in the way of craft and gives them, apparently, too small a burden to make craft necessary. Perhaps, too, Mr. Masters" failure is no greater than Housman's or Mr. Guiterman's. The failures of facility are bottomless.

A better clue may be found in Carl Sandburg's *The People, Yes;* I mean a better clue to Mr. Masters' failure. As a deliberate craftsman in verse Mr. Sandburg is at least as facile—at least as much given to taking the nearest and easiest way—as Mr. Masters or anyone else. But, and this is the gulf of difference, Mr. Sandburg is an unconscious master of the natural craft of the speech he hears and thinks; he knows by instinct very near exactly how much of it will go on paper or into formal discourse with the maximum of strength and the minimum of retained weakness. This is because Mr. Sandburg's sensibility operates neither higher nor lower than the level of the speech he uses. I do not mean to say that Mr. Sandburg is an unconscious artist: I do not believe there are any; but I think Mr. Sandburg would find it difficult to say at what point in a given poem he became conscious of using deliberate devices for specified effects. It is his initial advantage that his sensibility soaks up experience almost entirely in its native expressive aspect. His work has the air of coming from a mind that knows what it sees, believes what it sees, and is at home with what it sees. Hence his poems are full of positive affirmation, lyric aspiration, and a divine, almost a complacent, emotional conviction of rightness: with, on the other hand, no traces of struggle, no stigmata of irony, and no recognition whatever of the profound confusion of impulse and perception and necessity from which his exhilaration springs.

The confusion is there nonetheless, the lump, mass, and momentum of experience taken at its face value, and it is because he has done nothing to order it, integrate it, and make it radiant, nothing either to compose or plumb it, nothing to make it actual to the rational imagination —and thence ever available—that he is not a major poet. He has not seen the necessity. As the fullness of simple perception was for him all he needed of order and meaning, the mere indicative beautiful record ought to be enough for the poem and the readers of the poem. It is not enough. We have the record and see the footprint of affirmation and aspiration. Great poetry, if such is its purpose, is the enactment of aspiration: so that its apprehension is an inexhaustible and indestructible experience. *The Divine Comedy* is the only extended example we have. A comparison of Dante with Mr. Sandburg on this score should demonstrate—all sentimental enthusiasts to the contrary—that the poetry of Dante is inseparable from the philosophy, and the poetry of Mr. Sandburg is incomplete for the lack of a philosophy; and, further, to get back to our own point, should suggest that there is an efficient relation between the formal strength of Dante's poetry and its inspiriting philosophy, and that, analogously, some of the conspicuous formal weakness—the lack of location at a given moment, for instance—in Mr. Sandburg's poetry may be due precisely to the lack of an objectively felt philosophy.

Certainly, as it stands, a great part of Mr. Sandburg's poetry sprawls dangerously near the original level of its subject matter: experience at that level where it is taken to be its own expression. The danger is that of utter shapelessness: that the poetry, like the subject matter, will be extinguished the moment you take your eyes off it. The obvious locus for that danger is when the poetry becomes a catalogue, but is as clear, really, in the anecdotes—substantially not very different from those of Mr. Masters and just as poetically incomplete—which fill out a good half of the pages of this volume. No philosophy could save the poetry as it exists, but no sensibility affected with a philosophy could have created a body of poetry so innately beyond control. The other solution is just as inapplicable. If the felt philosophy of a Dante would not operate for control, neither would the major dramatic form of a Shakespeare. Major form, especially dramatic form, presupposes an extreme intelligence either at the center or at the focus of action; and that is exactly the presupposition impossible to find room for in a body of poetry given over to the fallacy of expressive form upon which Mr. Sandburg depends. (The fallacy, the most common of our time, consists in the belief that the act of expression creates its own adequate form.) The intelligence may be there, but only by accident, and fitfully; it does not participate in or modify the action; and it cannot be counted on to materialize when wanted or even to keep its eyes open; in short, a very poor instrument to compose or evaluate action. Mr. Sandburg does not, by a sound instinct, attempt the dramatic or any other intelligent form.

What he does do is run on, letting experience express itself as it will, trusting to the luck of juxtaposition and the specious unities of perception to come out right before the end. What saves the work and makes it have almost the value of poetry is the freshness of the surface of what he sees and not at all what he does with it. The freshness does act to establish a specious unity and forces a momentary sense of relationship between the elements of perception. More it cannot do. The unity *is* specious and lifts like a landmist before a nine o'clock sun; the relationship *is* momentary and disappears before the meditation of it can occur. That may be all Mr. Sandburg desires of his poetry; that it be like life at the ordinary expressive level where it is lived. That is a terrible, because unnecessary, limitation to put upon poetry.

Mr. Frederic Prokosch puts no such limitation upon his first volume of verse, called *The Assassins*. He puts no limitations on his work at all, nor has he found any to which he has felt bound to submit. He is Faust-like and geographical. The emotions of his poems are universal, dragnets for all experience, and their sites are widely distributed, mostly along the coasts of European seas. His work is, therefore, largely promise and very little performance beyond the measure necessary to establish the promise; but the promise is full, and is his own, with little obvious derivation. It is both welcome and suspicious to find a young poet whose best work is not immediately derivative; welcome for relief and surprise; suspicious because it suggests that he was unaware of his immediate ancestry in living poetry only because he was immersed in the stock ancestry of dead poetry both immediate and remote. With Mr. Prokosch the suspicion is partly gratified: his affective vocabulary is full of snakes and animals and distant places and enormous shores: full, that is, of stock expansive terms which must, without specification, be mostly dead. But the gratification is only partial and the welcome remains: he manages to produce out of each poem an emotional mood only tinted and not controlled by his stock vocabulary; and perhaps indeed his readers could not understand him—nor he understand himself—without the indicative, attention-calling tint. His great virtues are genuine depth and scope of feeling, a sense of the ominous and precarious and infinite, and a talent for phrasing; his defects are looseness of line and a general tendency to allow the number and variety of implications in his words to get beyond the control of his theme. There is an associated quality, sometimes a virtue and sometimes a defect, which rises from the use of a great number of conceptual words and names. He neither specifies his allusions nor certifies his concepts by representation in the actual instance; he rather invokes them. Meanwhile he is readable in the fragmentary sense, for the fragments which are lines and images and for the fragments which are his whole poems. He has more feeling for and has used more of the resources of poetic language—his words show more of the stress and forward rush for meaning and actually come nearer to making idiom—than any poet so far discussed in this review. Being content with the establishment of moods which, isolated, compose themselves if they are composed at all, he has no need for a compositional principle and has made no attempt at a major subject. The title poem is the best and presents a dominant mood of our time, rather like the mood of Yeats' "The Second Coming" but without its resource either in language or prophecy; the mood wherein we feel the imminence of chaos and the terrible precariousness with which every value is maintained.

Mr. Bynner, in his *Selected Poems* (edited and introduced by other hands) presents, as against Mr. Prokosch's beginning, the best and varied work of twenty-five odd years. Mr. Bynner should have been a great poet, and that he has not become one presents a problem for Van Wyck Brooks when he comes to write *The Budding of the 'Teens*. Mr. Bynner had in the beginning more drive, more verve, more obvious scope, and more presumed chance for maturity, than Eliot, Pound, Aiken, Moore, or Stevens—each of whom was comparatively a special case—ever showed. He has written more than any of them except possibly Aiken and has tried greatly with the noblest and most honest intentions. He remains fresh and easy to read, full of insight and inscape, of observation and landscape, everywhere competent, but without a trace of ultimate value. His inferiors in poetic imagination—Frost and Robinson—as well as his betters have outlasted him. He never grew in stature, only in competence and variety; he changed, often, and added to his girth, but he never deepened. His latest work has no more root in actuality than his earliest, and springs less in aspiration. Neither through his charm nor through his occasional ferocity did he ever reach the whirling point of mastery. Several sources of failure suggest themselves. Society, in the terms in which he was able to feel it, did not supply him with a theme demanding enough to exhaust his talent in his work; and he, for his part, could not change the terms of his feeling so as to take advantage of the *natural* themes that any society everywhere supplies: the themes of life as it is lived—the themes of Shakespeare and the great novelists, the theme of life made intelligible or actual by the power of the imagination. He required rather, always, an initial, reliable mode of belief, an *a priori* idealism, with which to test and determine the actual when he met it. He tried, again and again, to find such a mode, and found, I should say, increasingly intolerable versions of his own solitude. So governed, or rather failing of government, the sensibility of his verse was unable to cope with actuality when he discovered it. He could not assent to the actual, whether in the individual or in society, precisely because the need he had most cultivated was the need to transcend the actual, and he could not transcend it because he could not himself provide a principle of transcendence for a society that conspicuously lacked one. Hence he attempted to escape. His most important and distinguished poem, "Eden Tree," is the long, pathetic, and often lovely record of the different versions the escape took. In the end Adam, the protagonist, has neither escaped from Eve, who represents our knowledge of the wilderness of the world, nor found any satisfaction with any Lilith—with any intoxication of desperate inspiration; he is left, rather, profoundly disconcerted. Eden tree becomes the Cross, the Cross a bed to lie on, the bed the bed of death. Adam's death is the perfection of his loneliness.

Granted the type of sensibility, granted a society like ours where at the center if nowhere else things fall apart, Mr. Bynner's predicament is profound and insoluble. It is the predicament of the bottomless weakness of the human mind when it is at those stages that lack the rational imagination either to create a heaven out of need or to cope with the chaos of the actual from which heaven springs. Shelley was in that predicament and if we value Shelley above Mr. Bynner it is not because of his ineffectual resort to Plato and revolution but simply because he met the actuality of the felt predicament—not the actuality *behind* the predicament—in maturer verse than Mr. Bynner has ever been able to manage, so that his work at its best, if not his heart, had the rhythm of the rational imagination. It is bad enough to be born into a world without faith or unity and to feel increasingly the need for them, but it is worse to be born a poet in the same world and not have the means to express your aspiration. You miss then what unity there is in the apprehension of your experience, which is the most of unity and the only form of faith most worlds have to offer.

Let us plant here as firmly as may be the image of Alcestis fresh from the dead in English guise. She comes pat to Mr. Bynner's predicament, pat to the general predicament of the poetry of our time, and there is no hope for us if we cannot learn her lesson: which is the lesson of the irrational and the incredible made rational in the poetic imagination and so beyond the need of belief. It is a question whether the emphasis in Euripides is on the horrible human weakness of Admetus who dreaded God and fate, or on the extraordinary human strength of Alcestis who took Admetus' place in death and left him, for the time, a man without a fate, which is the condition of extreme human failure. The irony is, in either case—and in the irony is the composition of meaning and value—that it is through an intensification of his weakness that he receives Alcestis back from the dead at Heracles' hands and comes, as he says, on a new life, which is to say resumes his fate. It is only by breaking, under the ruddy and sensual persuasions of Heracles, the spirit of his vow to Alcestis never to take another wife, that Alcestis is returned to him. He must take her as another woman. Alcestis was his fate, his and no escape; but was it by enacting the excess of his weakness or of his strength? That Heracles, the strong man, the struggling man against the gods, was the agent of enactment only makes the value more ambiguous and seeming ultimate.

The point is that Euripides took a myth of human desperation which inhabited the Greek mind at an uncertain level of belief—a story that was perhaps still in Euripides' time capable of plastic and practical application—and transported it to a realm where neither the presence nor absence of belief matters, the realm where by the power of rational imagination in language and by no other power whatever, the myth became actual in the only possible terms of human value and meaning. It is in this sense that everything capable of being imagined is the truth, and only in this sense. It is the truth of experience forced onto the level of the actual, which is Mr. Bynner's lesson; and our lesson is—considering the extravagance and the literal preposterousness of Euripides' play—that any material is susceptible of imaginative actualization provided you approach it with a principle of composition and a care for detail. For Euripides the principle was the received myth. It is not through any scarcity of myths that our poetry lacks composition but rather through a tendency of the poetic imagination to become barbarous instead of rational, with the result that our poetry makes life mythical instead of making myths actual. That is a tendency which the example of Euripides should help reverse.

Of the particular translation of the *Alcestis* here presented by Mr. Fitts and Mr. Fitzgerald the worst that can be said is that it remains, here and there, a translation. The language is not always worked up to the poetic level called for by the action, and occasional resort is had to interpolated stage direction, which, in a poem, can only indicate and cannot control vocal tone and mood. Again it is a little surprising that the translators should have not more often and more nearly approached the norm of blank verse. My ear may be mistaken, but it seems to me that much of their verse is actually a loosened blank verse and demands of itself, for strength and lift, the occasional satisfaction of the normal overt meter. But these are carpings; the translation is cleanly made, without a trace of cliché, archaism, or stock language, and, most important, the verse is everywhere verse in its own right and never mere versification. There is, in short, little suspicion that we are being cheated of the original; there is an original on the page.

On one point, and on the very point of our emphasis, the example of Euripides must not lead to false counsel of ease in composition. Euripides is merely an exemplary seed; and if you plant him you will not bloom in composition forthwith; you will probably not bloom at all, but straggle and die of green rot like Stephen Phillips. The living imagination is its own germinal principle, and all it can borrow is a habit of growth, a tendency, a general direction; and in any case growth is difficult, and in the greatest cases suffers profound failure somewhere just short of perfection. *Hamlet* and *Lear* suffer such failure; so do *War and Peace* and *Moby*

Dick; in these works the very greatness of composition
testifies to the presence of undigested, unarticulated, disconcerted material, which without the composition
would have been lost altogether. The tragedy of imagination, like the tragedy of life, comes in its particular
overweening pride; the triumph of both is to represent
the actuality of failure.

I think it is because they share the conviction of something like what I have been saying that Conrad Aiken
and Wallace Stevens have in their work a compositional
drive and an ever-present particularizing intensity of
process that gives their best poems an objective and inexhaustible vitality, and leaves even in their poorer work
a residuum of genuine direction and implication. Each
is deeply concerned with the interminable labor and
single solace of the imagination.

> ah, can it comfort us,
> us helpless, us thus shaped by a word,
> sleepwalking shadows in the voice-shaped world,
> ah, can it comfort us that we ourselves
> will bear the word within us, we too, we too
> to speak, again, again, again, again,—
> ourselves the voice for those not yet awakened,—
> altering the dreams of those who dream, and shaping,
> while they sleep, their inescapable pain—?

And each knows that imagination has an end, and how,
and why, and where.

> To flourish the great cloak we wear
> At night, to turn away from the abominable
> Farewells and, in the darkness, to feel again
> The reconciliation, the rapture of a time
> Without imagination, without past
> And without future, a present time, is that
> The passion, indifferent to the poet's hum,

That we conceal? A passion to fling the cloak,
Adorned for a multitude, in a gesture spent
In the gesture's whim, a passion merely to be
For the gaudium of being, Jocundus instead
Of the black-blooded scholar, the man of cloud, to be
The medium man among other medium men,
The cloak to be clipped, the night to be re-designed,
Its land-breath to be stifled, its color changed,
Night and the imagination being one.

And each, finally, knows by what means the imagination
is to be resurrected.

We need a theme? then let that be our theme:
that we, poor grovellers between faith and doubt,
the sun and north star lost, and compass out,
the heart's weak engine all but stopped, the time
timeless in this chaos of our wills—
that we must ask a theme, something to think,
something to say, between dawn and dark,
something to hold to, something to love—

Medusa of the northern sky, shine upon us,
and if we fear to think, then turn that fear to stone,
that we may learn unconsciousness alone;
but freeze not the uplifted prayer of hands
that hope for the unknown.

To differentiate between the two men's methods and
manners is to establish their identity of purpose; to compare them is to make a measure of achievement. I hope
that my quotations above, of which the first and third
are from Mr. Aiken's *Time in the Rock* and the second
from Mr. Stevens' *Owl's Clover*, will by example release
me from what Henry James would have called the mere
weak specifications. But a few facts may be in order.
Both men have been obsessed, like Henry James, with
the theme of the human imagination at its daily work.

Each has struggled again and again to actualize the experience of the imagination—both in its action and in its characteristic inabilities to act—in poetic language at a very high, often excessively sophisticated and sometimes difficult level of intelligence; and again like James, the obsessive theme of imagination has gradually been made to include or to imply the whole diversity of normal themes. It is worth noting that the conscious emphasis upon the imagination as itself a primary theme is something of an anomaly in the history of the arts although not in the history of philosophy; it is another sign, I suppose, that the artist has himself to do the work formerly done for him by Church and State and the operative morale of society: he has to establish in the very process of his work what a mature society took for granted as it everywhere resorted to it, the nature and value of the imaginative act. In poetic practice—and here is the nub for us—the result is that satisfactory frames of composition acceptable both to the poet and to his presumed readers are almost impossible to discover, and that, as a consequence, almost all the work must be performed by the words themselves with the minimum benefit of composition. No wonder modern poetry is fragmentary.

Returning to Mr. Aiken and Mr. Stevens, there is a clue to the directions they take and the kinds of value they discover in the titles of one—*Harmonium*, and *Ideas of Order*—and in the general notion of Preludes in the other. Harmonium is a slightly flavored word for an instrument to make harmony; harmony is more than musical—there is, or is not, a harmony of the gospels, and there is a harmony in all things seen, or grown, together. Yet the word harmony itself would not, as a title, have carried its own implications; and it is a characterizing part of Mr. Stevens' talent that he should have used, with its flavor of self-mockery, the lesser word to produce the values of the greater. The title is itself a poem by Stevens. *Ideas of Order* contains just the measure of ambiguity—of double value in double meaning—to make itself self-explanatory. Ideas are principles, notions, clues, guesses, abstractions of hope, deposits of insight; but they are also things seen, both casually and deliberately envisaged. It is the function of poetry—or of Mr. Stevens' poetry—to experience ideas of the first kind with the eyes of the second kind, and to make of the experience of both a harmony and an order: a harmonium. Thus Mr. Stevens' values inhabit his words; and if he can make his words grow together he will be composing on his harmonium. The machinery of composition—the ways he uses words—is double; he fuses two separable vocabularies. There is the vocabulary of concepts or symbols—the nubs and cores and condensations of meaning—which is almost altogether dissimulated, by great craft, in the simplest and most familiar general terms of the language, in terms of the sun, moon, sky, clouds, in terms of sea and landscape, in the almost natural terms that cats and dogs can understand. And there is, forced into this, a vocabulary of difficult, striking, or puzzling words—as *gaudium* in the passage above—words that have to be looked up in the dictionary, and, looked up, always turn out to be the very instruments that make the general terms precise, predominant, and imaginatively actual. It is, then, with Mr. Stevens, the reality in the words themselves that is composed by the skill and precision with which the specific is made to work upon the general.

THE EXPENSE OF GREATNESS

With Mr. Aiken the situation is not exactly the reverse—it could not be when language is the medium,—
but as nearly so as the medium makes possible. If I
understand the formal notion behind the Preludes Mr.
Aiken has been writing in recent years, a prelude is a
beginning or approach, the taking up of a theme or the
search for a theme, a promise, but not, finally, the thing
itself except by implication. Both something else and
more of the same are always involved, at least in possibility, both before and afterwards. Formally separate,
like a prelude in music, no prelude ends in completion
but always in suspense and with a consequence: the
definition, as the subtitle to this volume attests, yet to
come. Like the dramatic monologues of Browning,
these preludes establish their composition by assenting
to their formal limitations. As soliloquies they must be
eloquent, persuasive, and apart; their crises must be built
of rhetoric but the elements of the rhetoric must be
concrete; and, above all, the binding force, the synergical
process, cannot be found primarily—but only immediately—in the words on the page. Mr. Aiken's machinery is not in his vocabulary—but in the attitudes,
almost the myths that underlie the vocabulary. The
dictionary and the general symbolism of language are
much less help in explicating Mr. Aiken than Mr.
Stevens. He writes with the habit and the assurance of
the traditional poet; his preludes, as he masters them, become, like the Elizabethan sonnet or the heroic couplet,
a definite and predictable form of thinking; and his
underlying meaning flows from the hidden predispositions of his time. If I am right and my ear is good, it is
such of these predispositions as his talent is capable of
receiving that transpire in the music of his verse, taking,

of course, their special and limited form. If the drama and the symbolism are often—to use a loose word—Freudian, so, I think, is our general moral imagination. But it is the Freudian made normal by extension and reduction and representation. It is no less Christian and, perhaps, no less Platonic, with similar qualification. It is always the poetic imagination that restores the speculative and abstract imagination to the condition of the concrete and the actual; because it is the poetic imagination that alone sees and feels the speculative at work in the composition of men and women. Mr. Aiken's preludes as they get suppler, as they delete more and more of the superfluous, the merely expansive, and the ornamental, and as the words come to find all their richness from their concreteness and their aptness, ought soon to deliver the definition they prepare, when the act of composition will, or will not, be completed. That is the direction in which Mr. Aiken works with increasing maturity of process, and, with Mr. Stevens and Mr. Eliot (whose *Ash-Wednesday* is the nearest to major composition our generation has yet come), it is in that direction that the fate of poetry may be looked for.

Nine Poets: 1939

THE COMPLETE COLLECTED POEMS OF WILLIAM CARLOS
  WILLIAMS. 1906–1938. New Directions. $3.
MIRRORS OF VENUS. A Novel in Sonnets. 1914–1938. Bruce
  Humphries. $2.50.
A GLAD DAY. Poems by Kay Boyle. New Directions. $2.
DEAD RECKONING. By Kenneth Fearing. Random House.
  $1.25.
LETTER TO A COMRADE. By Joy Davidson. Yale University
  Press. $2.
THE GARDEN OF DISORDER. By Charles Henri Ford. New
  Directions. $2.
THE FIVE-FOLD MESH. By Ben Belitt. Knopf. $2.
SEQUENCE ON VIOLENCE. By Harry Roskolenko. Signal Pub-
  lishers. $1.50.
THE COLLECTED POEMS OF LAURA RIDING. Random House.
  $4.

NINE books of contemporary verse running to over
thirteen hundred pages leave one both aghast and
agape. It is education by shock; the lesson, even after
reflection, confusing, and the value dubious. Not for
one's life would one repeat what one thought one had
learned. Far better, mouth open and teeth showing, a
conspirator caught, to stop at the shock. Let us see why.

Mr. Belitt says it is because you must try to integrate
yourself, make of your senses a single faculty and "loose
the inward wound to bleed afresh." But his labour at
integration ends, in 1938, rather more like vertigo:

Tranced as in surmise, lost between myth and mood,
Derelict, decoyed,
In some astonished dream of sailing. . . .

Dereliction is an important element in Mr. Belitt's sensibility; it is a function of sleep and dreaming, of a bird
and of human stragglers: at any rate we have derelict
claws of a singing bird and certain inexplicit stragglers
by the surge. One should not make too much a point
of it, yet it strikes sharp; that Mr. Belitt's poetry fails
of integrity less because it deals with the sentiment of
chaos and the moral of the abyss than because, in so
dealing, he prefers the dreamy, the quite somnambulistic
state to the waking representation. This is to indulge
in the dereliction—the reprehensible abandonment—of
poetic duty. He does not say—he does not represent—
what he is writing about; he only indicates, and forsakes,
what it was that led him to write.

Otherwise he does very well; his words work on each
other and carry each other along apace; it is a pleasure,
as sleep-walking goes, and at the right remove, to reach
his version of vertigo. With the work of Laura Riding
we have no such contact, no matter at what remove.
Her poems may, as she says in a long preface, be written
for all the right reasons, or for more right reasons than
anybody else's poetry, and her reasons may be mine as
well as hers, and that these reasons are all the reasons of
poetry, but I suspect just the same and with good reason
that the reason of all these reasons is the reason (buz buz)
she does not say once and for all Unreason, and then
add, for all the best unreasons that unreason is not not-
unreason. Perhaps she really does not not say so. Certainly she does not not say every now and then unre-
proach unharshed unloving unsmooth unlove undeath

unlife undazzle unmade unthought unlive unrebellion
unbeautifuls unzoological unstrange unwild unprecious
unbull unhurriedness unenthusiasm. Miss Riding is the
not star of un no not never nowhere. After page eighty
pretty well right through 477 pages she tells us what
she it they we you are not, and when she does not
tell us directly she tells us even more not clearly by not
not indirection. Many pages are not without fifteen
forms of the verbal negative; no page is without words
which produce negation. We have either

> There is much that we are not.
> There is much that is not.
> There is much that we have not to be

or we have such phrases as "native strangeness . . . Science, the white heart of strangers . . . the lionish landscape of advent." Here meanings beat against each
other like nothing but words; we have verbalism in
extremis; and end-product of abstraction without any
trace of what it was abstracted *from.* Automatic writing as featured by Gertrude Stein plus an obsession with
the *problem* (not the experience) of identity plus an
extraordinary instinct of how best to let words obfuscate
themselves here combine in the most irresponsible body
of poetry in our time. Miss Riding is not derelict; she is
jetsam: washed up; and just to the level that we are
washed up she makes excellent reading.

Mr. Kenneth Fearing's *Dead Reckoning* is not nearly
as good reading; for one thing a good deal of it is in
capital letters which are very hard to hear they are so
loud and not at all foxy and feminine like italics; and
for another thing much of it is in very long lines—some
of the lines are several lines long—with no pegs to hold

them up, so it is hard not to hurry to the end before they fall down or worse fall apart as indeed they often do both—down and apart, like the genealogies in the Bible and the catalogues in Whitman, and like what Mr. Fearing is writing about: the defeated people who live in cities and the present world generally and who want what is not to be had either in cities or the present world and want it very much almost exactly because they do not know what it is. We all of us have caught ourselves talking and sounding like Mr. Fearing's people showing what we are and what we want and hastily covering up the gap between. Mr. Fearing just says what it is like; his work is an example of Henry James' phrase: the platitude of mere statement: disturbing, apt, accurate; but in the end, no soap. Meanwhile, though one would rather read any poem by Fearing than any poem by Riding because he not only says what he is writing about but sticks to it, let us insist that there are certain obligations in the profession of poetry which if fulfilled leave the reader, not just in the same boat with the poet, but deeply in his debt. If Mr. Fearing wants to limit himself to the poetry of statements on the Whitmanesque line he will have to use that line for all it is worth; especially for phrasing and the control of speed such as are usually obtained by metre and rhyme; and further, and much more difficult, he will have to charge his lines so persuasively with his subject that every line will "tell" just in itself as well as in its major relations. In metrical poetry the filling may well be the bonding agent between the parts and inseparable from them; in non-metrical poetry the only bond is gravity and balance, what is only filling drops out.

Miss Boyle in *A Glad Day* gets round that difficulty

more or less in passing, partly she resorts largely to prose phrasing to keep her work moving, partly because her filling is indistinguishable at a given instant from her building material, and partly because she is apparently interested in using only the least amount of the vast possibilities her work declares. All that she does is penetrating, discriminating, devastating and decorative. She knows all about meanings without ever seeming to have experienced what is meant. This is the end of "In Defense of Homosexuality."

> Put under glass some of them could be worn as cameos
> Their femininity plumbed to the depths of
> A tedious vocation as engrossing as bee-raising
> And as monotonous to the outsider.

Her value lies everywhere, as in these lines, in the display of specialised and truncated perceptions: perceptions both so intelligent and so little tied to their locus that they can be used like postage stamps on anybody's mail; a feature which is perhaps representative of that general dissociative frame of intelligence called surrealism, or the addition to superimposed units of perception, superimposed but nowhere joined. Unlike Mr. Fearing she has nothing to learn because there is nothing in the world supplied by learning that she wants to do. Your sophisticate is only swamped by learning, cramped by form.

The outside of Mr. Ford's *Garden of Disorder* belongs to much the same school, the stretch of overt sonnets in the midreach of the garden doing nothing to belie the borders, as that in which Miss Boyle is mistress. The title poem is dedicated to Pavel Tchelitchew; hence one expects, and indeed is given, a flair for the commonplace seen as gusty because slightly twisted and distrait;

one is both amused and brought to the edge of discovery—where one is vaguely, and archly, taken aback:

When you were in the circus did the seals lie on their backs, piss straight up like hallelujah?

The archness makes it fun, and because it is fun it does not mean or need to be actual, and because it is not actual it must be taken either as not counting or as an escape from what does count. This is a splendid method, this verbalised nexus of the arch look and the thing seen, of voiding poetic responsibility at the moment that you feel it—splendid and fascinating, a very vice. In the poem called Plaint before a mob of 10,000 at Owensboro, Ky., which is quite the best poem in the book, Mr. Ford writes six magnificently direct lines which are all of his poem but its end; then he adds seven lines of arch filling which obfuscate precisely as they dictate the distich of ending. Let us compare two direct lines,

I, Rainey Betha, 22,
from the top-branch of race-hatred look at you

with two lines of filling—

The robins of my eyes hover where
sixteen leaves fall that were prayer.

The dignity and justness of the first metaphor is only reduced by the metaphorical (not the verbal) distortion of the personification. Perhaps it is the rhyme or it may be the sentiment that wreaks the injury; certainly there is corruption at work in the language, not the corruption from which we spring, but that in which we end, a corruption from which the archness of flavour is no redemption. The lines are simply offside, representing material out of control. When the robin eyes begin to hover the attention is distracted; it is the distraction, the specious haven, of irrelevance so often resorted to by the wavering intelligence, the selfish spirit, the vain craftsman before the invoked face of reality. That the resort is made as we say unconsciously—merely because at this nexus the poet thought of something or something suggested itself to put in—does not diminish the dereliction. The principle involved is practical and has a direct effect upon the degree of appreciation the poet can expect from his reader, namely: you cannot successfully write a short poem in either different modes of language or different modes of feeling unless you make sure that the different modes work together to a common advantage. Put the other way round, unity of tone is the best assurance of the affect of composition. Put generally: only within an order can you give disorder room. All of our poets so far have rather attempted to get along on vestiges of order in composition as in life, and are all examples of what Yvor Winters calls the fallacy of expressive form. The practical result is that as the poet does not keep to his subject and make it objectively complete neither does the reader keep to the poem.

Mr. Roskolenko, in his *Sequence on Violence*, has not yet, I think, begun to write poetry; he is rather a vast fascinating register of the mind as sensorium in which at any moment anything may occur. He has all the irresponsibile vitality of the immediate in sensation and of the frantic in perception; all governed, as is usually the case, only by vitiated convention, which is to say not governed at all. That is the rich material of sensation is not used to enliven convention; rather we have sensation and convention with very little connection between them. One level—that of the poems dealing with the politico-economical predicament—we see fresh sensation resolved into the convention of blanket anti-fascist terminology; on another level—that of the poems of personal revolt—we see it in the conventional negation of such final binding lines as those that end the last poem in the book:

> Love is only gall
> thus love offends us all.

But the lapse into vitiated convention shows most clearly, perhaps, on another level altogether—on the pervasive level where the detail of sensation or perception is supposed to acquire meaning or movement by jointure with the conventional word.

> You have seen *waves* and *rockets*—gerrymander
> the sightless shafts of air. . . .

The italics are Mr. Roskolenko's; the word here in question is gerrymander. In another poem we find "the spirit dismembered with elan," where the important word is elan. No stretch either of word or context in either poem will bring these words into definable vital (or organic) relation with the meanings wanted. They are so used as to be deprived of their ordinary cumuli of meaning without acquiring the authority of a new or special meaning. When you find this type of writing expanded so as to be the only circulating element in long and obviously serious poems, you will conclude that the writer was not only not in possession of his subject but that he gave in only to its most obvious temptations: of verbal vanity—the fluxion of words without knowledge or assumption of the dictionary.

Poetry is to be regarded as the use of one vocabulary

of the language. I have heard a medical man high in his profession assert that all medicine lay in an up-to-date medical dictionary; by which he meant that if he knew his vocabulary he could objectify his knowledge. It is the same thing with poetry, and with as much responsibility for life and death.

Of Miss Davidson's *Letter to a Comrade* there is less to say than of any of the books on our list. She is more evenly a poet than any but the two we have not yet mentioned; she has respect for the language, for the traditions of poetry, and for her own intelligence; she is forthright and what is more important she is candid. For the most part she writes with authority because she mostly limits herself either to what she knows or knows that she wants to know. She resorts neither to dogmas nor to any of the devices for stilling the consciousness, and succumbs only to those blueprint symbols of intellect and spirit natural to a growing mind affected by the megapolitan culture of this decade. The spirit which conceives and the intellect which articulates the predominant element of protest in her poems are not entirely hers, not digested, not matured, but are a non-incorporated framework borrowed perhaps from the land of the *New Masses* where the best of these poems previously appeared. She has, that is, permitted her sensibility to be violated by the ideas which have attracted her. This is because the technique of her verse is not yet strong enough or plastic enough to cope alone with the material her sensibility has absorbed, and takes meanwhile any help it can get. There is nothing surprising in this; the very forms of our education, and the very formlessness of our taste, seem fairly designed to set us in immaturity by preventing us, so to speak, from the

maturity we had only to assent to to inherit. Miss Davidson gives as her greatest promise that she has within her
the ability to make that assent.

With Mr. Wheelwright's *Mirrors of Venus* and Dr.
Williams' *Collected Poems* we come upon one man who
insists upon his inheritance and attempts to make the
most of it and another man who, looking at the botch
of the half-inherited, denies that there is anything to inherit. The difference is clear. In Mr. Wheelwright you
get the sense of perceptions powerfully backed, fed,
and formed; shaped otherwhere, celebrated here; a pattern not repeated but rediscovered. In Dr. Williams
at his best you get perceptions powerful beyond the
possibility of backing; the quotidian burgeoning without trace of yesterday; the commonplace made unique
because violently felt. Dr. Williams of course inherits
more than he thinks and Mr. Wheelwright not unnatu-
rally suffers from what he inherits. *The Mirrors of
Venus* lack richness, the *Collected Poems* lack culmina-
tion. Dr. Williams is full of tags that he knows nothing about; Mr. Wheelwright knows too much about his
tags and by over-deliberation occasionally uncovers a
void. Mr. Wheelwright moves towards the kinky, the
special, the wilful, the sport of thought and spirit and
form because he is so much aware of the general; Dr.
Williams moves towards the flatness of the general because he takes every object, uninspected, as fresh. Mr.
Wheelwright deals with moral and spiritual struggle;
Dr. Williams deals with the same struggle before it has
reached the level of morals and touches on the spirit
only by accident. Mr. Wheelwright reaches the explicit through abstraction, by celebrating the fulfilment
of pattern:

THE EXPENSE OF GREATNESS

Habit is evil,—all habit, even speech;
and promises prefigure their own breach.

Dr. Williams reaches the implicit through the concrete,
by acknowledging what he sees:

It's a strange courage
you give me ancient star:

Shine alone in the sunrise
toward which you lend no part!

There are facts about these two poets which implement
our respect for their poetry and put iron in the bias of
our general regard for them as figures in the world of
our present sensibility. The facts have nothing to do
with magnitude, which is a gift of heaven, and of which
our appreciation depends as much on distance as on use.
We are concerned here merely with the facts of poetic
character. There is, to begin with, the fact that Dr.
Williams writes exclusively in free verse of an extraor-
dinarily solid and flexible species. Further he despises
traditional English metres; the sonnet he thinks good
only for doggerel, subverts most intelligences, and has as
a word a definitely fascistic meaning. I do not doubt
that he may be right for himself; which goes to show
only that his intellect is in him so badly proportioned
that it interferes with the operation of his sensibility. He
needs to work, as it were, under cover; needs to find his
work seemingly already done for him when he takes it
up. The depth and rightness of his instinct for himself
is shown by the mastery in at least twenty poems of
varying length of a form adequate in every respect to his
poetic purpose. Yvor Winters says that this is the form
of free verse, and that it scans, has outer rules and an

inner scheme. I refer the reader to Winters' *Primitivism and Decadence* where the technique of Dr. Williams' free verse is fully discussed; I cannot follow the discussion myself, preferring to believe (until I can follow it) that Dr. Williams' astonishing success comes from the combination of a good ear for speech cadence and for the balance of meaning and sound, plus a facility for the double effect of weight and speed. When Mr. Winters (in the *Kenyon Review*, January 1939) compares Dr. Williams to Herrick as equally indestructible, the justice of his comparison, if there be any, must lie in the comparison of incongruities; for the older poet spent his life refining his sensibility in terms of his medium, precisely as the younger has evidently insisted on his sensibility at the *expense* of his medium.

However that may be, what remains of Dr. Williams' medium has been so successful for himself, that many have thought it would be successful for anybody. We are accustomed to think of him as a fertile poet—as fruitful in poems for other poets to read. The pages of the poetry journals every now and then show the results; curiously, the imitation is almost always of the poorer or more crotchety poems. The fact is, it seems to me, that Dr. Williams is a product of fertility. All the signs and recognitions of fertility in his work point backward. He is almost a reduction not a product, a reduction to a highly personalised style to express personal matters—a remarkable, but sterile, sport. You can imitate him, as you can imitate anything; but you cannot incorporate him. In short, his work adds to the sentiments but not to the sensibility.

One reason is that almost everything in Dr. Williams' poetry, including the rendering, is unexpanded notation. He isolates and calls attention to what we are already presently in possession of. Observation of which any good novelist must be constantly capable of, here makes a solo appearance: the advantage is the strength of isolation as an attention-caller to the terrible persistence of the obvious, the unrelenting significance of the banal. Dr. Williams perhaps tries to write as the average man—that man who even less than the normal man hardly exists but is immanent. The conviction which attaches to such fine poems as The Widow's Lament in Springtime, Youth and Beauty, or the first section of Spring and All, perhaps has its source, its rationale, in our instinctive willingness to find ourselves immanently average; just as, perhaps, the conviction attaching to tragic poetry is connected with our fascinated dread of seeing ourselves as normal. Dr. Williams has no perception of the normal; no perspective, no finality—for these involve, for imaginative expression, both the intellect which he distrusts and the imposed form which he cannot understand. What he does provide is a constant freshness and purity of language which infects with its own qualities an otherwise gratuitous exhibition of the sense and sentiment of humanity run-down—averaged—without a trace of significance or a vestige of fate in the fresh familiar face.

The facts about Mr. Wheelwright are very much on the level of significance and fate; they make the matter of his preoccupation; and as they are delivered or aborted they make the failure or the success of his poems. The subject is the significance of friendship and the fate of friends: "the mirror of Venus reflects loved ones as each would be seen." The emphasis—the feeling for pattern—is protestant-christian; divine but apprehended by the individual. The form is that of the sonnet, varied, twisted, transformed, restored: some inverted, some in couplets, some Shakespearean, some in free-verse, some in blank-verse; for Mr. Wheelwright feels that a sequence of "perfect" sonnets would produce hypnosis in the reader instead of demanding and controlling full attention. That may be so; but I observe that all the nine sonnets that seem to me almost wholly successful depart least from one or other of the stricter sonnet forms, and that those which seem to me to abort their subject matter are in free or metrically unequal verse. (Those which seem to me successful—nine out of thirty-five—are Abel, Sanct, Father, Holy Saturday, Lens, Plus, Phallus, Mirror, and Keeper. The worst failures, Kin, Parting in Harlem, and Village Hangover, seem to have been put in for structural reasons without becoming part of the architecture.) Whether the imposition of external form is responsible for the emergence of a whole pattern in these poems, I do not know. The interesting thing is that we have the form and we have the pattern, while elsewhere in the books under review we have neither. It is at least suggestive, that had Mr. Wheelwright everywhere mastered his form, then his pattern would everywhere have been clear. But diagnosis is not cure; and it may be the other way round. None of us to-day, none even with the full strength of Christian or Marxist belief, can take full advantage—full nourishment—of our heritage, whether of enlivening form or enduring pattern, without extraordinary and almost impossible luck—like that of Thomas Mann in his novels. Without such luck, without that gift, the struggle is too much to the individual and against the society in which he lives. Success seems to involve concession to oneself as well as to society. One is the product as well as the victim of the damage of one's lifetime. We are in the predicament of the protagonist in Mr. Wheelwright's sonnet Sanct; protestant to the last drop.

> We know the Love the Father bears the Son
> is a third Mask and that the Three form One.
> We also know, machines and dynamos
> —Preservers in motion; Destroyers in repose—
> like visions of wheeled eyes the addict sees
> are gods, not fashioned in our images.

> Then let us state the unknown in the known:
> The mechanism of our friendship, grown
> transcendent over us, maintains a being
> by seeing us when we grow lax in seeing,
> although without our sight it could not be.
> (One states, one does not solve, a mystery.)
> This human Trinity is comprehended
> when doubt of its divinity is ended.

Not only protestant, but also heretical.

> Turn by an inward act upon the world!
> An innocence like our Creator's faith
> is younger than my doubt. You give it birth
> who, seeing evil less veiling than clear rain,
> see truth in thought as through a lens of air.

That is, both inimical and foreign; trying for the scope of the normal rather than the closeness of the average. I fear that the readers of this review may have difficulty with Mr. Wheelwright and none with Dr. Williams; yet I am certain that when he finds that he has understood Mr. Wheelwright, and enjoyed him, he will understand much better what he misses as well as what he enjoys in Dr. Williams. There is room for both poets.

"It Is Later Than He Thinks"

THE IDEA OF A CHRISTIAN SOCIETY. By T. S. Eliot. New
York: Harcourt, Brace and Co. 104 pages. $1.50.
OLD POSSUM'S BOOK OF PRACTICAL CATS. By T. S. Eliot.
New York: Harcourt, Brace and Co. 46 pages. $1.25.

OLD POSSUM had other things than cats on his mind
when he batted out his practical rhymes, and Mr.
Eliot, too, had some of Old Possum drowsing within
him when he constructed his idea of a Christian society.
Who can say which is which, and how much both at
one time and also at another time, and whether asleep
or waking, and can say it in time—he will know the
riddle that cats and society make when put together, and
will know that to know the riddle is better than to pretend to know the answer. It is the business of possums
to sleep, to pretend dead, to cry aloud as it were by
critical silence, as the very proof of vitality: *Non Possummus!* The Old Possum is the old Adam in deliberate
disguise: worn to hide the defeat within which he
huddles.

Well, all of us are defeated almost to the degree that
we try, and there is every reason to let ourselves enjoy,
with hands thrown up but without alarm, Mr. Eliot's
practical fun about cats through the possum non pos-
sumus part of our sensibility; and when we stop enjoy-
ing we can turn the cats over to the children, on the
amusing notion that they will enjoy what we did not,

and will not enjoy—because not old enough to take defeat as fun—what we did.

It is one thing to put cats in first place, a thing quite spontaneous to do, and another thing to *put* God in first place, which is not spontaneous at all but a deliberate act of desperation, and the more desperate because it is an act that cannot be completed. To put cats in first place merely reduces one's humanity; to *put* God in first place is to strip humanity bare. It is the loss of God which procures his exaggeration. If God is not already in first place, as well as in all other places, then to put him there is to put him out of reach.

It is true that for certain sensibilities in certain situations there may be no alternative; the mind may be forced to any extreme of self-privation in order to circumvent assent to defeat; and indeed something of that sort has been Mr. Eliot's situation. Living and participating in a society which has been emphatically unable to cope either with the evil and loss of value which itself generated or with the threat of an alien society with positive but intolerable values, he has been driven further and further into complete dependence upon the idea of God as it appears, or ought to appear, in the Anglican Church. The astonishing—perhaps it is only the illuminating—aspect of his motion is that it has been his profound sense of the actual—all that has made him a poet—which has brought him into the haven of an ideal separated from the actual, as he himself says, not only now but for a long time to come, and indeed, for many of the societies that make up the world, separated for a length of time that cannot be foreseen. If I were a theologian, and I have no disrespect for theology, I might say that the separation was radical, and risk the assertion

that the ideal from which he proposes to draw sustenance, is Erastian in reverse—that is, by default—and
quote his own words against him. If his Church had
anywhere the authority he would everywhere require
for it, it would be identified with the State in the sense
that it controlled it. "By alienating the mass of the
people from orthodox Christianity, by leading them to
identify the Church with the actual hierarchy and to
suspect it of being an instrument of oligarchy or class,
it leaves men's minds exposed to varieties of irresponsible
and irreflective enthusiasm followed by a second crop
of paganism."

But I am not a theologian, and prefer to retreat upon
the lesser language of the law, and upon that language
only in its lay sense: *Non Possummus*. We are not able;
it will not happen. Mr. Eliot's ideal of a Christian
society—his idea of what is aimed at—cannot be realised
in this world and I should imagine would be unsuitable
in any probable world, just as I imagine that it would
be superfluous in the heavenly world. He is right in
insisting that he is not proposing utopia; he would be
righter if he did not make his proposition at all. I do
not mean to oppose Mr. Eliot's thought and, what I
respect more, his constructed emotion, with either assertion or evasion. But I cannot help believing with a
conviction only less than his own, that a Christian state,
a Christian education, a Christian philosophy, are as outmoded as the Christian astronomy which accompanied
them when they flourished. To be outmoded in this
sense is to be aside from both the modes of understanding and the springs of action. Specifically, magical access to the authority of any supernatural *order* has
disappeared, and without magic any claim of rational

access is bound to be discounted like any other. It does not follow that Christianity has disappeared, but only what long custom and accident had made seem its inherent authority over matters it had really, like a sponge, only absorbed. The means of re-absorption do not appear to exist in any visible Church or body of Churches, and if the matters cannot be absorbed the authority cannot be asserted with any prospect of obedience; with the prospect of anything but mounting indifference to the authority the Church does properly assert.

There remains for Mr. Eliot the possibility of regeneration. Some one, some group, some Church, may yet be able to build out of what is common to the actual life of this time and the actual life of all times—and build with neither simplification nor privation of any phase of reality—a new church of Christian truth. That was the labour of the Christian Fathers. Meanwhile we have merely the assertion of the "truth of Christianity" without ever being shown what it is made of, what it is, and how the two are, or ought to be, the same. I mean—and I do not think I am alone among those who endure a sense of immanent peril beyond present decay—that when Mr. Eliot invokes Christian truth or Christian ethics I actually do not know what he means and have no way of finding out. I think it is too late to say.

The urban, suburban, industrialised, lower-middle-class society—neutral or pagan—which Mr. Eliot decribes, has other ears to the ground: it listens to itself, all other voices failing. Mr. Eliot could tell it a good deal of what it hears, and has, but in the wrong language. Better, he knows what sort of person could tell, and be both persuasive and understood; yet he insists on hinting at it in a tongue which because of *his* education and *his* predilection, is partly alien and a little pompous. Here is an example. He has been making some pertinent and acute observations about Parliamentary and revolutionary political parties, and proceeds, speaking of the permanent value of Aristotle. "Just as his views on dramatic poetry were derived from a study of the existing works of Attic drama, so his political theory was founded on a perception of the unconscious aims implicit in Athenian democracy at its best. His limitations are the condition of his universality. . . . Thus, what I mean by a political philosophy is not merely even the conscious formulation of the ideal aims of a people, but the substratum of collective temperament, ways of behaviour and unconscious values which provide for the formulation." Mr. Eliot believes that this formulation can be made in terms of the central insights of Christianity; and he is right just so far as Christianity is itself the result—the imaginative expression—of an Aristotelian study and perception of the true nature of the western world. But beyond that point the mind which does not find itself compelled to submit to a supernatural order in natural things, cannot go; for to such a mind, the voice of the supernatural order must too often seem merely the gospel of that inner voice which Mr. Eliot has himself several times reprehended, the voice of enthusiasm, fanaticism, and partisanship—or as he once characterised it, the voice of vanity, fear, and lust. That Mr. Eliot tries to forstall or minimise that possibility by setting up a "clerisy" or "Community of Christians" composed of all those showing unusual intellectual and/or spiritual superiority, and by inviting the services of those "individuals who, with great creative gifts of value to mankind, and the sensibility which such gifts imply, will yet remain blind, indifferent, or even hostile" to Christianity, only makes his Idea of a Christian Society seem more implausible; for it is a confession of the actual impossibility of complete resort to the supernatural order. I do not mean what Mr. Eliot means when he says that a religious culture is necessarily imperfect; I mean a critical vitiation of thought and act. *Non Possummus!*

For the rest, there are two things to remember. Mankind has in the bulk never been able to scrutinise the moral world, or think itself in control of the political world, except by the aid of an inscrutable authority; without such aid observation falls apart, values are confused, and principles compete. It is not surprising that Mr. Eliot should share and exemplify the common experience. It is only surprising, when as he says "ignorance is ubiquitous," that he should attribute a relation other than imaginative to his authority. For after all, even for him, it is only as it is *imagined* in terms of his actual "total harvest of thinking, feeling, living and observing human beings" that he can himself understand, and judge, and use the authority which he invokes. If he thinks otherwise, we shall have to remember that it is later than he thinks, as late for us in our day as it was for Aristotle in his.

The Letters of Marian Adams

THE LETTERS OF MRS. HENRY ADAMS. 1865-1883. Edited by Ward Thoron. Boston: Little, Brown, and Company. 587 pages. $5.

T HE interest of these letters is triple without being anywhere divided. There is the historical interest of the letters from Washington; there is the social interest of all but the early travel letters; and there is, predominantly, the interest of a developing sensibility and an emerging character. What unites the interest, apart from the fact of authorship, is the accident that all but the first of the letters—which is really a descriptive essay on the Grand Review of Grant's and Sherman's Armies in 1865—are private or personal letters, and of these all but four or five are addressed to one correspondent. These are a daughter's letters to her father— the letters of Marian Hooper, wife of Henry Adams, from Europe, Egypt, and Washington to Robert W. Hooper a retired Boston doctor. They parade a person not a cause, exhibit a sensibility not a position, and have as their single motive the nurture of a deep human relationship during long periods of interrupted contact. They make, if you like, an informal and unconscious work of art; they make a long serial fiction, always based upon the reality provided at the moment by person or place or deed, but often escaping or sacrificing reality, too, in the interest of the amusing or the picturesque or the extravagant, in the interests, finally, of the human relationship involved. These letters are, then, the objective or substituted form of a felt intimacy; and it is only through that guise, which must first be appreciated in its human warmth, that we may discern our own interests at whatever level we choose to find them.

With such an approach the personal quality of the letters becomes a principle of illumination rather than a formula of distortion. The politicians and diplomats and private persons coming in and out of Mrs. Adams' Washington house, the balls and receptions and conferences and conversations, all add up to a personal response, all unself-conscious and candid and prejudiced, to the Washington scene under Hayes and Garfield and Arthur. The Star Route fraud, the long attack on Blaine, the trial of Guiteau, and the Ponca affair, are, as Marian Adams explicitly makes use of them, only the vehicle of personal reaction. They keep her going; activate her sensibility and stabilise her point of view; and her letters show both her sense of motion and her access of conviction. They show her growing up. For emphasis, Washington was politics as New York was money and Boston dying culture. People counted in Washington primarily as they gyrated in relation to power and the corruption of power; Mrs. Adams recorded her daily experience of that relation, and as we read we feel Leviathan twitch and tremble.

The historical interest is for us precisely in that personal sense, achieved cumulatively from letter to letter but nowhere conspicuous in the instance, of what Leviathan felt like. The feeling was evidently composite—confused and ominous and exciting—futile and necessitous, intolerably corrupt and inescapably fascinating—the feeling both of a waking nightmare and a steady march. It is an advantage, this feeling, that had Mrs. Adams' approach been intellectual or philosophical or historical, instead of immediate, prejudiced, and personal, she would never have given us: the advantage of judgment by instinctive taste. That the taste was founded upon integrity and that the integrity was the product of a scrupulous but sophisticated culture, is for the reader to remember. Marian Adams came from Boston, and so brought judgment in her blood. But the Boston she came from was out of power—as it seemed, for the moment; in fact forever—and she served admirably the critical function of pitting against the common American spectacle of irresponsible power an innately responsible sensibility undepraved by power.

For the rest, for the so-called facts behind the personal response, the reader may be at once sent to the general histories and referred to Mr. Thoron's excellent apparatus of footnotes and appendices. The histories will provide extension and perspective for the appetites roused by Mrs. Adams and, as it were, certified, dated, and stamped by Mr. Thoron. Especially useful are the certifications provided by Mr. Thoron's running extracts from the *Nation*, which represented the Adams or liberal reform side of the politics of the time, and the citations from the *Education of Henry Adams*, which represent the matured, but selective, intellectual judgment of later years.

Similarly—and this makes a good transition—Mr. Thoron's biographical notes and citations do a good deal to heighten the interest of Mrs. Adams' letters as an inadvertent social study of the English and American scene; the notes provide the flavour and prop of identification and so satisfy that instinctive superstition which holds even the scantest genealogy as a firm aid to understanding. Here—for the social interest—it is again the assured Boston blood that energises the operation of Mrs. Adams' taste. Boston blood was, as always when not too thin or fanatic, perceptibly salt; it was constitutionally aware of the smart of things, and no smart was so obvious as the smart of pretense or smuggery, or snobbery or cheapness, in itself or especially in others. Marian Adams' blood was of an unusually rich solution; richened by travel, by native rebelliousness, by opportunity taken, and by her husband's extraordinary intellectual power as constant weeder and cultivator. Her blood, so richened, was her social taste, and her wit was the weapon of her taste; as a certain residual intolerance, an occasional blindness,—qualities invariably emphasised in strong character—was her defence of taste violated or uninformed. She rejected Lilly Langtry and Oscar Wilde because their morals were intolerable, and she rejected Whistler's painting because she was blind to its effect. But she was hardly ever taken in, or not for long, by any person or pattern she did accept. Her taste when it worked was accurate; an expression, more than a measure, of value. What she thought, and the principles of her thought, were either tacit or in abeyance before the magnificent opportunity to see and feel. If she lacked the profound general insight into character and history which her husband expressed at his best, she also lacked the ponderous disadvantage of that insight which is inept because it is merely intellectual. Her taste was resolute, quick, and shrewd in action; sharp for the ludicrous, unerring for the vain and the sham; exquisitely sensitive of detail; and founded ultimately upon a sweet, warm, animal intelligence—the intelligence men think of as feminine, and some women call poetic, an intelligence gracious, vivid, and charming without loss of the rational.

She had a balanced mind, a poise of sense and being, instinct and training, which had so grown and prospered by 1882, when she was thirty nine, that Henry James, on the hour of sailing for Europe, made deliberately his last farewell to her, saying that she seemed to him "the incarnation of my native land." Mrs. Adams herself said of Henry James that "it's not that he 'bites off more than he can chaw,' . . . but he chaws more than he bites off," and she professed herself dubious of James' tribute.   James exaggerated; other types incarnated America more conspicuously; and as an incarnation of anything—even Boston—Mrs. Adams was exceptional; but James had a sound value in mind.   It was not the value of her good table, her fine house, her pictures and books and friends, her love of flowers and dogs and horses, her clothes and charm and conversation—nor even, as he was an inspiriting part of her, her extraordinary husband.   To be amusing, to be precious in any easy sense, was never enough for James.   The live thing was the important thing, and the live thing in a woman was intelligence showing as residual charm, as quickness or slowness, but always as deep or vivid response.

Nothing so shows such an intelligence as habitual overt characterisation: a talent which Mrs. Adams had to the extreme of assurance, an assurance, quite beyond either snobbery or intellect, that freshens as it validates the language used and gives it idiomatic twist.   I trust that the following quotations will obviate by example much discussion of sociology and manners, will make plain the variety and scope of Mrs. Adams' sensibility, and send the reader scurrying to the book from which he ought never to have been distracted.

Characterisation is not limited to persons, as the sense of a smile is not restricted to the lips; there is a fundamental buried sense in us which is the agent of all response, and which we may find as well touched by landscape as elsewhere. We have a Paris sun in winter which "hangs like a white frost-bitten ball in the sky." Again, also in Paris, there is the image of "an asphalt *plage*, with human surf beating on it." Speaking of the new red brick houses in London: "The smoke and soot softens them at once, so that they look as if they had grown on the spot from seed." For the same discriminating depth of sense there is this about a Titian in the Prado, which "looks as if it were painted with powdered jewels soaked in sunshine." Shifting from the colour of paint to the tone of personality we have "a nice, sweet, good woman but not too deep for wading;" we have Browning "who tapped me familiarly on the arm and said, 'I'm coming to see you,' in the tone of 'keep up your spirit.' " We have the Duchess of Somerset who "kept throwing up her chin, as if the check-rein were too tight." We have Mr. Welsh, the American Minister in London, "a quiet Baptist deacon style of man, with no nonsense and no charm;" and for purely physical description becoming sharp characterisation, there is Mrs. Mackintosh— "fat, rosy, placid, torpid, like a nerveless feather-bed." For a combination of satire and observation there is a sketch of three senators in action: "Bayard is not an orator, is not quick and has a disagreeable nasal twang, and Sherman swallows his sentences, perhaps fearing no one else will. Mahone looks like a weasel, is very small,

proud of his feet, one or both of which lie on his desk."
For a pure quip, a propos of being home late to dinner:
"One great advantage in coloured cooks and waiters
is that they never look black at any unpunctuality—a few
shades browner one does not notice." For malice of
language without meanness of spirit but rather the riches
of caricature, I give two examples. Passing   through
New York to Washington, Mrs. Adams "tumbled plump
on the very most lurid of all our pyrotechnic friends,
—or acquaintances rather,—Mrs. E., a lady with a most
plethoric past, a precocious present and a future which
would baffle and bankrupt any clairvoyant." At a London cattle show she saw the beautiful Mrs. Ronalds, who
had been a Boston girl. "I think she would easily euchre
Becky Sharp; has taken a house in Sloane Street, and, I
am told, sent for her mama and papa to enact sheep
dogs!" For pure luxuriance of created observation—observation that quite transcends the object—there is this
from a Royal Academy reception, to describe the ladies'
costumes: "fat fugues in pea-green; lean symphonies in
chewing-gum colour; all in a rusty minor key"—which
brings us almost back to the landscape sense from which
we started, and brings us up, for a conclusion, to the
following paragraph, which seems to me to present
nearly all the elements of Marian Adams' sensibility in
compact and vivid form.

Yesterday I went to consult Mr. Worth about a gown to
go with my Louis XIV lace, which he admired extremely,
as I knew he would. He was standing pensively by the
window in a long puce-coloured dressing gown with two
exquisite black spaniels—twins—sitting on two green velvet
chairs. This is what he wants me to have: the main dress
gold colour, the velvet only to lay the lace on and at the

bottom in front. I have become bored with the idea of getting any new gowns, but Henry says, "People who study Greek must take pains with their dress." If I were a bonanzaine I would sail in and make a business of it, but an occasional venture is too much trouble.

If there is one quality to be emphasised beyond others, and beyond the personal quality, in these letters, it is, I think, the quality that goes with the shrewd, quick, constant sense of social elan: the smart *and* rush of things.

The Expense of Greatness

Three Emphases on Henry Adams

W HERE your small man is a knoll to be smoothed
away, Henry Adams is a mountain to be mined
on all flanks for pure samples of human imagination
without loss of size or value. That is the double test of
greatness, that it show an attractive force, massive and
inexhaustible, and a disseminative force which is the inexhaustible spring or constant declaration of value. As
we elucidate our reaction to the two forces we measure
the greatness.

In Adams the attractive force is in the immediate relevance that his life and works have for our own. The
problems he posed of human energy and human society
are felt at once to be special and emphatic articulations
of our own problems. The disseminative, central force,
which we find objectified in his works, may be felt and
seen as the incandescence of the open, enquiring, sensitive, and sceptical intelligence, restless but attentive, saltatory but serial, provisional in every position yet fixed
upon a theme: the theme of thought or imagination conceived as the form of human energy. We feel the incandescence in the human values and aspirations that were
fused by it, from time to time, in persuasive form; and
the cumulus of his life and works makes a focus, different as differently felt, whereby the particular values actually rendered shine concentrated as it were in their

own best light. We make the man focus upon himself, make him achieve—as he never could for himself in the flux and flexion of life—his own most persuasive form. To make such a focus is the labour and the use of critical appreciation.

The approaches to such a labour are varied and must be constantly renewed and often revised. No single approach is omniscient or even sufficient. Here, in this essay, I want to take Henry Adams in a single perspective and submit it to three related emphases. I want to regard him as he often chose to regard himself, as a representative example of education: but education pushed to the point of failure as contrasted with ordinary education which stops at the formula of success.

The perspective is worth a preliminary emphasis of its own. It was as failure both in perspective and lesson by lesson that Adams himself saw his education. Success is not the propitious term for education unless the lesson wanted is futile. Education has no term and if arrested at all is only arrested by impassable failure. Surely the dominant emotion of an education, when its inherent possibilities are compared with those it achieved, must strike the honest heart as the emotion of failure. The failure is not of knowledge or of feeling. It is the failure of the ability to react correctly or even intelligently to more than an abbreviated version of knowledge and feeling: failure in the radical sense that we cannot consciously react to more than a minor fraction of the life we yet deeply know and endure and die. It is the failure the mind comes to ultimately and all along when it is compelled to measure its knowledge in terms of its ignorance.

Most failures we have the tact to ignore or give a kinder

name. That is because we know by instinct at what a heavy discount to put most proffered examples of failure. There was no effort of imagination in them and only private agony, where for great failure we want the utmost unrelenting imagination and the impersonal agony of knowledge searching the haven of objective form. Most failures come too easily, take too little stock of the life and forces around them: like the ordinary failure in marriage, or business, or dying; and so too much resemble the ordinary success—too solemn and scant and zestless for realisation. A genuine failure comes hard and slow, and, as in a tragedy, is only fully realised at the end. A man's success is in society, precarious and fatal; his failure is both in spite and because of society— as he witnesses its radical imperfection and is himself produced by it, its ultimate expression. Thus in a great man we often find inextricably combined the success which was his alone, though posthumously recognised, with the failure which as we feel it is also our own in prospect.

Let us take for our first emphasis Adams as a failure in society. If we assume that an education means the acquisition of skills and the mastery of tools designed for intelligent reaction in a given context, it will appear that Adams' failure in American political society after the Civil War was a failure in education. Society was bound for quick success and cared only for enough intelligence to go on with. It cared nothing for political mastery, and commonly refused to admit it had a purpose beyond the aggregation of force in the form of wealth. The effect on Adams as a young man was immediate but took time to recognize. If *vis inertiae* was enough for society, any education was too much; and an Adams—with the finest education of his times—was clearly useless. The question was perhaps not initially of Adams' failure but of society's inability to make use of him: its inability to furnish a free field for intelligent political action. Washington was full of wasted talent—of able young men desperately anxious to be of use—as it is now; but no one knows what talent might accomplish, then or now, because talent has never been given a chance without being at the same moment brutally hamstrung.

The discovery—that he was to be wasted whether he was any good or not—was all the bitterer to Henry Adams because he had three generations of conspicuous ability and conspicuous failure behind him. Every Adams had ended as a failure after a lifetime of effort—marked by occasional and transitory success—to handle political power intelligently. Their intelligence they had kept; none had ever succumbed to the criminal satisfaction of power on its lowest terms—whether power for interest, or, worst of all, power for its own sake: the absolute corruption, as it seems to a scrupulous mind, of giving in; but all equally had failed at the height of their abilities. If times had changed for Henry it was for the worse. Where his ancestors found in a combination of scruple and temper an effective termination of useful public careers, Henry found his scruple alone enough to preclude a public career altogether. Scruple is sometimes only a name for snobbery, stiffness, or even an inner coldness—all, forms of disability; but in an Adams scruple was the mark of ability itself, and its limit, as it made intelligence acute, responsible, and infinitely resourceful, but a little purblind to the advantage of indirection. An Adams could meet an issue, accept facts, and demonstrate a policy, but he could never gamble with a public matter. Jefferson's epitaph for John applied to them all: as disinterested as his maker. If the odds grew heavy against an Adams he resorted to an access of will—or, if you choose to call it, a wall of stubbornness, which is merely will grown hysterical. But acts of will or stubbornness are merely the last resorts of minds compelled to act scrupulously against the unintelligent or the unintelligible.

Thus it is that many great men, if seen as examples of intellectual biography, seem either sports or parasites upon the society that produced them. They were compelled to act against or outside it; and our sense of radical connection and expressive identity is only re-established in the examples of their works aside from their lives. Certainly something of the sort is true, with different emphases, of Whitman, Mark Twain, Henry James, Melville, and in our own day of Hart Crane and George Santayana. They stand out too much from their native society: all outsiders from the life they expressed and upon which they fed. If all knew the ignominy of applause, applause from the wrong people, for the wrong thing, or for something not performed at all, it only accented their own sense of eccentricity and loneliness. That is how Adams stood out, but without much applause ignominious or otherwise, eccentric and lonely; but within him, as within the others in their degrees, was an intelligence whose actions were direct, naked, and at their best terrifyingly sane.

If, as I think, it was the scruple of his mind that made Adams an outsider and that at the same time gave precise value to his eccentricity, then the scruple should be defined both for itself and in terms of Adams. It is what I have been deviously leading up to: as it represents the single heroic and admirable quality of the modern and sceptical mind as such; and a quality not called for by the occasion but crowning it, even when disastrously.

Scruple, generally speaking, is the agent of integrity, what keeps action honest on the level of affairs, or on the level of imagination when actuality or truth is the object. The etymology of the word refreshes the meaning I emphasise, where we have the Latin *scrupulus*, a small sharp stone, a stone in one's shoe, an uneasiness, difficulty, small trouble, or doubt. Scruples differ with the type of mind and education. Most men either get rid of them or show pride in their calluses. In either case the process of thought is made easy and reaction insensitive; you give in, you are practically carried along, but you get nowhere except where you are taken, and you know nothing at all of what you have been through, or of its meaning.

Specifically, with Henry Adams, scruple of thinking and thence of action was the whole point of his education for public life. Men without scruples either victimised power or succumbed to it; and if you had the wrong scruples you succumbed, like Grant, without knowing it. Political education was meant to supply the right scruples at the start, to teach sensitiveness to new ones as they came up, and to ingrain a habit of feeling for them if not apparent. It is scruples that compel attention to detail and subordinate the detail to an end. When excess atrophies the mind, whether of scruples or the lack of them, it is because either an impossible end or no end was in view. In science the adjudication of scruples is called method and taken for granted; but the whole test of the democratic process is whether or not the seat of power attracts the scrupulous intelligence and gives it rein.

Here we may conceive Henry Adams as a provisional focus for that test.

In a sense no test is possible. Adams never held office. He only made himself embarrassingly available in the near background of Grant's Washington. Power was what he wanted, but on his own terms: the terms of his training. Perhaps he offered too much; perhaps his offers seemed too much like demands; at any rate he got nothing. But if we take him as a type—whether of 1868 or 1932—we can see that he was in the predicament of all young men whose abilities seem to lie in public life but who refuse waste motion. Society has no use for them as they are, and the concessions it requires are fatal to self-respect and taste, and lead either to futility, the treason of submission, or an aching combination of the two.

Both Adams and society saw politics was a game, but the difference in their angles of vision made their views irreconcilable. Adams saw the game as played impersonally with, as ultimate stake, the responsible control of social energy. Since ultimate value was never sure, every move ought to be made with the maximum intelligence and subject to every criticism your experience provided. If you stuck scrupulously to your intelligence you had the chance to come out right in the end under any scruples, democratic or not. You had a chance to put your society in control of itself at the centre of its being. That was Adams' idea of the game, the idea of any honest young man.

Society played differently. The stake was immediate power, the values were those of personal interest. Thus the actual stake—control of social energy—was left for the ventures of interests irresponsible to the government

meant to control them. Society in its political aspect
cared more for chaos than unity; and the democratic
process was an unconfessed failure, obliviously committing itself to social anarchy. Yet the failure remained
unconfessed; the society lived and gathered energy; it
was omnivorous, rash, and stupid; it threatened to become uncontrollably leviathan; it seemed occasionally on
the point of committing suicide in the full flush of life.
Always it had been saved, so far, by its vitality, its prodigious capacity for successive ruination, or by the discovery of a new and available source of power.

There was the young man's predicament. Should he
assume that society was no field for intelligence and that
its own momentum was sufficient to its needs? Should
he rather enter the field, outwardly playing society's version of the game, while inwardly playing his own as best
he could? Or should he work on society from the outside, accepting his final defeat at the start, and express the
society rather than attempt to control it?

The first choice is the hardest; taken mostly by weak
minds, it resembles more the dullness of indifference than
disconsolate impartiality. Most men of ability, fortunately, make the second choice; it is they that make the
administration of society possible and intermittently tolerable. Individually, most of them disappear, either lose
office or succumb to it; but the class is constantly re-
plenished from the bottom. A few survive the struggle
in their own identity, and these are the ideals the young
men hope to cap. J. Q. Adams was one of these, Gallatin and Schurz are clearly two more, as Senators Walsh
and Norris make two examples for our own day. Men
like Cleveland and Theodore Roosevelt are partial sur-
vivals. Adams thought his friend John Hay not only

survived but succeeded in establishing a sound foreign policy; history is a harsher judge than friendship. As a general thing promise in politics not only dies early but is resurrected in the corruption of party or unwitting interest, which is what happened to Adams' friend Lodge. For the most part Adams' reiterated sentiment remains apt: "A friend in power is a friend lost." Small men might pass unnoticed to honourable graves but the great were lost.

Henry Adams lacked the dimensions suitable to a small man in public life and lacked the coarseness of will and ability to dissimulate to seize the larger opportunity, had it offered. Hence he made gradually the third choice, and brought the pressure of all the education he could muster upon society from the outside. It took him seven to ten years to make the choice complete. The first form of pressure he exerted was that of practical political journalism, of which the principal remaining results are the essays on "The New York Gold Conspiracy," "The Session, 1869-1870," and the essay on American financial policy called "The Legal-Tender Act." The second form of pressure was also practical, and combined the teaching of history at Harvard with the editorship of *The North American Review*. Already, however, the emphasis of his mind was becoming imaginative and speculative. Seven years in Cambridge taught him the impossibility of affecting society to any practical extent through the quarterly press, or through any press at all. Two of his essays were made campaign documents by the Democrats—their import reduced to the level of vituperative rhetoric—and then forgotten; so that by the test of the widest publication possible their practical effect was nil. There remained a third form of pressure

not so much indirect as remote, and that was pressure by
the imaginative expression, through history and fiction
and philosophy, of social character and direction; and
the aim was to seize the meaning of human energy by
defining its forms and to achieve, thus, if it was possible,
a sense of unity both for oneself and one's society.

Expression is a form of education, and the form that
was to occupy the rest of Adams' life, the subject of our
second emphasis. Put another way, society had failed
to attract Adams to its centre, and Adams undertook to
see whether or not he could express a centre for it. Unity
or chaos became the alternative lesson of every effort.
Here we have gone over or climbed up to a second level
of failure, which is the failure of the human mind, pushed
to one of its limits, to solve the problem of the meaning, the use, or the value of its own energy: in short the
failure to find God or unity. What differentiates
Adams' mind from other minds engaged in the same
effort is his own intense and progressive recognition of
his failure; and that recognition springs from the same
overload of scruples that made him eccentric to the society that produced him. What he did not recognise
was the ironical consolation that the form his work took
as a whole was itself as near the actual representative of
unity as the individual mind can come; which is what
we have now to show.

Henry Adams' mind acquired, as his work stretched
out, a singular unity of conception and a striking defi-
niteness of form. It was the idiosyncrasy of his genius
to posit unity in multiplicity, and by exploring different
aspects of the multiplicity to give the effect, known to be
false or specious but felt as true, of apprehending the
unity. In reading *The Life of Albert Gallatin*, so suc-

cessfully is the effect of Gallatin's career composed, we have to think twice before realising that it is meant to show one aspect in the story of the failure of the democratic process to unite American society. Published in 1879, when Adams was forty-one, it so well struck the theme of Adams' whole career that it can be bracketed with Adams' own autobiography and be called "The Education of Albert Gallatin."

As important here, striking his theme gave Adams his first mature prose. The previous essays had been comparatively metallic, brittle, and rhetorical, and carried a tone of intermittent assertiveness rather than of cumulative authority. It was the subject perhaps that matured the style: Gallatin was the best in character, ability, and attainment that American history had to offer. At any rate, the biography of John Randolph, which came in 1882 and portrayed the worst waste in ability and personal distintegration in American history, showed a reversion to the earlier immature style. If Adams was, as Hay said, half angel and half porcupine, then it was altogether the porcupine that got into this book. The tragedy of Randolph was personal eccentricity, his constant resorts hysteria and violence, and Adams brought those elements over into his own style. Later, in his History, Adams repaired his injustice and treated him with charity of understanding, as an energetic sample of his times.

Meanwhile and just afterwards, in 1880 and 1884, Adams published his two novels, *Democracy* and *Esther*. These suffer about equally from Adams' incompetence as a novelist, and the reader can take them best as brilliant documentary evidence of Adams' insights and pre-occupations. To intrude the standards of the art of fiction would be to obviate the burden the books actually carry. *Democracy* exhibits a political society full of corruption, irresponsible ambition, and stupidity, against the foil of a woman's taste and intelligence. So brilliant and light is Adams' execution, it is hard to decide which vice is worst of the three.

Madeleine Lee, Adams' foil, is struck a heavy blow in the face by her first and only presidential reception. She stands fascinated and aghast at the endless wooden procession. "What a horrid warning to ambition! And in all that crowd there was no one beside herself who felt the mockery of this exhibition. To all the others this task was a regular part of the President's duty, and there was nothing ridiculous about it." It was Adams, not Mrs. Lee, who felt the full force of the blow. He remembered what he had seen at Devonshire House a few years back when Mme. de Castiglione, the famous beauty of the Second Empire, entered.

How beautiful she may have been, or indeed what sort of beauty she was, Adams never knew, because the company, consisting of the most refined and aristocratic society in the world, instantly formed a lane, and stood in ranks to stare at her, while those behind mounted on chairs to look over their neighbors' heads; so that the lady walked through the polite mob, stared completely out of countenance, and fled the house.

In *Democracy*, Mrs. Lee received a second blow, which we may obscurely feel as a consequence of the first, when, after his corruption is discovered to her and she taxes him with it, her suitor, Secretary of the Treasury Ratcliffe, defends himself by minimising his offence, passing it off as commonplace, and asks her to purify American politics through marriage to him and with his aid.

The audacity of the man would have seemed sublime if she had felt sure that he knew the difference between good and evil, between a lie and the truth; but the more she saw of him, the surer she was that his courage was mere moral paralysis, and that he talked about virtue and vice as a man who is colour-blind talks about red and green; he did not see them as she saw them; if left to choose for himself he would have nothing to guide him.

Which blow was the harder to bear? Was corruption, like stupidity, only an atrophied form of intelligence? Given the system and the society, did not the practice of politics necessarily produce one form or the other?

Adams himself did not feel the full force of the second blow until twenty years later when Theodore Roosevelt inherited office from McKinley. Secretary Ratcliffe in *Democracy* was the archetype of all he hated and Roosevelt represented an approximation of a good deal he admired. Ratcliffe was about the worst you got and Roosevelt was the best you could expect. But the lesson the two men taught about the disease of power was much the same, however they taught it on different levels. At heart Roosevelt, as a type, was more source of despair than Ratcliffe.

Power is poison. Its effects on Presidents had always been tragic, chiefly as an almost insane excitement at first, and a worse reaction afterwards; but also because no mind is so well balanced as to bear the strain of seizing unlimited force without habit or knowledge of it; and finding it disputed with him by hungry packs of wolves and hounds whose lives depend on snatching the carrion. Roosevelt enjoyed a singularly direct nature and honest intent, but he lived naturally in restless agitation that would have worn out most tempers in a month, and his first year of Presidency showed chronic excitement that made a friend tremble. The effect of unlimited power on limited mind is worth noting in

Presidents because it must represent the same process in society, and the power of self-control must have limit somewhere in face of the control of the infinite.

"Here," Adams goes on, "education seemed to see its first and last lesson." Certainly it is part of the lesson of the second Roosevelt as well as of the first; and certainly it is a lesson that in one form or another can be drawn not only from Presidents, but from every concentration of power in single hands. Power is greater than the hands that hold it and compels action beyond any tolerable volition. No wonder men make a game of it, as they make mathematics of time and space, since it is only as converted into a game that the experience of fatal struggles is commonly found tolerable.

But the lesson had other forms, as the energy it attempted to express took other forms than the political. There is the well of character, the abyss of science, and the aspiring form of religion, all expressions of human energy, and a wakened and scrupulous mind was compelled to respond to them all. Experience is only separated into its elements in the *tour de force* of expression, and as in *Democracy* Adams separated the bottom level of political experience, in *Esther* he separated the highest level of religious experience he could find in America and measured it against the response of a woman's intelligence. The question asked and the lesson to be learned were simple and fundamental and desperate. Assuming the Christian insight in its highest contemporary form, could the Church supply a sense of unity, of ultimate relation with God or the sum of energy, to which intelligence could respond? If the Church couldn't—and the Church had no other motive for being—nothing else could, and the soul was left on its own and homeless. Or so it seemed to Adams; hence the desperateness of the question; and hence the disproportionate importance relative to its achievement that Adams himself assigned to the book. Writing to John Hay from Japan in 1886, he suggests that it was written in his heart's blood, and again to Elizabeth Cameron from Papeete five years later, he says: "I care more for one chapter, or any dozen pages of 'Esther' than for the whole history, including maps and indexes." The nine-volume history represented the predicament of the society he had abandoned, and *Esther* represented his own predicament in relation to that God or unity the hope of which he could never in his heart altogether abandon. Like Spinoza, Adams was god-intoxicated, like Pascal god-ridden. His heart's hope was his soul's despair.

That the responding intelligence in *Esther* as in *Democracy* should have been a woman's, only reflects a major bias of Adams' imagination. Women, for Adams, had instinct and emotion and could move from the promptings of the one to the actualities of the other without becoming lost or distraught in the midway bog of logic and fact. Impulse proceeded immediately to form without loss of character or movement. More than that, women had taste; taste was what held things together, showing each at its best, and making each contribute to a single effect. Thus the argument of a woman's taste dissipated every objection of logic, and at its highest moments made illogicality itself part of its natural charm. Taste was the only form of energy sure enough of itself—as all non-human energies may be—to afford beauty; elsewhere the rashest extravagance.

Thus Adams tried everywhere to answer great questions in terms of a woman's taste and intelligence. Who else but Esther Dudley could form the centre of the book she named? Only the strength of her instinct could accept the Church if it showed itself alive, and only the courage of her taste could reject it if it proved dead or a shell. That she might be confused in instinct and unconscious of her taste, only made the drama more vivid and its outcome more desperate. The problem was hers, but an artist could help her solve it, and perhaps a scientist, too, if he felt the struggle as an artist feels it. So Wharton, the artist, puts the question to her and answers it. "It all comes to this: is religion a struggle or a joy? To me it is a terrible battle, to be won or lost." The object of the battle is Nirvana or paradise. "It is eternal life, which, my poet says, consists in seeing God." The poet is Petrarch, and his words: *Siccome eterna vita è veder dio.* Strong, the scientist, for his part tells her: "There is no science that does not begin by requiring you to believe the incredible. I tell you the solemn truth that the doctrine of the Trinity is not so difficult to accept for a working proposition as any one of the axioms of physics." Between them—between art as it aspires to religion and science that springs from the same occult source—Esther might have been able to accept religion as that great form of poetry which is the aspiration of instinct and informs the whole of taste; but the Church itself, in the person of the Reverend Mr. Hazard, her lover, failed her both in persuasiveness and light. Power in politics and pride in the Church were much alike.

The strain of standing in a pulpit is great. No human being ever yet constructed was strong enough to offer himself long as a light to humanity without showing the effect on his constitution. Buddhist saints stand for years silent, on one leg, or with arms raised above their heads, but the limbs shrivel, and the mind shrivels with the limbs.

There is a kind of corruption in the best as well as the worst exemplars of each—which I suppose the Church would admit sooner than the state; a corruption in each case that makes for the self-falsifying effort of fanaticism. Hazard in his last argument appeals neither to instinct, intelligence, nor taste; he appeals to Esther's personal desperation and fear and so shows the ruination of empti- ness within him. Esther can only answer him from the depth of revolted taste. "Why must the church always appeal to my weakness and never to my strength! I ask for spiritual life and you send me back to my flesh and blood as though I were a tigress you were sending back to her cubs." Although she loves him, the inadequacy of his church to its own purpose compels her to dismiss him, but neither for science nor for art, but for despair. That is the blood in whch the book was written.

As *Democracy* foreshadowed the major theme of the *Education*, the theme of *Esther* is given deeper ex- pression throughout *Mont-Saint-Michel*, and, as well, in at least one place in the *Education*. *Esther* is a rep- resentation of the failure in fact of American society to find God in religion. As he grew older, especially after the tragic death of his wife, and felt more and more that society had abandoned him, Adams grew more preoccupied with the ultimate failure of imagina- tion itself, as illustrated in every faculty of the mind, than with the mere indicative failure of fact. Not facts which could be met but their meanings which could not be escaped were his meat. The meaning of *Esther* is intensified and made an object of inexhaustible medita- tion in the meanings Adams found in the monument

Saint Gaudens made for his wife in Rock Creek Cemetery. Part of the meaning lay in its meaninglessness to most of those who saw it, and part in the horror of the clergy who saw in it their defeat instead of their salvation. In a letter, Adams gave the monument the same motto he had embedded in *Esther*: *Siccome eterna vita è veder dio;* you could, in a gravestone, if you had the will, see what life needed but never provided. In the *Education* Adams suggests that the monument mirrors to the beholder whatever faith he has.

In *Mont-Saint-Michel and Chartres* the problem of *Esther* is made at once more universal and more personal. There Adams made an imaginative mirror of his own effort towards faith in terms of the highest point of faith—that is, of effective unity—the world had ever seen: the Christianity of the great cathedrals and the great intellectual architecture of the schools. The Virgin dominated the cathedrals as a matter of course; and Saint Thomas dominated the schools by an effort of will; but without the Virgin the schools would merely have paltered, as the cathedrals would never have been built. The Virgin was pure energy and pure taste, as her spires and roses were pure aspiration. Adams' book is the story of her tragedy; not that she was destroyed or even denied, but that men no longer knew and loved her, so lost their aspiration with the benefit of her taste, and no longer felt any unity whatsoever. The Virgin herself is still there, "but looking down from a deserted heaven, into an empty church, on a dead faith." She no longer gave orders or answered questions, and without her the orders and answers of Saint Thomas were useless; and similarly, for Adams, the orders and answers of all later authorities.

Thus the education that led Adams to the Virgin was

the greatest failure of all; the highest form of unity was, in effect, for the modern man, only the most impossible to recapture. Where Esther had very simply repulsed the church because it appealed only to her weakness, Adams was in the worse ail of having no strength with which to seize it when it called for all the strength there was: he had no faith, but only the need of it. The Virgin's orders were the best ever given; obeyed, they made life contribute to great art and shine in it; but he had nothing with which to accept her administration. Her answers to his problems were final; she was herself the cumulus and unity of energy, and she removed, by absorbing, all the contradictions of experience; but seven centuries of time had made life too complicated for the old answers to fit. The same energy would need a new form to give the same meaning.

The failure of education was the failure of the unity which it grasped; the pupil was left with a terrible and weary apprehension of ignorance. Thinking of the Virgin and of the Dynamo as equally inexplicable concentrations of energy, Adams was led into the last phase of his education in the application of the mechanical theory of the inevitable change of all energy from higher to lower forms. What he wrote may be found in the later chapters of the *Education*, and in his two essays "A Letter to Teachers" and "The Rule of Phase Applied to History." It was, I think, the theory of a desperate, weary mind, still scrupulous in desperation and passionately eager in weariness, in its last effort to feel—this time in nature herself—the mystery in energy that keeps things going. It was the religious mind applying to physics on exactly the same terms and with exactly the same honest piety that it applied to the Virgin.

The nexus between the two was shown in the need for either in that fundamental condition of the mind known as *ennui;* and Adams quotes Pascal, the great scrupulous mind of the seventeenth century.

"I have often said that all the troubles of man come from his not knowing how to sit still." Mere restlessness forces action. "So passes the whole of life. We combat obstacles in order to get repose, and, when got, the repose is insupportable; for we think either of the troubles we have, or of those that threaten us; and even if we felt safe on every side, *ennui* would of its own accord spring up from the depths of the heart where it is rooted by nature, and would fill the mind with its venom."

Nature was full of *ennui* too, from star to atom. What drove it? What made energy change form in *this* direction and not that? Adams tried to find the answer in the second law of thermodynamics—the law that assumes the degradation of energy; the law which sees infinite energy becoming infinitely unavailable; and he tried hard to *feel* that law as accounting for change in human society. The attempt only put his ignorance on a new basis. As analogues, the laws of physics only made the human predicament less soluble because less tangible. You might learn a direction, but physics prevented you from feeling what moved.

Reason, in science, as Adams had discovered earlier in *Esther*, deserted you rather sooner than in religion; and the need of faith was more critical. Had Adams had the advantage of the development of the quantum theory from the thermal field to the whole field of physics, had he known that all change was to come to seem discontinuous and that nature was to reveal a new and profoundly irrational face, he would have given up his last effort before he began it. A *discontinuous* multiplicity cannot be transformed into unity except by emotional vision. Adams had earlier said it himself. "Unity is vision; it must have been part of the process of learning to see. The older the mind, the older its complexities, and the further it looks, the more it sees, until even the stars resolve themselves into multiples; yet the child will always see but one." In 1915 Adams wrote to Henry Osborn Taylor that "Faith not Reason goes beyond" the failure of knowledge, and added that he felt himself "in near peril of turning Christian, and rolling in the mud in an agony of human mortification." But he had not the faith; only the apprehension of its need which made him struggle towards it all his life.

Failure is the appropriate end to the type of mind of which Adams is a pre-eminent example: the type which attempts through imagination to find the meaning or source of unity aside from the experience which it unites. Some artists can be content with experience as it comes, content to express it in the best form at hand. Adams gives LaFarge as an instance. "His thought ran as a stream runs through grass, hidden perhaps but always there; and one felt often uncertain in what direction it flowed, for even a contradiction was to him only a shade of difference, a complementary color, about which no intelligent artist would dispute." Shakespeare is another instance. In such artists failure is incidental, a part of the experience expressed. But Adams, by attempting to justify experience and so to pass beyond it had like Milton and Dante to push his mind to the limit of reason and his feeling to the limit of faith. Failure, far from incidental, is integral to that attempt, and becomes apparent just so soon as reason falters and becomes abstract, or faith fails and pretends to be absolute. Aside from the question of magnitude, one difference between Adams and his prototypes is, to repeat once more, just this: that his scrupulous sophistication made him emphatically aware of his own failure; and this awareness is the great drive of his work.

Here is our third emphasis. The failure of Adams in society—or society's failure to use Adams—was perhaps self-evident when stated. The singular unity of Adams' subsequent efforts to express the unity he felt has, I hope, been indicated. There remains the question of Adams' special value in the light of his avowed failure. The value is double.

The greatness of the mind of Adams himself is in the imaginative reach of the effort to solve the problem of the meaning, the use, or the value of its own energy. The greatness is in the effort itself, in variety of response deliberately made to every possible level of experience. It is in the acceptance, with all piety, of ignorance as the humbled form of knowledge; in the pursuit of divers shapes of knowledge—the scientific, the religious, the political, the social and trivial—to the point where they add to ignorance, when the best response is silence itself. That is the greatness of Adams as a type of mind. As it is a condition of life to die, it is a condition of thought, in the end, to fail. Death is the expense of life and failure is the expense of greatness.

If there is a paradox here, or an irony hard to digest, it is not in the life experienced or the failure won, but in the forms through which they are conceived, in the very duplicity of language itself, in the necessarily equivocal character, earned by long use, of every significant word. Thought asks too much and words tell too much; because to ask anything is to ask everything, and to say anything is to ask more. It is the radical defect of thought that it leaves us discontented with what we actually feel—with what we know and do not know—as we know sunlight and surfeit and terror, all at once perhaps, and yet know nothing of them. Thought requires of us that we make a form for our knowledge which is personal, declarative, and abstract at the same time that we construe it as impersonal, expressive, and concrete. It is this knowledge that leads to the conviction of ignorance—to the positive ignorance which is the final form of contradictory knowledge; but it is the triumph of failure that in the process it snares all that can be snared of what we know.

The true paradox is that in securing its own ends thought cannot help defeating itself at every crisis. To think straight you must overshoot your mark. Orthodoxy of the human mind—the energy of society in its highest stable form—is only maintained through the absorption into it of a series of heresies; and the great heresy, surely, is the gospel of unity, whether it is asserted as a prime mover, as God, or, as in art, as the mere imposed unity of specious form. In adopting it for his own, Adams knew it for a heresy. Again and again he describes unifying conceptions as working principles; without them no work could be done; with them, even at the expense of final failure, every value could be provisionally ascertained. That is the value of Adams for us: the double value of his scrupulous attitude towards his unifying notions and of the human aspirations he was able to express under them. To feel that value as education is a profound deliverance: the same deliverance Adams felt in the Gothic Cathedral. "The delight of its aspiration is flung up to the sky. The pathos of its self-distrust and anguish of doubt is buried in the earth as its last secret." The principles asserted are nothing, though desperate and necessary; the values expressed because of the principles are everything. For Adams, as for everyone, the principle of unity carried to failure showed the most value by the way, and the value was worth the expense.

A Feather-Bed For Critics

Notes on the Profession of Writing

THESE notes have definitely an ulterior purpose which it is to be hoped will become clear, and not only clear but measurably acceptable to a few readers. What that purpose is cannot now be said, and cannot in all probability ever be said, by this writer, in a short form of words: it will show, if at all, as the result—call it meaning—call it frame of mind—of the elements here put together. It may be said briefly enough, though, with what this purpose has to do: With the profession of writing, only implicitly with criticism as a separate form of writing, more especially with the obligation of the critic to use what little power he can borrow to establish the idea of the writer as a man with a profession. It is a labour then, frankly hortatory, tactlessly moral; and it is undertaken because of those feelings, in a rising gorge, of stress, unease, and perfidious futility which form the base of immediate reaction to the general impact of writing in America. The reader not used to considering writers as having a profession and writing as a living, growing institution, will be on the right track if he merely goes on thinking, if he does think, of society as a whole in his usual terms. For there is a profession of society, and there is a sense, here hoped for as present, in which the profession of society and the profession of writing are the same. It is this focal identity, for example, that makes the untenable positions gotten into by our legislators and those assumed by our writers, notably on the war, deeply comparable though superficially at wide variance. Both classes, representative of the whole society, act from a defect of professional responsibility, with whatever unquestioned personal sincerity, and hence act, as they live, beyond their means, moral, intellectual, and emotional.

It is under the pressure of this felt conjunction—wherever the focus may lie—of the profession of society and the profession of writing that these remarks will compose themselves if they can. Assuming that the writer's business is to write, and that only by writing can he affect society, it is then necessary for him to envisage under what conditions, towards what nearly impossible ambition, he had best move to secure the maximum responsibility in his work. He must ask himself, too, what constitutes that inward mastery which alone makes his work objectively authoritative. And he must reflect, constantly, that in making these definitions and these decisions, whether for his own work or for work already produced, and whether positively in recognition and discovery, or negatively in judging and explaining a deficiency,—he must reflect that he is performing the most arduous critical act of which he is capable; and he must be aware that he is not performing that act alone, or anyhow wilfully, but together with many as the product of the tension of a lifetime, his own life seen in the life of his society.

Your honest writer, so committed, in this respect resembles the Popes: that in the exercise of their authority —what we call more familiarly their authorship—they are indeed but *servi servorum dei*. The burden of understanding is matched only by the burden of ignorance, and these are only less exacting than the burden of passing between them. The exaction, it may be said in passing, is loss of faith: seen in critical practice as the constantly increasing incredibility of *any* given intellectual bridge-work. However that may be, these burdens, with their native exactions, are present one way or another in every writer's word, and are tangible so to every critic with the least developed sensibility, and are nameable—and therefore manipulable—under the terms of any intellectual approach or prepossession willingly undertaken. The difficulty is to make others, who lack time or training or who do not see the need, pay attention. We know enough or too much; only, as I. A. Richards once remarked, we do not know enough to settle matters by debate or to persuade by argument; which is why, here, a different type of composition employs itself: that of delivery, as in a poem, it is to be hoped with every rational prepossession, but without much logical fancy— which may betray the weakness as well as expose the intent of this writer.

Weakness is something too, and there is a radical goodness in its estimation. If you ask how this weakness— this unused, this perhaps unavailable strength—is to be delivered—well! in an order not entirely fortuitous, the order, if we can manage it, in which the elements of our problem are exposed in the second paragraph above. We will take it, then, pretty much phrase by phrase, no more evenly than necessary, and see how it adds up.

Assuming that the writer's business is to write. The whole social question bristles in this assumption like an acre of oat stubble; which means, as a rule, that we dismiss the assumption along with the question, either by that indifference which regards questions as self-solving and basic assumptions as automatically carried out, or by that uneasy form of deep interest which expresses itself by putting things off. The fact is, that writers *devote* very little of their ability exclusively to writing; and one's surmise in explanation is that society neither requires nor perhaps permits more than the least devotion—just enough to keep the uniform recognisable, not enough to warrant respect for it. Such a condition at any rate explains why your economically and socially successful writer both looks and acts like a business-man whose business is anything but writing; he may show the earmarks of a tweed suit or a worried air, but he seldom shows the stigmata of an inward devotion, as the best lawyers, doctors, and mechanics do. More seriously, barring the extraordinary, the great, and the fanatic, who are above the count of these notes, your average successful writer, your run of the mill selling writer in the bookstores and magazines, gains his success by conceding as little as possible to the exigencies of his trade and only what is necessary to its tricks. It neither adds nor detracts from their social usefulness to remember that neither Mrs. Rinehart nor Mr. Edmands, say, can be criticized or appreciated as writers; neither above nor below, they are aside from any possibility of that concentrated attention which amounts to criticism and places enjoyment. Mr. Lewis of late years and Miss Ferber perhaps furnish sharper examples of the shapes wrought or inflated by social pressure—as Miss Millay furnishes a more intolerable example—out of writers whose work is no longer susceptible of critical enjoyment. Think of Balzac, George Sand, Christina Rosetti, as analogues from another society whose pressure was differently directed or differently resisted. The difference between Zola and Dreiser, Rousseau (of *The Confessions*) and Wolfe, is not only a difference of talent; it is a difference, too, in the quality of the operative force of the whole social institutions which they willy nilly represent. We might put it that the demand together with the capacity for informed seriousness in high level popular novels has fallen off. Again, it could rather be said that the demand and capacity for fact, excitement, urgency have overwhelmed the high seriousness that might otherwise have fostered good writing. *Grapes of Wrath* and *Native Son* are perhaps as far as we can profitably go in the direction of serious writing, and it is no accident that the first has been compared with *Uncle Tom's Cabin* and the second has been so widely accepted as a document. This is said without denigration of Mr. Steinbeck's imaginative abilities which are great, or Mr. Wright's extra-literary predilections which are conspicuous—and to both of which we shall return.

But let us disregard the profit motive, and remind ourselves of that considerable band of serious writers who lack only a theme or a living, or, what is the excruciation of poverty, both; for surely an adequate theme is itself as slow and hard to find as a living, and much harder to recognise when found. (Which is why your young writer, mistaking mere possessions for riches, and the immediate for the urgent, so often *begins* with autobiography.) Here society is again at work, securing the dissipation of energies before they reach concentration. The work is variously subtle and brutal: offering themes of endeavour in teaching and lecturing, in publishing and editing, now and again in quasi-public life, and enforcing the offer by exposing the blank necessity of acceptance if a living is to be made at all. You meet a serious writer to-day, and you ask him where he teaches. It is no blushing matter either; for if he doesn't teach, the chances are he does something else, far more exhausting and no less irrelevant to his writing—if he still does any: as, working for Mr. Luce, which appears to be a kind of fur-lined purgatory, where either the itch or the ability to write seriously is gradually rubbed out, when the candidate is ready to leave, more empty than he is pure. It is better to teach, in the double hope of good pupils and eventual freedom; which is a Pauline saying, if ever.

But "better" things are snares, and need desperate sensibilities, like Paul's, to advocate, and wearied sensibilities, like those of the first century, to accept. One hardly knows whether to emphasise or to straddle the parallel; the doubt is part of our ignorance, in this direction, of everything but our combined sense of termless strain and sourceless guilt. Such large considerations may well be treated as digressions. Immediate concerns only can be felt as direct.

What is direct here is the "better" lot of the writer attached to a university or a college. It is obviously better than any other lot possible in this country, better even, probably, than the lot of the government post resorted to by the French; it furnishes better than average subsistence and provides better than average opportunity for what is called leisure to write. On the face of it, the social institution being what it is, writers have no complaint and every reason for gratitude to a university system flexible enough to make room for them and kind enough to overlook their frequent disability as teachers. When burning is in question—by which I mean when one of the more supine forms of prostitution is the alternative—teaching is better; for the plain fact is that, at any given time, only a few serious writers can make a living entirely by writing, and you do not yourself decide whether or not you are one of that few for this year or this generation. You cannot call yourself Hemingway, no matter how good you are, without the great likelihood that you will turn out to be Wilson or Dos Passos; and even if you were right and Hemingway you will probably find yourself working for *Esquire* or the North American Newspaper Alliance more than is good for your writing. But burning is not here the question of will, any more than it is the question of superior value. What we want—what all of us want together—is not to save a few individuals, but to secure and elevate the profession, to save and improve the professional habit of the whole possible band of serious writers, from which the individual appears and without which he cannot survive his apparition even the meagre remnant of his lifetime.

What happens generally is that writers take in each other's writing, which is a bad example to the public and encourages many, vain of so sure an audience, to become writers without other sign of calling, and which is a worse example to the writers themselves because it either aggravates that bane of devotion, the snobbish form of professionalism, or makes a very hall of mirrors of one's sense of personal futility. Writers write, at least secondarily—which is to say by habit, in practice, and with the maximum of craft—for the great world, which however sparsely peopled is always great enough. This is where the university comes in, at least indirectly, to help reestablish the writer, *in his profession*, as an effective force in the great world; not by giving him the leisure to write—for in a sense he always has leisure for writing if he wants it—but by buying some of his leisure, of which he has plenty to begin with, so that he can use his time— those passages amidst leisure which are as likely rare and exhaustible as common and availing—actually to write. The shift in emphasis is important, but not, in these days, radical: it puts the writer upon exactly the same basis that the great medical schools put some of their doctors and the great scientific schools some of their physicists and chemists: they teach, in their leisure, not physiology, crystallography, and tar compounds— which are good subjects and need to be taught—but teach rather, actually, the art, the invoked quality of the profession of medicine, physics, chemistry. That is what is required of them. That is what ought to be required of writers brought to a university: to teach, in their leisure, the profession of writing. If the consequence were only to renew generally the respect felt in the 18th and early 19th centuries for men of letters, there might well again come to be a race of men of letters, and a race of writers (for these need not always be the same) who were educated as well as handy in their profession.

I am not thinking of residential poets, nor of chairs like the Norton chair at Harvard; for these are special posts given, quite properly, to men whose professional position is already secure. To the professional man they constitute a reward or an easing; but they do little to strengthen the profession itself. I am thinking, to repeat, of something comparable to a research instructorship or assistant professorship in the sciences; and it is an irony of our educational system in relation to our society, that the matter should not be thought of the other way round. Surely it is a natural development of the function of a university or college devoted to liberal education to take up when society leaves off the preservation, maintenance, and insemination of the *profession* of letters. The arts have always flourished best in connection with some institution of society; it is only rarely that they have flourished at all as institutions by themselves—notably and precariously in the last century in the first flush and tide of popular education, which being the immediate past seems the standard, when it is the exception. Today under the forms of capitalist democracy, indeed under any political-cultural forms likely to appear, there is no public institution of the state itself able to afford an integral connection for the profession of writing—however it may be for painting, architecture, and music. The university is at least the only obvious overt institution both sturdy and elastic enough, capable and remotely willing to furnish such a connection. I say capable, because it would require only development and modification of existing modes and habits; and willing, because there are already, here and there, jobs and set-ups that require of their incumbents thorough-going professional standards and proved competence in professional practice, quite apart from the work required to be done in what is, relatively, leisure from that practice but without release from those standards. It is not for nothing that serious writers gravitate—thinking of gravity as positively felt force—into teaching; and it is not for nothing at present that most of them disappear, as writers, into the larger mass and reappear if at all as professors without, for them, a profession. They teach English, a highly interesting and widely diversified occupation ranging from freshman grammar to Gothic grammar, with problems and aggravations of its own, but having no connection whatever with the business of writing or its leisure. The best that can be said for such teaching is that it is a waste of talent when talent exists and an indifferent kind termination for the waste effort of talent that only thought it existed, permitting, as it does, the delusion to persist without much gainsaying production.

It is not that the university, even when properly employed, furnishes the ideal guarantee of the writer's profession; not at all—too many mistaken choices, too much misled energy are certain to appear; but it is the thing at hand, and it is the business of the positive critic, when he can momentarily bring himself to exist as positive, to lead writers where they necessarily are going. The independent profession drawing sustenance from the broad base of society remains the "natural" ideal— the ideal or projected form of actual inclinations. Your successful great writer and also your successful merely serious writer—remember that a writer need no more be blamed for the accident of success than for the commonplace of failure—seem the enactment of the ideal. Really, so far as the profession is concerned, his independence is exactly as accidental as the possession or use of an inherited income. The serious writer choosing such independence in advance or in the first part of his career is like the man who hopes without ground for a fat legacy or a rich wife. The unknown uncle or the millionaire's widow may turn up, but the policy rates are high on the off chance, and the writer who can survive the waiting wear and tear, both moral and financial, is uncommon, for he thus deliberately exposes himself to all the meannesses and limitations of his profession, with no immediate return but self-felt prestige. For the uncommon writer—he who gets the legacy, even when much smaller than expected—it is worth it; prestige alone, one thinks, is worth little, unless, as is the case, the writer who battens upon it is more an actor than a writer. (We may have here, parenthetically, a partial explanation of why so many devoted writers, otherwise of matured sensibilities, exhibit so distorted a view of society, so inveterate a fear of the normal, quite as if they were saints *manqué*.)

What we have been saying is that the profession of writing cannot be expected to prosper as an independent institution if its sole resource lies in a series of accidents. More or less of its members—depending on the quality of popular education at the moment and the consequent nature of popular direct connection with imaginative literature—more or less and usually most of its members will have to participate in some living institution, not limited to the profession, perhaps in order to endure at all, but more especially to achieve their own coherence and secure their own aims. The priest requires the church, which has many functions beside the priestly, even when he is outside it and against it, in order to preach at all. The lawyer requires the courts, with their multiplicity of vested or executive interests, in order to reform and envisage law. The doctor requires the hospital and the school, which are so much devoted to mere custodial treatment and routine pedagogy, for the very medium of his practice. Serious men require the institutions of society almost more than they require to change them to fit their will and imagination, require them sometimes in the offing and sometimes at hand. Serious writers are no different; for them it would seem to-day that the university is the only available institution, whether in the offing or at hand cannot certainly be said, except by the university itself. I think at hand.

But what is at hand is only the next step, most likely useless and astray, unless there is an end coming into view, a shaping force felt pressing from behind, not so much for the individual writer, who writes what he can —the nearer, as he is a good writer, to what he just *cannot* write—as for the profession as a whole, which needs, for compactness, for identity, for social relation, exactly the double sense of source and direction; a statement which brings us immediately upon the other half of our preliminary assumption about the writer: *that only by writing can he affect society*. Here almost the story might smugly stop on a foregone conclusion, were it not for the violence everywhere abroad and the collapse everywhere within: the present war and the probable peace. For it is war seen as disorder paramount, order imposed by *adventitious* force, that uproots first the self-evident, the dependable, the convenient, the customary: all the outward signs of inward order, all the drive that goes by use. Thus the whole regiment—the ruling habit—of our practice comes into artificial and torturing question—as in a nightmare the act of breathing becomes questionable and voice is only possible as a scream.

Mr. MacLeish—in his *The Irresponsibles*—has recently brought the practice of writers into question and has provided a minatory answer, rather more prophetic than critical, to the effect that the irresponsibility of the imaginative reactions of writers to the last war and its ensuing peace has infected the young of this generation with an irresponsibility towards the present war and indeed towards society itself. I have no wish to take issue with Mr. MacLeish—he has the good of the profession in his head as well as his heart, and besides he is at least partly right on the facts; and I have no intention of making him appear to sit in corners he would never consciously occupy; but his remarks have both roused reactions singularly inappropriate to his intentions and raised considerations, of vital import, that seem to have escaped him and most of his readers as well. Mr. MacLeish himself only shares the common guilt of that rash sincerity which speaks out of a mind not fully made up, perhaps only half made up, and yet speaks with full urgency. Half way is always hell. It will be understood then, that the following remarks are addressed to the question itself and not particularly to anything he said in raising it. His essay is a point of departure.

The departure is backwards, if we can make it so; backwards into an earlier and more primitively abstract view of the relation of the writer to his society, from the vantage of which Mr. MacLeish's concrete indictment of contemporary writers seems very like wishful thinking if not positive vainglorying about the writer's position and influence in the operation of a culture. If a small group of imaginative writers can affect, by their own authority alone, the general moral fibre of their time, and can then, under Mr. MacLeish's suasion or another's, undo that damage and again alter the fibre by a simple change of heart or shuffle of the will, then the position of the writer is supreme. I do not say Mr. MacLeish believes this or would be agreeable to saying it; but many of his readers have reacted as if he had said and did believe it: it is what many of the readers already either negatively liked or positively hated to believe. It is such a compliment as leaves little else in the world to flatter; neither educa-

tion, nor church, nor legislature can stand to a novelist
or a poet with his dander up. The grain of truth that
lies in this reaction, shows itself plain on reversal of emphasis. A writer's sensibility is the joint product of his
education and of the general (relatively uneducated,
rather *minted*) sensibility of his time. What he writes
depends on the time, the direction he pushes it in depends primarily upon his education, on his craft only in
the deep sense, the process of his feeling alone depends
on himself. Anything else is largely personality or cultivated idiosyncrasy, and that too is largely a matter of
education and perhaps religion, or the absence of these.
If what Mr. MacLeish's readers believe about the influence of writers is true at all—if the writers of our time
have been irresponsible—it is only true either because of
the accidental evil of uneducated writers (now presumptively *being* educated) or, and I think this is the grain
that made the pearl, because education and religion and
rational piety towards society have fallen apart specifically rather faster than imaginative writers as a class generally have: which if it is the case leaves the writers more
or less right in the first place, and in the second place
discovers them as central to an emptied society, but in
the third place both right and central to an insignificant
degree, and quite without moral authority or, as writers,
political will.

This is precisely not what the general run of thinking
has come to be about the possible effects of the writer
on society and his obligations towards it. He is expected
to be both a political philosopher and a district leader in
a cultural Tammany Hall; to create values and also to
undermine them; to be, as it were, the very heresiarch of
orthodoxy; to be a moral publicist, to hold positions, and

take sides; and all this while telling an amusing story or composing a musical poem. The articulate part of society, in short, seeing the centre fall apart, tends to make the writer, who showed him the fact, deliberately a false god, and then call him responsible. The next thing they will want to hang him, like California Mr. Steinbeck, and no doubt upside down.

But all this is a weak fiction, a desperate fable, and, provided writers will go on writing, or resume it if they have left off, will collapse of its own structural weakness under the steady impact of the art it sought to enslave. Yet we want a fiction about the writer and society, and want one especially whose verisimilitude and native root-system will strengthen the writer to withstand the convulsions of his society. We should put it together as if it were the truth, which it may be—though truth in this kind has no great longevity, only an endless capacity for resurrection. At any rate we should include, in order to be persuasive and whole-hearted, most of the elements of the fable we wish to set aside. Let us say then that in the nature of things—by their urgency—a writer somehow combines in his person some of the attributes of the publicist, the moralist, the preacher if not the priest, in general the attributes of the social reformer as well as those exclusively of the writer; that is why we call him a writer, here, rather than more properly a poet—which is only what he ought to be. It is worth adding that the lawyer and the doctor also generally share these attributes, and, to the extent of their cultivation, the mason, the carpenter, and the mechanic—indeed every person submitted to a sidewalk interview or a radio quizz. There is no escape, anywhere, from imputed omniscience and implied responsibility. My point is, that it is only because he is as a rule abler in the use of words than the others that the writer is pushed forward as the scapegoat of general necessity; and this because of the universal practical confusion of ideas with the words which are only their vehicle, and the worse confusion of words with ideas, which in fact exhaust only a fraction of the power of words. Actually the ideal or administrative moral authority of the imaginative writer, like that of the mechanic, stems only obscurely from his craft; plainly from his education, his religion, his rooted prejudices. Otherwise a great writer would be—whenever his drama was conceived on moral terms—necessarily a great moralist; which is regrettably not the case, as we see in D. H. Lawrence, Thomas Hardy, and the later Tolstoi. Morals, as I think T. S. Eliot once remarked, are only a *secondary* consideration for the writer, as they are only a *primary* consideration for the saint; whose full consideration they may be I will not say, unless it be that statue of butter the citizen: that is, yours, and mine, and yours too.

It is not meant to assert here as a part of our fable what is so often asserted of the experimental scientists, that one's work is superior to moral valuation merely because the individual worker is not responsible for the evil purposes to which his invention is put. Good and evil are, I take it, in the world of value, inextricable. To think otherwise is a stimulating, or often a consoling heresy, which must be reabsorbed into common sense. The best, the keenest heresy is only brilliant as it flashes against the background of orthodoxy, illuminating it in a new light never afterwards to be forgotten. The dream of absolute freedom of imagination, of utter moral independence, is the most haunting and most illuminating heresy that the writer—any artist—can entertain; which is why it is brought up here, as the stigmatising preface to a declaration, without which the declaration might seem flat and the rote of stale habit.

The material of the writer is morals; as the de Goncourts said, ethics in action; inescapably: not creative morals, not ideal morals, but actual morals of behaviour, whether projected or real. The writer cannot help taking society as he finds it; his difficulty and his obligation as a writer consist in the attempt to see what he finds as actual, remembering always that the fantastic and the illusionary may be as good witnesses of the actual, if seen in the buff, as the quotidian and the undeluded, and very likely better. His difficulty as a man and his obligation towards society consist in the attempt to be honest in distinguishing the actual—never failing to separate what can be felt from the mere wilful imperative of what ought to be felt, and never using an imperative at all except in a subordinate position outside the focal interest. To combine conceptual honesty and the act of vision is the constant athletic feat of the artist, requires all the poor talent he can muster, and of course most often stops short at failure—showing mere honesty or mere vision or mere mechanism. The test of success is enduring interest; and there, in enduring interest, lies the writer's whole authority and his sole moral strength. It is perfidy to the actual that weakens a writer and disintegrates his writing, and it is fidelity to the actual that strengthens him and gives his writing its only effect on society.

If we look at Dante we will see this plain. It is his mastery of the actual at every pertinent level, from the colour of dusk to the vision of God, from simple lust to heavenly love, and by mastery I mean provisionally his ability to compel our interest and take away our attention—it is *this* mastery, and not his mastery of Tomist philosophy, that has affected all Christian society since he wrote. The Divine Comedy was the actual morals of a whole society before it could be Tomist theology, which was yet responsible, somehow, for the boundaries of the poet's vision; it was, in short, Christianity grounded. Conversely, since we have mentioned them, Hardy and Lawrence and the later Tolstoi may be said to fail, relatively, just in the degree that they fail to compel our interest except in terms of wilful imperatives at just those points where the actual was needed. Hardy intruded the mechanical irony, Lawrence the dark blood-stream, Tolstoi his "literal" Christianity, as the overt form of their dramatic crises, when they should, at most, have instigated the crises, and preferably should have been left to one side, framework discarded. Present and emphatic, these emotional and intellectual devices substituted for the enormous powers to render the actual which these writers possessed, and fatally hindered the moral strength which came from the exercise—when it occurred—of those powers.

Mr. Steinbeck too was mentioned a few pages back, and his *Grapes of Wrath* makes a very good example indeed of your more ordinary serious work, where conceptual honesty and the act of vision, both existent, were not so much combined as exhibited in parallel, so that both suffer from the charge of distortion and incompleteness. There is actuality enough in the Joad family and its adventures to affect society with the deepest and most incontrovertible form of evidence: the represented, qualified, concrete instance; but there is also a good deal of substitute mechanics—lay figures and puppet passages —which impair the evidence, impeach the actuality, and dishearten the interest. One suspects that Mr. Steinbeck's sensibility was not mature enough, not grounded enough, not *slowed* enough by its subject-matter, to avoid the intermittent temptation to hasten its effects by taking up a series of positions, known to be either sympathetic or aggravating, without first making them tenable by actualisation. It is the commonest and most explicable failure of the serious writer.

Mr. Wright was mentioned along with Mr. Steinbeck because of the accident of similar popular success, and it seems fair at this point to separate the two men as types of writer. *Native Son* is one of those books in which everything is undertaken with seriousness except the writing. One needs only to compare it with *Crime and Punishment*, which insofar as it is a *novel* it resembles, to see how frivolous, how external the motor violence is by which alone the drama is pointed. For the rest, for the movement of the thesis of the book as distinct from the drama, Mr. Wright depends on a social fairy-tale of the class struggle which is so far from being grounded in the folkways of American society that its operation is felt as mechanical and deprives even the violence of its native significance. In explanation it may be hazarded that the book is a product of a sensibility so jaded by desperation that it could not reach the condition of imaginative honesty (personal or political honesty—mere sincerity, for writing—is not in question); with the result that though there was an overwhelming actuality behind and beyond the book, there is none in it.—Is not one here encouraged to wonder, as a kind of digression made in order to get back, whether it is not precisely this absence of the actual which has afforded *Native Son* so much less social effect than *Grapes of Wrath?* To think so would be both a tribute to the power of writing and to the reading public.

On that notion, we move another step further towards the centre of our discussion: to the consideration of the modes and manners by which the writer secures—what Mr. MacLeish and all the rest of us want—*the maximum responsibility in his work*. Stephen Dedalus had the nub partly in hand when he felt, with a lift, at the beginning of his now altered career as a writer, that he might yet come to be the conscience of his race. The whole of *Ulysses* is indeed the expressed, utterly actualised example of the agen-bite of inwit. He had another part of it too, when he defined sentimentality as the unwillingness to assume the enormous responsibility for a thing done. The quotations are not exact; never mind; they serve to suggest the image of James Joyce as the writer of the generation just gone who showed the maximum responsibility in his work. On another level there is Gascoigne's remark that "the verse that is to easie is like a tale of a rosted horse." We can pull these remarks together pretty well by drawing from them a conclusion: that to feel responsibility is to feel the pang of experience, and to act from responsibility is to put that pang into one's writing. To get out of this some of the wanted sense of debt to one's material (or, almost indifferently, obligation to society) we can add the savory of Yeat's remark to the effect that good poets write with difficulty what bad poets write easily. There is no more facility ever, in live writing than in a live conscience, and no less absolute, achieved speed. (The reader who understands the notion of speed will forgive the rest.)

Now these sentences make more a sentiment than a definition; the dictionary will have none of us in this mood, and what the dictionaries will not have the schools, which we aim at, will abuse. But we can rise to translation, and be above abuse; for the dictionary—that palace of saltatory heuristics—is quite on our side, with a jump: saying that he who is responsible may be called to account, may be made to reply, in short to respond; and to respond, if we jump back a little, is both to perform the answering or corresponding action, and to show sensitiveness to behaviour or change; and again, with another jump, this time into Skeat, we find invoked for further discovery the word sponsor: a surety, a god-father or godmother, one who promises, with a probable alliance with the Greek words for treaty or truce, and for pouring a libation, as when making a solemn treaty. The development is interesting: he who is responsible swears, and swears, and answers just the same. We can bring that down without marring it much. This polite fellow keeps tight on what he values and says what he saw. Not everybody can tell him what he values—his politeness is the finished look of his education; and no-body can tell him what to see without blinding his vision or filling his mouth with toads. Society gave him his ideas of value and, as he is a writer, he tests his ideas—the phrase is Allen Tate's—by experience. The result, to be useful, to be responsive to the facts—to be responsible—must be as objective, indeed almost as anonymous, as any activity of the Bureau of Standards.

Here is where the twinning notions of response and sponsorship come in. They need not be pushed in the face but dangled a little, not forced food but bait: a very appetiser to the operative imagination, whereby habit is led out of itself to become a conscious, because everywhere freshened, act. To be sponsored, as both the catechism and the WPA tell us, is to be asserted provisionally whole and good, a thing impossible on its face, which is why it is reserved to the god-parents, to the ideal which stands in the place of the actual, and yet also is a thing deeply to be desired and aimed at: a new home in the wilderness. To be sponsored then is to be provided, here in the actual world, with a sense of allegiance. As the soul forms, the sensibility grows, or the project is finished—all operations in the actual world —either the allegiance must come to permeate the agent, thus reaching into the actual, or limbo—damnation, if you want to be stiff about it—ensues. Once the soul is formed, the sensibility matured, the bridge used, your god-parents are not enough, you have to work for your inheritance—the object of allegiance—in order to know even what it is, and in order especially to know whether it is what you were told. To work, in the case of a writer who has achieved or is trying to achieve mature sensibility, is to respond, which is primarily to see and feel, secondarily to place; to respond, in terms of his allegiance, to as much as possible of the actual he knows, and a bit more. As he succeeds he will have stretched his sense of the actual, by illuminating it, and his sense of allegiance, by actualising it. As he fails—as he retires upon his god-parents by rote—he will have lessened either one sense or the other, or commonly both. It is on a parallel with these remarks that we can understand Joyce's "uncreated conscience of his race"—the bite, the pang, of knowing together the idea and the actuality; and it is on another parallel that we see how it is we derive from great writers our deepest sense of the ideality of action and our clearest sense of the fact of allegiance. One need not push it, as a third parallel, that these quickening works have been almost indifferently received by the existing imagination—popular or official—either as the next word on the tongue or as irresponsible assaults upon the foundations of society, or that still others seem likely as centuries pass to be candied over till eternity. Epego, as Montaigne says, I will hold back; but it is part of the bait. Besides, as Montaigne also said, "the human mind cannot keep rambling in this infinity of shapeless ideas; it must compile them into a certain image after its own model."

How, aside from emulation of those whom he admires, a serious writer can do much by himself to secure the conditions of maximum responsibility for his own work, I do not know. A writer does little but the physical act of writing by himself. The profession—the tradition and institution of letters—does more, much by rote. Society as a whole does still more—providing motives, of which it both enables and impedes the enactment. There is something indefeasible about impedimenta, whether to an army on the march or to a writer hunting a theme; whence the shameful selectiveness of victory. Perhaps the writer by himself can do no more than attempt to be as initially conscious of his insights and his feelings, and as finally unconscious, as he is of his words and the tricks of his trade. Certainly he can do no less; for to do less is to avow half-mastery enough—is tantamount to saying that if you know *how* to do, *what* you do will take care of itself—is indeed an example of that profound alienation of human powers which consists in the substitution of fanaticism for conviction.

Fanaticism—to quote him who used to be anathema

upon it; fanaticism, says Santayana, is when you redouble your effort having forgotten your aim. Aims
remembered modify the periphery of action. Fanaticism, all periphery, can modify nothing. Conviction,
we may hazard, is when you redouble your effort in
terms of your aim. Your fanatic writer has a need which
cannot be satiated and an obsession which is insolent:
both fractional to his nature and its pattern. Your convicted writer has a need which may be envisaged as
satisfied and a preoccupation which is radical: both func-
tional to his nature and an actualisation of its pattern.
Your fanatic writer may show every competence and
every violence; he is beside or beneath himself. Your
convicted writer may show possible mastery and eventual strength; he is inside and beyond himself. We
glance at extremes, and exceed the provision before us;
but only in order to return to the average out of which
we may construct a normal case, to use the phrase in our
topic paragraph, of *that inward mastery which alone
gives a writer objective authority in his work.*

Conviction is again the word we jump for. Surely it
is a fertile and stimulating definition, quite with a speed
of its own, which says that when a writer feels conviction he feels an inward mastery of the outward materials
of experience. He has passed in his conceptual ardour
beyond the realm of ideas: Conviction is *that* mastery.
What is conceived is taken again into the mind and is
there submitted to the conscience—to that pangful process of being known together; thence by grace there may
come about that final human feeling towards experience
called conviction: that it has been conquered together.
These are words, no less; running their aptest errand, to
bring us news of the reality of what we thought and

felt, but could not surely know until they came to convince us. Conviction, then, is inward mastery of the outward materials of experience.

How may a writer come by it? An artificial question, like all the rest, if the answer wanted is expected to be helpful. How does he come by experience? Is it not by assenting to it? And is not assent the immanent form of conviction, its pervasive, remaining form before it reaches particular articulation? One assents to a thing not so much because it is true or false, appropriate or banal, but because it is so, is what it is, and is, exclusively and ambiguously, for good and for evil, its own meaning. Such is the beginning of conviction. It can be cultivated exactly as if it were a habit, and improved with use, but unlike your ordinary habit if you stop cultivation it dies or becomes another thing; for there is another definition, incomplete like the others, which says that conviction, or the deep assent that ends in conviction, is only the supreme act of attention: that attention which keeps not only the trees but also the woods always and at once in full mind; and that attention, too, which turns both outwards and inwards, upon what confronts the sensibility no more than upon the process—the modification—of the sensibility receiving it. It is the attention of a man in love. Even that attention slips without provocation, flags from excess of its own zeal, only to be roused again when the sensibility is startled or jogged.

In a way, that is what has happened to Mr. MacLeish, and to many more. The war has startled sensibilities everywhere, not so much to a renewal of the act of attention perhaps as to a realisation of the lack of an anterior conviction—operative sensibility—which would have kept the attention in focus. In other sensibilities, those incapable of conviction, the shock of war has obliterated the inward attention while raising the outward intolerably: when we get hysteria or fanaticism or a monstrous sport of these. We need not praise war more for the one consequence than the other. We should rather complain that the war caught us with our conviction inchoate instead of formed, our attention dissipated instead of focussed; for in war it is only the rudimentary forms, the saving remnants, never the full expressive virtue, of the convicted imagination that can be used. War with its violence and its imposition of adventitious order only shows us what we already lacked, or had let go, or ignored. If patriotism, as Santayana said, no more springs from war than ideal love from debauchery, neither does the conviction that enlightens both.

In making this complaint we remind ourselves that in all his concern with the convicted imagination, in looking for it, determining it, finding its lack, the writer must reflect that he is performing *the most arduous critical act of which he is capable.* He is endeavouring, so to speak, to keep himself in a steady startled state: as if one were about to be haunted: as if one were never to get used to, and hence never to let down, one's powers of vision, one's resources of feeling, and had yet, in such suspense, to judge, to decide—and so to express—the actuality of the job in hand. It is in this sense that the composition of a great poem is a labour of unrelenting criticism, and the full reading of it only less so; and it is in this sense, too, that the critical act is what is called a "creative" act, and whether by poet, critic, or serious reader, since there is an alteration, a stretching, of the sensibility as the act is done. The cost of criticism is, if I may borrow and restrict a little a phrase I have used before, the expense of greatness; as its earnings are in the sense of conviction pervading the job done. Thus it is judgment that ends in conviction.

The expense is too arduous to be borne by the individual writer, nor can he earn the way of conviction alone. He can neither judge nor make anything of the actuality and the facts and the idea, by himself. Culture is not private, unity is not idiosyncratic. The critical act is performed, if at all, *together with many, as the product of the tension of the writer's lifetime, his own life seen in the life of his society.* To say this is to pause, take breath, and say everything at once; and is to run the risk, too, of saying nothing.

The reader will make up his mind about that. All or nothing then is this. Without the profession of writing behind him the individual writer is reduced to small arms; without society behind it, the profession is impotent and bound to betray itself. A deep collaboration is necessary, a collaboration in which the forces are autonomous and may never consciously co-operate, but which is marked by the unity they make together and by the culture which the individual, by the act of his convicted imagination, brings to light. The individual writer is nothing himself, but there is nothing without him. In the gap between lie all the kinds of writers in the world showing through diversity of interests and inexhaustible variety of modes a common character, or a failure to achieve it, for serious writing. I do not know what that character is; but take away Dante, Shakespeare, Tolstoi, Aeschylus, it is what is left that they illuminated. To persuade writers—and readers too—of that character today: to bring them to full consciousness of their profession, and to situate the profession in society; that is the major possible labour of the professional critics, a race hitherto more ornamental than necessary. But now, in the first society of the western world not based upon the religious imagination but based directly and precariously upon the secular and experimental imagination, so far as it is based at all, it is a race that seems more necessary than it is possible. It is this fact taken as a sentiment that makes notes such as these, previously irrelevant or supererogatory, not only an appropriate exercise but a major preoccupation both for the poet as critic and for the critic as poet. The reader who doubts the necessity or thinks it arrogant may be asked what state, what church, is there that shows enough polity or enough piety to the actual society they administer to give the writer the bread and wine of conviction. Yeats was much troubled by this question in his last years and came very near in his prose, where he was uncritical, to giving in to the adventitious conviction of force and marching men; but in his poetry, which was completely critical, he looked at the actual to the end, though with increasing desperation.

> Here is fresh matter, poet,
> Matter for old age meet;
> Might of the Church and State,
> Their mobs put under their feet.
> O but heart's wine shall run pure
> Mind's bread grow sweet.
>
> That were a cowardly song,
> Wander in dreams no more;
> What if the Church and the State
> Are the mob that howls at the door!
> Wine shall run thick to the end,
> Bread taste sour.

Desperation is not required; the props are gone, the values remain. There is society itself which has produced state and church from everlasting, and will do so again at the next moment of mastery, when its convictions are made plain. Meanwhile the writer has merely the greater labour to do of seeing with supreme attention not only the actual but also, what had previously been largely given him free of attention by church and state, the values that enlighten the actual as the actual grounds the values. This is critical labour; desperate in process, the end is possible; and to think of the possibility only puts a different conclusion to an observation of T. E. Lawrence, who felt our predicament a little ahead of us. "The everlasting effort to write," he said, "is like trying to fight a feather-bed. In letters there is no room for strength." To the responsible writer, conviction turns everything to strength. But that is to range within peril of the ideal; which we have meant to.